The Function and Use of TO and OF in Multi-Word Units

The Function and Use of TO and OF in Multi-Word Units

Michael Pace-Sigge
University of Eastern Finland

First published 2015 by
PALGRAVE MACMILLAN

Palgrave Macmillan in the UK is an imprint of Macmillan Publishers Limited, registered in England, company number 785998, of Houndmills, Basingstoke, Hampshire RG21 6XS.

Palgrave Macmillan in the US is a division of St Martin's Press LLC, 175 Fifth Avenue, New York, NY 10010.

Palgrave Macmillan is the global academic imprint of the above companies and has companies and representatives throughout the world.

Palgrave® and Macmillan® are registered trademarks in the United States, the United Kingdom, Europe and other countries.

ISBN 978–1–137–47030–0

This book is printed on paper suitable for recycling and made from fully managed and sustained forest sources. Logging, pulping and manufacturing processes are expected to conform to the environmental regulations of the country of origin.

A catalogue record for this book is available from the British Library.

Library of Congress Cataloging-in-Publication Data
Pace-Sigge, Michael, 1970–
The function and use of TO and OF in multi-word units / Michael Pace-Sigge, University of Eastern Finland.
pages cm
Summary: "The highly frequent word items TO and OF are often conceived merely as prepositions, carrying little meaning in themselves. This book disputes that notion by analysing the usage patterns found for OF and TO in different sets of text corpora. Looking at historical roots and earlier corpus linguistic research, this study demonstrates that both OF and TO have clear semantic and pragmatic functions. The book analyses corpora from three types of text: spoken, semi-prepared spoken such as speeches, and written fiction to explore how the two words are used in English overall and what genre-specific characteristics stand out"— Provided by publisher.
ISBN 978–1–137–47030–0 (hardback)
1. Corpora (Linguistics) 2. Functional discourse 3. Grammar, Comparative and general—Prepositions. 4. Grammar, Comparative and general—Syntax. I. Title.
P285.P33 2015
425'.7—dc23   2015018333

Typeset by MPS Limited, Chennai, India.

To Katie, my heart's better head

Also, to Zoe McGarry and Larissa Wang,
the coming generation

Contents

List of Figures and Tables

Figures

Tables

Acknowledgements

I thank Professors Paul Baker (Lancaster) and Michael Hoey (Liverpool) for encouraging me to pursue this line of research. Also, many thanks to Professor Doug Biber (Northern Arizona) whose research clearly influenced me. I also thank Libby Forrest at Palgrave Macmillan for helping me complete the project. Thanks must also go to the anonymous reviewers and to Andrew Hardy (Lancaster), Jingling Ma (Tianjin Chengjian University) and Toar Sumakul (Satya Wacana Christian University) for their useful comments, and to Poppy Patterson for her interest.

This work would not have been possible without access to a great variety of corpora. I would especially like to thank Katie Patterson (Liverpool), who kindly let me use her corpus of nineteenth-century British literature, and Amanda Cardoso (Edinburgh) and Marten Juskan (Freiburg) for letting me use their Liverpool English transcripts. Furthermore, I thank Dawn Carroll (National Museums Liverpool), Paul Carson (BBC) and Tom Williams (London School of Economics) for granting me permission to use their podcast material. I extend thanks to the ESRC (Economic and Social Research Council), which enables access to materials produced in course of their funded projects.

Last but not least, my thanks go to Palgrave Macmillan's Production Team and, in particular, Katie Patterson and Jess Pope for their patient copy-editing.

List of Abbreviations

2w, 3w, 4w	2-word, 3-word, 4-word: referring to the length of a word cluster
3S	3 Sources corpus: combined figures for 19th-centry British Fiction, ANC Written Fiction and BNC Written Fiction data
4CC	4-Corners Corpus: Spoken Lancaster, Liverpool, London and Newcastle English Corpus
19C	Corpus of 100 texts of 19th-century British fiction
ANC-F	ANC-Fiction/Prose American National Corpus sup-corpus
AUX	Auxiliary Verb
BASE	*British Academic Spoken English* corpus
BAWE	*British Academic Written English* corpus
BBC	British Broadcasting Corporation
BNC-C	BNC-Spoken-Conversation British National Corpus sub-corpus
BNC-F	BNC-Written-Fiction/Prose British National Corpus sub-corpus
CANCODE	*Cambridge And Nottingham Corpus of Discourse in English*
F or FREQ.	Frequency of occurrence: number of occurrences
ICE	International Corpus of English, University College London
Inf.	as in *to*-Infinitive: *to*-Infinitive form
LL	*log-likelihood* (value); statistical testing
LSE	London School of Economics
MSM	Multiple Speaker Material: Q&A and panel material; podcast – sub-corpus
MWU	Multi Word Unit
N	Number of occurrences
NML	National Museums Liverpool

NML-m	multiple-speaker/plenary session transcript section of the NML sub-corpus
OED	Oxford English Dictionary
Q&A	Question-and-Answer sessions held after BBC Reith and LSE public lectures
R	Rank of occurrence
Reith	Reith Lectures, a series presented yearly by the BBC since 1948; podcast – sub-corpus
Reith-Q&A	Question-and-Answer session transcript section of the Reith sub-corpus
SSM	Single Speaker Material: speeches delivered by a single speaker; podcast – sub-corpus
tot.	total
VAR	Various Sources: a selection of single- and multiple-speaker presentations collected from various sources; podcast – sub-corpus.
VAR-m	multiple-speaker/plenary session transcript section of the VAR sub-corpus

1
Introduction

> Linguists are accustomed to seeing the language as divisible into coherent units such as phrase, group or clause. The simple frameworks proposed here are intended to raise consciousness of the many different and eminently sensible ways we might develop to present and explain language patterning. We have sought to demonstrate that two very common grammatical words, one on either side, offer a firm basis for studying collocations.
>
> (Renouf and Sinclair, 1991: 142)

1.1 What this book wants to achieve

This book looks at the usage patterns found for the highly frequent items *of* and *to* in different sets of corpora. The book disputes claims that these two items can merely be referred to as *prepositions* and carry little meaning in themselves. Instead, looking at historical roots (cf. Brorström, 1965; Hook, 1975) and earlier corpus linguistic research (Sinclair, [1970] 2004), the aim is to demonstrate that both *of* and *to* have clear semantic and pragmatic functions. In order to achieve this, corpora from three types of text will be explored here: spoken (BNC Spoken Conversation and more recent material); semi-prepared spoken (public speeches as found in the BBC Reith and LSE public lectures but also Q&As and plenary-led speeches); and written fiction (BNC; 19th-century British and early 20th-century US full text).[1]

Drawing on material first presented by Sinclair (1991), Gries (2003), Hoffmann (2005) and a wide collection of spoken data, this corpus-driven investigation shows that *of* and *to* carry specific roles within larger *lexical items*.

1

This book shows that it is crucial to recognise that *of* and *to* are not only highly frequent items by themselves; they are also highly prominent in the most frequent bigrams, trigrams and even longer clusters in prepared and semi-prepared spoken utterances. It is crucial to be aware of the fact that (as pointed out by Sinclair, 1990; Francis, 1993; Stubbs, 1996) certain word forms predominantly appear in one single construction. This needs to be taken into account in our understanding of language. Furthermore, the unconscious specific usage pattern for the particular sub-set of English language use described here mirrors findings by Biber (2000) and Hoffmann (2005), and is seen as further support for the lexical priming theory (Hoey, 2005).

This book has two aims. First, this investigation wishes to demonstrate that both *of* and *to* have clear semantic and pragmatic functions. Guéron (cf. 1990: 161 and 164), who states that particles and prepositions have an inherent locative content, concurs here, up to a point. Yet I seek to demonstrate that "inherent semantic content" exists for a wider range of items. Drawing on material first presented by Gries (2003) and Hoffmann (2005), it will be shown that *of* and *to* are far less easy to classify than is generally assumed. Second, these particular words fulfil specific roles within larger *lexical items*, which reflect both their roots and their communicative functions. Through their frequency, *of* and *to* provide a key argument as to why language should not be seen as single-word units which have autonomous categories and functions: English, characteristically, is dominated by what John Sinclair terms *lexical items:* single and, in particular, multi-word units. *Of* and *to* should be seen as an integral linking part of important formulaic clusters found in the English language. Of particular importance for corpus linguists is the fact that traditional forms of classification seem to struggle to describe or determine what and when the items are used. Hill admitted that "no one classification or order can be considered perfect" (1968: vii), and therefore he refers to his own classifications as "interim". In fact, it could be pointed out that no classification can ever be complete – the more data one looks at, the finer-graded the classification could become. This would be a task as futile as measuring the length of the British coastline.[2]

As a result, it can be argued that there is no need to chart every single possible function an item could feasibly have: this book sees its primary task in providing an insight into the predominant functions in which *of* and *to* are found.

1.2   Structure of the book

In this book, six corpora will be focused on: Fiction corpora are a collection of 19th-century full-length novels (19C) and 20th-century fiction found in the BNC Written Fiction (BNC-F). For the prepared spoken material, single-speaker speeches (SSM) are compared to material coming from post-lecture Q&As and plenary public events – that is, multiple-speaker material (MSM). Finally, casual spoken English comes from the BNC Spoken Conversation (BNC-C) and a collection of regional transcripts – from Lancaster, inner and outer London, Liverpool and Newcastle (four corners of England – 4CC). These sub-corpora have been arranged in a way that they are roughly equal in size. Chapter 2 will offer a brief recourse to the historical use for *of* and *to* before giving an overview of more recent, mainly corpus-based work. The following chapters present a arch of use from written material in Chapter 3, which compares 19th-century British fiction with 20th-century British and American fiction, via the semi-prepared spoken (both speeches and plenaries/discussions) in Chapter 4, to a description how *of* and *to* are being used in casually spoken British English corpora in Chapter 5. Chapters 3 to 5 look in detail at whether there are specific forms of use for *of* and *to* that are prominent in any of the sub-corpora that make up the main corpora. Chapter 6 presents the discussion of findings. Here the usage of the two items is firstly investigated based on genre and secondly investigated across genre boundaries. In Chapter 6, only the British fiction is taken into account. This means that 100 19th-century full-length novels (19C) are compared to excerpts from 20th-century fiction found in the BNC Written Fiction (BNC-F).

Chapter 7 provides a brief overview on research into the use of corpus-based findings and teaching English, and provides valuable links between the research results provided here and how they can be used in the teaching of English.

Chapter 8 concludes the investigation with a summary of the main differences found for the usage of the items *of* and *to* based on the data.

All wordlists and concordances in this book were produced using WordSmith Tools (Scott, 2012–2015). Statistical testing was conducted using the log-likelihood calculator devised and provided by Paul Rayson (n.d.).

The book focusses on bigrams and trigrams, and will refer to longer clusters found only where these occur in sufficiently high numbers. For reasons of space, not all calculations undertaken for statistical testing have been given in full: where needed, log-likelihood results are being referred to in the text simply as *differences are statistically (not) significant*.

Finally, please make good use of the endnotes. They usually provide further information and statistical data which might be seen as very useful further information to the reader.

2
The Background: From Historical Descriptions of TO and OF to Contemporary Corpus-Based Evidence

2.1 Introduction

The occurrence pattern items *of* and *to* should be of interest to every corpus linguist, as they are amongst the most frequent items in every corpus of English. The items have been investigated, in their function as preposition, with recourse to corpus data by both Sebastian Hoffmann (2005, looking at the British National Corpus (BNC) and Thomas Hoffmann (2011, looking at two parts of the International Corpus of English – ICE-GB and ICE-EA). In my research, however, I shall take my cue from the OSTI report (Sinclair et al., [1970] 2004) and, in particular, John Sinclair's discussion on the item *of* in Chapter 6 of *Corpus Concordance Collocation* (1991), as well as my own work on *to* (Pace-Sigge, 2013).

It is an often overlooked fact that every language undergoes change. Written English, at least in Britain and the USA, is largely codified and standardised; the English we speak and write today – Contemporary Modern English – is a non-permanent stage within this ongoing change. It can be argued that use by a larger number of people, the need to communicate beyond geographical and language borders, codification of the written language and so forth have all slowed the speed of change. Indeed, it might be seen as relevant that what we call "Modern English" coincides with the reign of Henry VIII, and the greater centralisation of power within a nation state and the community of English speakers. Though there were far fewer speakers of this Northern Germanic language during that time, the strong reliance on oral transmission rather than the written record and the variations due to history, geography and circumstances can be seen as reasons for wider divergence.

Tyler and Evans, with reference to the OED, say that "owing to the influence of Latin and then French in medieval England, *of* was employed in translation in place of the French *de*, further cementing the displacement of the native genitive case marker" (2003: 209). Brorström points out that "... in the transition period between Middle and Modern English, the prep[osition] *of* was used in a large number of constructions different from (normal) present-day usage" (1965: 66). He highlights that today we tend to use words like *at*, *about*, *for*, *in* and others, where *of* had been used in 15th-century correspondence.

As for *to* as the *to*-Infinitive, Fischer (2000: 153) discusses the "widespread belief that the development of the original preposition *to* before the infinitive into a meaningless infinitival marker follows a well-known grammaticalisation channel". Tracing the development of usage from Old English (OE) to Middle English (ME), she finds that, amongst other things, the *to*-Infinitive starts being found after prepositions other than *for*; with split infinitives being attested in the 14th century. Fischer finds that, unlike Dutch *te*, English *to*-Infinitive is more purposeful and carries "inherent future meaning". With reference to Traugott (1993) and Plank (1984), she says that

> there has been formation of new modal auxiliaries in English consisting of a matrix verb that has semantically inherent future reference and the *to* element that belongs to the infinitive following the verb, as in *to be going to/gotta, to want to/wanna, to have (got) to/gotta* etc. (Fischer, 2000: 161)

Fischer (2000: 163) concludes that "grammaticalisation need not be a process driven purely semantically"; instead a number of factors, over time and specific to English, forced a grammaticalisation of the item. Hence *to* as an infinitive is formed "by universal iconic constraints or patterns such as persistence and isomorphism".

Similarly, we can see that *too* and *to* are not simply (present-day) homonyms, they are also linked semantically: "*Too* entered ModE as an emphatic form of *to*, meaning 'in addition to'" (Hook, 1975: 89), which is a poignant demonstration how a sounding of one particular word was mirrored in its (still retained) spelling. This, briefly, gives an impression of how words change their collocations and meanings through usage. This is as true for the so-called "grammatical" (as opposed to "lexical") words like *of* and *to* as it is for items where we have seen clear changes of meaning, word-field and collocational neighbours – *wireless* and *gay* come to mind.[1]

2.2   The historical use of prepositions, with a focus on OF and TO

There is a huge apparatus on the development and usage of prepositions in the English language. It is not seen as the role of this book to review the literature concerned in detail.[2] Instead, the aim is to give an impression of some of the discussions and, it is felt, incongruences of the research that is presented without recourse to corpora.

Contemporary Modern English only has minimal inflection which, in turn, means that semantic and tempus nuances need to be expressed through lexical variation. Given the historical development from a highly inflected prototypical Germanic language to a Saxon-Nordic-Norman creole that is the basis of the present-day variant, it is unsurprising that previously minor elements have become crucial for the smooth operation of the present form:

> ... prepositions of a thousand years ago often have to be translated with different prepositions today. Prepositions became increasingly important when inflections were reduced, because what had formerly been shown by case endings often required prepositions. Instead of adding a large number of new prepositions, however, the language simply tended to employ each existing preposition for more and more meanings, and sometimes meanings shifted from one to another. (Hook, 1975: 164)

This would explain the rather large number of possible uses and meanings *of* and *to* have, as described in Hill (1968), who, in the Palmer-Hornby tradition of providing a pattern grammar (revived with corpus data by Hunston and Francis), listed, in 1968, 63 usage patterns and meanings for the item *of;* in the same volume, 96 usage patterns and meanings were listed for the item *to*.[3] Denison (1985) focussed on the surface-structure of clauses that use prepositions. Looking at OE texts, of which there are a finite number available, he finds support for his claim that the "prepositional passive" (e.g. (a) *It was set fire to* (b) *She won't be made a fool of*) is not recorded in OE. At the same time, any use of such terms as *of* and *to* etc. can be seen in ME first. Denison presents evidence that this form was not used (nor, I imagine, would it be deemed grammatical) before the thirteenth century. He gives a detailed review of how the use of prepositions has evolved. Denison takes care to point out that not all the changes seen over the last thousand years can be explained: "As far as word order is concerned, there remains the problem of explaining the

existence of prepositional passives with P-V order, an apparent reversion
to a surface word order associated with the older underlying word order"
(Denison, 1985: 203). Brorström also makes extensive use of existing
texts, comparing early Modern English texts with present-day usage.
He concurs with Denison: "it is rarely possible to explain why a certain
preposition in a certain phrase gradually comes to be dropped or ousted
by another preposition or other prepositions" (1965: 66). He merely
observes that "in earlier Modern English, the prepositions *at, for* and *of*
seem seldom or never have been interchangeable with *about*" (1963: 323).
One interpretation he gives, however, is that

> There can hardly be any doubt that the large reduction of *of*-
> constructions in later [Modern English] is, to some extent at least,
> connected with the *polysemantic* character of the preposition *of.* In
> many contexts, a more 'expressive' preposition (e.g. *about, by, from*)
> seems to have been preferred to the often ambiguous *of* for reasons
> of clarity. (Brorström, 1965: 66)

The concept of polysemy continues to be discussed, with more recent
publications by Tyler and Evans (2003), or Van der Gucht, Willems and
De Cuypere (2006). Like Brorström and Denison, yet unlike a great many
other grammarians, Lindkvist can claim that his findings are based on
"2600 excerpts made from British and American literature" (1972: 11). He
complained that "A common defect in some earlier treatment of English
prepositional usage seems to have consisted in employing too wide a
definition of categories and too general a description of usage" (1972: 10).
Although this may make procedures easier, details are easily being dis-
pensed with. Unfortunately, the opposite is also true: Where the focus is
on minute detail, there is blindness to the wider structure, and to broad
patterns. Furthermore, it then becomes a contentious issue of what to call
any of these short, highly frequent items and how to define them:

> Depending on their conceptual frameworks, ... scholars have used
> a bewildering variety of names to classify [these forms] including
> the following: preposition, particle, adverb, locative auxiliary, sta-
> tive predicate, predicator, modifier, preverb, adprep, verbal adjunct,
> aspect marker, satellite, intransitive preposition, transitive adverb.
> (O'Dowd, 1998: 8)

This is described in even more detail (and by displaying a certain,
sarcastic, tone) by Jacobsson (1977). These different names refer to

the different functions that grammarians have found for items like *of* and *to*.

As early as 1938, Harold Palmer's *Grammar of English Words* divides the use of the item *to* into two major categories: (1) *prepositions* and (2) *particles marking the infinitive* (1938 [1961]: 227f.).[4] Heaton (1965: 10) says that "adverbial particles are special kinds of adverbs, most of which have the same form and meaning as their corresponding prepositions. Many are, in fact, prepositions used as adverbs." Jacobsson (1977: 42) goes further in making distinctions: "*To*, for example, which is normally used as a preposition only, is semi-adverbial in *What's this world coming to? ...* and fully adverbial in *Push the door to.*" Guéron (1990: 153), quoting Edmonds, describes a particle as "an intransitive preposition". However, given that he looks at only a small selection of so-called common prepositions (about, out, to, up) with only a few chosen examples, one can doubt whether there is any value in generalising his findings. Cappelle (2004: 25) does, indeed, dispute Guéron's claim and shows in his work "that directional particles are different from directional prepositional phrases". Furthermore, there are claims that some of these items, like *of*, can appear in one function, but not another:

> Certain prepositions (of, at, from) never function as particles, while certain adverbial particles (for example, away), never function as prepositions. Only a certain subset of forms ... seems to have dual membership in both categories. (O'Dowd, 1998: 6)

Like O'Dowd, Jacobsson, appears to be critical towards the idea of categorising these items. Nevertheless, he contradicts O'Dowd categorically: "Some particles are always transitive; this group includes the 'pure' prepositions *at, from*, and *of*" (Jacobsson, 1977: 41). Frank Lebas (2002: 63), discussing the preposition *in*, claims that "It is possibility of interpreting their semantic material in a special way that motivates the intuition of a special category for prepositions".

So who is right – and when? All of this highlights the key issue of this book: "why should the same lexical form ... have membership in two different lexical categories?" (O'Dowd, 1998: 4).

It appears that, indeed, both *of* and *to* can be found to have simultaneous membership in even more than two lexical categories: Quirk et al. (1985: 653) give examples where "the distinction between preposition and adverb is not quite clear" and refer to uses like "close to" and "near to". Similarly, Biber et al. (1999: 76), in their corpus-based Longman Grammar, highlight that "there can be an overlap between prepositions and other word classes". This, to me, triggers the doubt of whether it is at all useful to employ such categories to reflect the fact that "today's unabridged dictionaries may distinguish literally scores of different meanings or shades of meaning of any of the most common prepositions, such as *of*" (Hook, 1975: 164).

This short overview shows that there are clear deficiencies in the treatment of the types of words usually referred to as "prepositions" – *of* and *to* included. There is little agreement concerning what these items do and how to class them. Confusion is even stronger when the same token can be ascribed to a number of categories. A further contentious issue is created where scholars use made-up material, allow intuition as a guide or focus on a rarely used form found in a literary text. Forgoing the chance of looking at percipient use, this allows them to support any type of view that fits their particular theory advanced by them. Jacobsson's idiosyncratic view on the issue seems to highlight these problems:

> At the outset of our discussion some doubt was cast on the value of a grammar in which everything is either this or that. The conclusion to be drawn from this study, and many others, is that such a grammar cannot cope with the facts of English or, for that matter, any other natural language. It may be objected that grammarians have known this all along and that there is no point in flogging a dead horse. The fact is, however, that the horse is far from being dead. (Jacobsson, 1977: 60)

While more recent research by semanticists and cognitive linguists (see 2.3 below) appears to indicate more awareness of these issues, there is still an overwhelming tendency to look at specific cases or uses, rather than trying to undertake a deeper investigation of the surface-structure or looking at how far these highly frequent items can be seen to form part of characteristic formulaic patterns.

2.3   OF and TO empirical and corpus-based descriptions

In this section, the discussion of literature will come in two distinct parts. Firstly, investigations on the two items undertaken by (mostly) researchers interested in cognitive, pragmatic and semantic properties will be looked at. In the second half, the focus will be on corpus-led research, starting with initial findings presented by Sinclair et al. in the OSTI report back in 1970.

2.3.1   Early issues with non-empirical data

Lindkvist (1976) describes that he assembled evidence for his work, which amounted to 50 000 items of the post-1945 period of British and American Literature. He first published on this subject in 1950, and his, Brorström's, Hill's and Palmer's books are all based on data painstakingly assembled by hand. There is no indication by the authors of how long (in modern parlance: how many man-hours) it had taken them to collect their material.

He is one of the early critics of (1960s) dictionaries, saying that "the prepositional construction of certain adjectives and verbs is rather arbitrarily dealt with in dictionaries" (Lindkvist, 1976: 322). As an example, *warn about* is more frequent than *warn of* or *warn against*. Likewise "the verbs *inform* and *remind* are construed solely with *of* [judging from the dictionaries]. This may be true of the 19th Century but definitely not of English today" (ibid.: 323). Similarly, Bybee (2003) writes about historical change and how the *repetition effect* brought about grammaticalisation of forms.

Being able to match, replicate, test and compare data, and then go well beyond in a matter of weeks with present-day corpus methods, can rightly be called progress. Yet we must not fail to acknowledge that quantitative, evidence-based language investigations existed long before the advent of computer-readable corpora. The big shift, however, lies in the analysis of the figures computed.

2.3.2   Corpus-based investigations

Baker (2011) calls the preposition *to* a *lockword* – "a word which may change in its meaning or context of usage when we compare a set of diachronic corpora together, yet appears to be relatively static in terms of frequency". Why this is not the case for *of* has been discussed in 2.2. This book is concerned with the *formulaicity* of language-in-use. I refer the reader to Wray and Perkins (2000), who have described the previous publications on this issue. Proportional frequencies, number-based probabilities and statistical tests are being applied in order to trace the patterns of occurrence, rather than merely describing the patterns found. Snider (2010) undertook an in-depth investigation into the occurrence patterns for the items *at* and *to* as prepositions. In his research, he highlights how far their usage indicate "participatory or non-participatory goals" and points out that only *at* is employed where non-spatial non-participatory goals are indicated. *To*, however, appears for spatial, participatory goals only in rare cases.

Looking at preposition placement, Thomas Hoffmann (2011: 278) claims that "even the in-depth corpus and experimental studies presented in [Hoffmann, 2011] were not able to exhaustively cover all preposition placement phenomena. Furthermore, individual speakers will obviously have entrenched different constructions to different degrees."[5] Nevertheless, Hoffmann's and other research data reveal a pattern that, beyond personal idiosyncrasies, points to a high degree of formulaicity (cf. Wray, 2002) of multi-word-units. One key set of data on the structural behaviour of *of* compared to *to* has been already provided by O'Keeffe et al. in 2007 (cf. pp. 65ff.): the authors provide lists of the 20 most frequent two-, three-, four-, five- and six-word clusters in the five-million-word CANCODE corpus. Going through this data, Pace-Sigge (2013: 191) highlights that "both OF and TO are prominently used words. However: OF appears the more frequent the longer the cluster [is, whereas] TO usage decreases in frequency the longer the cluster [is. We can therefore assume that] TO appears to prefer occurrence in short chunks of English."

Similarly, Biber (2000) indicates that the item *to* should be seen as part of a set of words, rather than looked at as single, free-standing entity. This is strongly underlined by Sebastian Hoffmann's (2005) work on prepositions, as seen in Table 2.1. What is shown here are those complex prepositions occurring with high frequency in the BNC. Given that

Table 2.1 The most frequent complex prepositions in the BNC: OF and TO

COMPLEX PREPOSITION – TO –	N IN BNC	COMPLEX PREPOSITION – TO –	N IN BNC
IN TERMS OF	10 060	IN RELATION TO	4 668
IN FRONT OF	6 118	IN ADDITION TO	3 426
IN FAVOUR OF	3 528	IN RESPONSE TO	2 004
IN RESPECT OF	2 932	WITH REGARD TO	1 656
ON BEHALF OF	2 713	WITH RESPECT TO	1 330
IN SPITE OF	2 703	IN CONTRAST TO	877
ON TOP OF	2 516	BY REFERENCE TO	660
IN CHARGE OF	1 630		
BY MEANS OF	1 617		
IN VIEW OF	1 507		
BY WAY OF	1 419		
IN SUPPORT OF	1 083		
IN SEARCH OF	980		
BY VIRTUE OF	953		
IN EXCESS OF	835		
IN PLACE OF	775		
IN NEED OF	774		

Source: Adapted from Hoffmann, 2005: 23.

Hoffmann's list gives the 30 most frequent complex prepositions in the BNC, it is fairly clear that *of* appears in the majority of the phrases listed here, followed by *to*. Seventeen of the 30 include *of*, seven include *to*. Far less frequent are complex prepositions including *with* and *for*. This is in line with the findings given above. Such data from various sources adds relevance to focus on these two target items and we shall see, in the course of this research, if and in what way the corpora used for this investigation match or diverge from this list, which is based on a single, general collection of texts.

Furthermore, it shall be investigated whether it is the prepositional use that is dominant for these two items or whether a more multifaceted picture (as, say, O'Dowd indicated) appears.

Sinclair et al. (1970 [2004]: 157) highlight the fact that *of* collocates with *kind, type, sort, one, some* and *most*, which "carry the meaning of classification" and are deemed as "ambiguous, and we may expect that collocation with *of* will be a good indication of this particular meaning" (ibid.). Fittingly, the preceding nouns of this early corpus study were identified as: *part, amount, number*.

Sinclair (1991: 83) gives a further description of the usage pattern for *of*: "The selection of *of* is governed by the choice of verb, and *of* is again sensitive to what precedes more than to what follows." When we look at a highly frequent *of* cluster, Sebastian Hoffmann (2005: 167) highlights the stable use, implying a high degree of fixed nesting (cf. Hoey, 2005 and Arnon & Snider, 2010) for *of*: "In 96 per cent of all cases, language users leave the complex prepositional phrase *'in terms of'* intact ... It can be assumed that the units as a whole are stored in the user's mind and are recalled subconsciously."

This mirrors claims made by Hoey (2005: 13) as part of his Lexical Priming Theory, namely that "every word [or *sets of words* are] is *primed* to occur with particular other words and in particular grammatical and semantic sets". With regards to the usage patterns of *to* discovered in their investigation, Sinclair et al. describe the following:

> The most noticeable feature is that the prepositional aspect of *to* is overshadowed by its use preceding a non-finite verb. In the scientific text, there are no significant noun or pronoun collocates at position N+1, and in the conversation, the total number of occurrences with *America, her, me* and *the* [sic] at N+1 is only 62, whereas there are 218 collocations with verbs. (Sinclair et al., 1970 [2004]: 157)

Biber (2000: 297) looked at the genre-specific distribution of *to* clauses. He describes *that* use as common in conversation, while not very common in academic prose. *To* clauses, however, are moderately common in both. Biber reasons that only a few verbs control both types of clause. The verbs that control *to* clauses have "different lexical associations" (ibid.) to those found with *that*. Thus, the agreement of verb and *to* construction can be deemed as genre specific. According to Biber (2000: 298), the most common verbs controlling a *to* clause in conversations are *want, try* and *like*. Within academic prose, prominent verb-collocates are *like, tend* and *appear*. In Chapter 3, the structural use in public speeches and academic presentations will be compared to see whether they are similar or diverge.

Looking at the pragmatic aspects of *to*-usage, de Smet and Cuykens point out that

> Just like *used to* and *tend to*, 'like/ love + to-infinitive' involve a to-infinitive form, whose to element tends to coalesce with the preceding verb. Just like the auxiliaries *would* and *will*, which can also be used to express habit, 'like/love + to-infinitive' have volitional uses that are historically prior to their other uses. (de Smet and Cuykens, 2005: 31)

This links to Sinclair's and Biber's findings that *to* appears to prefer verbs as collocates. The authors look at a less formal use – *like/love to* – and show that the construction mirrors the more formal *tend to* (whereas *used to* is fairly common in spoken British English – cf. Pace-Sigge, 2013). Having looked at the historical development of the construction, de Smet and Cuykens found evidence of *pragmatic strengthening* in their corpora, something that "is typically—if not exclusively—associated with ongoing processes of *grammaticalization*" (de Smet and Cuykens, 2005: 24).

2.3.3 The idea of *multi-word-units*

While there are other names for *multi-word-units* (MWUs) – for example *compound words, extended units of meaning, lexical bundles, multi-word expression, n-grams* – I shall retain the wording chosen by John Sinclair throughout. Although MWUs can be idiomatic, indeed, can be phrase-like (cf. Cheng, 2012: 110), they must not be confused with figures of speech. Sinclair developed this idea in the 1990s and, where such MWUs form meaningful entities, he described them as *lexical items* – see Sinclair, [1996] 2004 and Sinclair, [1998] 2004. Initially, Sinclair investigated the concepts of the *open-choice principle* and the *idiom principle*, and the focus was on lexical words like eye (*naked eye*), brook (*brook no interference*), etc. – see Sinclair [1996] 2004. However, in his conclusion he widens the scope: "One possibility is a type of item based on a grammatical core rather than a lexical one. 'Collocational frameworks' were proposed by Renouf and Sinclair (1991) .... In these the core is one or more frequent grammatical words, usually discontinuous, like *the ... of'* (Sinclair, [1996] 2004: 39). Such *discontinuous collocational frameworks* have been found in the course of my research and will be reviewed in Chapters 3 and 6. Based on this earlier research, Sinclair moved on and says that

> Current models [of language] do not overcome the problem of how a finite and rigidly formalized lexicon can account satisfactorily for the apparently endlessly variable meanings that arise from the combination of word choices in texts. I have suggested that the word is not the best starting point for a description of meaning, because meaning arises from a word in particular combinations. (Sinclair, [1998] 2004: 147f.)

One result of this was the *Linear Unit Grammar* (Sinclair and Mauranen, 2006), where evidence from both written and spoken language are considered. At the outset, the authors describe a set of questions they address, namely what role chunks play in the analysis of texts and, furthermore, what range of texts types can be chunked. The answer to the former was given as a "central and pivotal role in the early stages"; as for the latter, it was confirmed that any text typed can be chunked (cf. Sinclair and Mauranen, 2006: xvi). The reason for this is the fact described by Sinclair and Mauranen towards the end of their book. They note that "PUBs [Provisional Unit Boundaries] often separate prepositional phrases from the preceding text, thus distinguishing them from the same words counting as adverbs" (ibid.: 146). Furthermore, they give the example of the three-word phrase *a number of*:

> a common three-word phrase in English, well known to any fluent speaker [which represents a case of a] mismatch between the chunking of a particular text and the provisions of a general grammar. [Therefore] the analyst is alerted to the likelihood that the prepositions are components of lexical structures that take precedence over grammatical ones. (ibid.: 147)

The approach thus taken – looking at chunks to provide a basis for further analysis of text and to consider a variety of text types and not only a single genre – is echoed throughout this book.

When *to* usage is observed not as a historical development but as part of the process of language acquisition, it can be seen that children understand, process and produce utterances with *to* as part of multi-word-units. Rice (1999) undertook a corpus analysis of 32 English-speaking children's first usages of the prepositions *to* and *for*. The insights gained are quoted in full below:

> Although *to* and *for* are both considered allatives in English, there are major differences in the kinds of particular semantic relations they are associated with, as well as differences in their specific syntactic contexts, so it should not be surprising that there are differences in when and how they are acquired. There are points of overlap, but these bear less on the cognitive expectations than on other factors. Cognitive simplicity or other purely semantic factors like concreteness of reference or transparency contribute little to early mastery of a sense type. Instead, (1) frequency of exposure, (2) co-occurrence preferences, or (3) experiential utility seem to be responsible for the sequence of emergence of sense types. Moreover, (4) abstract usages of both prepositions first emerge in stock expressions and other collocations with specific lexical items. (Rice, 1999: 275)

The issue raised as item (4) highlights a point that is important for this study, namely how the short, highly frequent items "emerge in stock expressions and other collocations with specific lexical items" (ibid.). Points (1) and (2) appear to describe the same phenomenon that Hoey (2005) refers to as *lexical priming*. Hoey describes the concept of *priming* as used by him as follows:

> We can only account for collocation if we assume that every word is mentally **primed** [sic] for collocational use. As a word is acquired through encounters with it in speech and writing, it becomes cumulatively loaded with the contexts and co-texts in which it is encountered, and our knowledge of it includes the fact that it co-occurs with certain other words in certain kinds of context. (Hoey, 2005: 8)

Hoey expands the concept to include both *words* and *sets of words* and, moreover, sees this claim to be valid for colligational structures of items as well. Hence, "the same applies to word sequences built out of these words; these, too become loaded with the contexts and co-texts in which they occur" (ibid.). Hoey, with reference to Krishnamurty, calls this particular property *nesting*. It is stressed that *priming* is neither a fixed nor an exclusive characteristic of (any) language. Primings drift, they change as language usage shifts, as one learns a new language, etc.

primings reflect one's personal grammar – for example, a phonologist will have a different set of primings mentally available than a neuro-surgeon. Primings are, in concert with general language acquisition, first encountered by way of receptive primings, and feature as productive primings only at a later stage.[6]

Taking into account the approaches to language given by Sinclair and Hoey in particular, this book aims to provide a corpus-driven approach to the usage of the items *of* and *to*. By this I mean to present their occurrence patterns in the way that Francis (cf. Francis, 1993: 2ff.) described the Collins COBUILD grammar project. Firstly, I shall provide only real data: secondly, the aim is to compile, as far as possible, a *non-contrastive account* of *of* and *to*, showing how each item is used, and in which constructions it appears in its own right. Thirdly, the defining feature of the research of this book is that it is *data-driven*: the data of each corpus comes first. The final, fourth characteristic is that the *lexical approach* will be given preference over any *grammatical approach*.

This investigation will look into how far the earlier observations can be said to hold true for the genre of public presentations and whether *to* is, or is not, a less interesting item to study. After looking at the data from different text forms in Chapters 3–5, we shall investigate the validity of the prior research presented in Chapter 6.

3
OF and TO Usage in Fiction

3.1 Introduction

For this chapter, the focus will be on the occurrence patterns found in *fiction text* sub-corpora. Three such collections will be used to investigate *of* and *to* usage.

On the whole, the material is fairly evenly split into a corpus that is based on a broad selection of material – namely, the BNC (Written) Fiction sub-corpus (BNC-F hereafter) which gives samples of around 40,000 words of 432 texts published between 1960 and 1993.[1] This will be a broad representative of contemporary use of words in British fiction. The other half of the research material is based on complete texts from the period of 1800–1913. The main component here is British 19th-century fiction (19C hereafter) sub-corpus (Patterson, 2014). This consists of 100 full-text novels, designed in a way that it contains no more than two separate novels per writer. The third corpus is the far smaller in scope and size as its main function is to provide a US comparator. This is the small ANC-F[2] Fiction sub-corpus (ANC-F hereafter) which contains the full texts of 11 novels published between 1901 and 1913 from the publisher Hargraves and Eggan. This chapter will also be the only one in the book to make use of US-American material.

All the material together has been researched for evidence of consistent repeat usage of the same or similar clusters: furthermore, each corpus has been analysed separately so to be compared to the other sub-corpora. See Table 3.1 for the make-up of the material used. This shows that the two target items are amongst the most frequent words in all three corpora.

Table 3.1   Sub-corpora used

Sub-corpus	Files (no.)	Tokens	OF	OF %	TO	TO %
BNC-F	432	15,686,705	336,291	2.14	415,828	2.65
19C	100	12,716,669	369,172	2.90	356,042	2.80
ANC-F	11	837,647	22,584	2.69	22,481	2.68
3 Sources (3S) Total	543	30,518,650	728,047	2.49	794,351	2.60

The interest in the items *of* and *to* here is threefold:

1. Does the usage pattern of the items reveal content, pragmatic and stylistic structures which are particular to fictional texts?
2. Is there an inherent stability of how the items occur? In other words, are fixed chunks (or clusters) a salient feature specific to the genre?
3. Can evidence be produced that the usage of the two items is highly frequent beyond their genre? In other words, do *of* and *to* appear in specific multi-word units (MWUs) that are independent of their pragmatic use?

The last point will be discussed, in detail, at the end of this book. Points one and two will require a look at whether collocational, colligational and nesting patterns which are found in the three sub-corpora.

Written text, particularly texts of the genre imaginary writing, have one very specific feature. Unlike online speech production (see Chapter 5), where a speaker can produce and respond directly to the discourse partner/s and unlike public speaking (see Chapter 4), which is produced with a specific target audience in mind, any writer writes "into the dark" – he or she cannot reliably predict who the readership will be. Neither can a writer of fictional text include extra-lingual information directly. As a result, two features emerge: firstly, the writer has to try to be (beyond the style and the particular sub-genre) as unambiguous as possible: the reader cannot check things that are unclear. Secondly, the writer will have to include descriptions that go beyond simply talking, as one would find in speech-based texts. The tone of voice and extra-lingual features, amongst others, should be described. Consequently, one could expect that the sets including *of* and *to* in fiction texts to be different to the text types discussed later.

This chapter moves from the general to the specific. First there will be a broad overview on how *of* and *to* occur, followed by a look at how the items are used in bigrams. Moving on, the most consistently meaningful clusters, trigrams and longer chunks will be looked at. Finally, any characteristic uses within the three sources will be highlighted.

3.2 Salient features across the sub-corpora

In this section, I shall look at the bigrams, trigrams and longer clusters across the three sub-corpora (to be referred to as 3S). Table 3.1 shows that *of* and *to* occur with roughly similar frequencies, though in BNC-F, *of* is less frequent than *to*. The aim here is to highlight features that are less-than-expected. Consequently, we could discount the most frequent bigrams for *of* and *to*: *of the* and *to the*. In 3S, *the* is by far the most frequent item (it occurs 1,541,023 times – 5.05 per cent of all words). This is nearly twice as frequent as the second-most frequent item (*and* – 2.82 per cent of all words). Yet, as Table 3.2 shows, even just the comparison of the most frequent clusters for *of* and *to* indicate some structural difference as well as convergences between the items. The table gives percentages as a fraction of all uses of *of* and *to* respectively.

Table 3.2 gives some interesting insights. Though the base figures are the same, *of the* appears in more than one-fifth of all uses of *of*, whereas *to the* is found used in every tenth occurrence of *to*. The dominant use of *of the* is also highlighted by the fact that this is by far the most frequent cluster, the second-ranked *of a* appearing nearly five times (4.7) less often. This is in stark contrast to the bigrams *to the* and *to be*. This, already, hints at the separate grammatical constructions, or the colligations, in which these two items seem to appear.

Before I shall look at the items individually, one collocate has to be noted: the personal pronoun *her*. *Of her* is ranked fourth most frequent bigram (3.48 per cent) while *to her* is ranked third (though with a lower relative frequency – 2.64 per cent of all *to* uses). *Her* and *she* are indeed fairly frequent – appearing in 1.07 per cent of all words.[3] In these bigrams, *of his* is clearly more frequent than *of her*; on the other hand, *to her* occurs 20,987 times, while *to him* occurs only 13,157 times

Table 3.2 3S most frequent bigrams for OF and TO

Rank	3S 2w OF	N	%	3S 2w TO	N	%
1	OF THE	165,163	22.69	TO THE	80,579	10.14
2	OF A	34,474	4.74	TO BE	52,463	6.60
3	OF HIS	32,662	4.49	TO HER	20,987	2.64
4	OF HER	25,179	3.48	TO DO	15,910	2.01
5	OUT OF	24,575	3.38	TO SEE	15,533	1.96

(1.66 per cent – ranked 11th). This seems already to indicate a certain pragmatic function that is thus displayed. We shall look at this in more detail later.

3.2.1   OF bigrams in fiction texts

Even just a cursory look at the *of* bigrams is rather revealing. Table 3.3 shows *of* and *determiner* within the 20 most frequent bigrams. *Of the* is clearly dominant – being not just five times as frequent at the second – ranked *of a*. Also, *the* is just over twice as frequent, compared to *a*: 5.05 per cent compared to 2.12 per cent.[4] Other determiners, in particular pronouns, are highly preferred, appearing in seven of the 20 most frequent bigrams. "Determiners indicate the type of reference made by the noun phrase (e.g. definite, indefinite, possessive)" (Carter and McCarthy, 2006: 322). This usage can be seen as a fairly salient characteristic of *of* in fiction texts.

Looking at Table 3.4, *of* seems to fulfil a rather different function. Two bigrams, *of course* and *sort of* seem, indeed, not to point at a possessor – they seem to be (vague) discourse markers, indicators of spoken language. Other uses shown in Table 3.4 are directional (*out of*); related to a place or process (*end of, part of, side of, of all*), and referring to a part or fraction (*one of, part of, of all, some of*). This, in itself, seems to point to at least two, if not four different functions for the item *of* in its most frequently occurring bigrams.

Table 3.4 highlights one other issue which has to do with frequencies and ranking. The first three bigrams – *out of, one of, of course* – are ranked in consecutive order and appear with higher frequencies than the rest of the list which are far closer in frequency. To be more precise, *out of,* indicating directionality, is, overall, the second-most preferred *of* use here, after the most frequent determiner bigrams. In this light, *of course,*

Table 3.3   3S – 20 most frequent 2w determiners for OF

R	3S 2w OF	N	% tot	% OF
1	OF THE	165,163	0.54	22.690
2	OF A	34,474	0.11	4.740
3	OF HIS	32,662	0.11	4.486
4	OF HER	25,179	0.08	3.475
8	OF MY	11,283	0.04	1.550
9	OF THEM	10,954	0.04	1.510
10	OF THAT	7,599	0.02	1.040
11	OF THIS	7,510	0.02	1.033
12	OF THEIR	7,381	0.02	1.015
17	OF HIM	5,728	0.02	0.767
20	OF AN	5,215	0.02	0.716

Table 3.4 3S – 20 most frequent 2w non-determiners for OF

R	3S 2w OF	N	% tot	% OF
5	OUT OF	24,575	0.08	3.375
6	ONE OF	19,521	0.06	2.681
7	OF COURSE	13,304	0.04	1.827
13	SORT OF	7,136	0.02	0.980
14	PART OF	6,350	0.02	0.872
15	OF ALL	6,108	0.02	0.831
16	END OF	5,775	0.02	0.790
18	SIDE OF	5,415	0.02	0.744
19	SOME OF	5,342	0.02	0.733

the discourse marker, can also be classed as a relevant form. If, however, we look at types, we can see that reference to a part or fraction (i.e. *one of, part of, of all*, etc.) forms the largest group of *of* bigrams apart from the determiners. Such "post-modifying *of*-phrases" are being described as having the use of "partition" in Quirk et al. (1985: 703).

When looking at trigrams and longer clusters later, it will be seen in how far these bigrams form relevant parts of longer chunk in the texts.

3.2.2 TO bigrams in fiction texts

Bigrams for *to* seem to split into two main categories. There are the group of *to* and *determiner*, mirroring what we found in section 3.2.1. The other group are *to* and *Infinitive* which split into the second category – general verbs (with *to* and *have*-lemma as the dominant subgroup). There is a minor third category referring to directionality: *back to* and also some uses of *going to*.

Table 3.5 indicates that, amongst the 20 most frequent bigrams, *to* and determiner use is not as prominent as we find it with *of*. For example, *to the* is proportionally half as frequent as *of the*. As a clear preference we find *to* appearing as part of an infinitive construction, and, within these, prominently with the prime verbs *be, do* and *have*. This is shown in Table 3.6. Three other things are notable – the strong use of *to be*, which is unexpectedly frequent, compared to *to the*. *The* appears as 5.05 per cent of all words in this collection of fiction texts. This means it is ten times more frequent than *be* (0.52 per cent). *Be* is therefore not much more frequent as *have* (0.47 per cent) either, something that the bigrams seem not to reflect. In fact, *be* occurs 157,493 times, *have* 143,243 times. This means, *to be* is used in about one-third of all uses of *be*, yet *to have* and *have to* combined make up less than one-fifth (17.0 per cent) of *have* occurrences. Also, *to do* is fairly prominent, given that *do* appears only 69,983 times in the 3S corpus. *To do*, consequently,

Table 3.5   3S – **20** most frequent 2w determiners for TO

R	3S 2w TO	N	% tot	% TO
1	TO THE	80,579	0.26	10.14
3	TO HER	20,987	0.07	2.64
6	TO ME	14,964	0.05	1.88
7	TO HIS	14,612	0.05	1.84
10	TO A	13,760	0.05	1.73
11	TO HIM	13,157	0.04	1.66
19	HIM TO	9,873	0.03	1.24

Table 3.6   3S – **20** most frequent 2w TO and *verb-Inf*

R	3S 2w TO	N	% tot	% TO
2	TO BE	52,463	0.17	6.60
4	TO DO	15,910	0.05	2.01
5	TO SEE	15,533	0.05	1.96
9	TO HAVE	13,983	0.05	1.76
10	TO GO	11,555	0.04	1.45
11	TO GET	10,957	0.04	1.38
12	TO MAKE	10,928	0.04	1.37
13	HAVE TO	10,475	0.03	1.31
14	WANT TO	10,262	0.03	1.29
16	TO SAY	9,926	0.03	1.25
18	HAD TO	9,377	0.03	1.22

represents 22.7 per cent of all occurrences of *do*. It must also be noted that the majority of bigrams are *to*-Infinitive, yet *have to, had to* and *want to* form the majority of such constructions.

This seems to indicate a specific use, which ought to be realised where *to be* is part of larger chunks.

It can be seen though that certain verbs are strongly prominent in fiction texts, in particular, *see, make, want* and *say*. These items seem to point to pragmatic functions within this type of texts.

Table 3.7 carries the title "non-determined" largely because of the bigram *going to*. This could indeed be a **verb-INF+*to***, a reference to future action, a discourse marker or reference to direction. Which of these are predominant can only be determined through the look at larger clusters. *Back to*, on the other hand, is neither *to*+determiner nor *to* with the infinitive, it would be seen as indicating directionality: functioning as a preposition.

Table 3.7 3S – 2w TO non-determined

R	3S 2w TO	Freq.	% tot	% TO
8	GOING TO	14,153	0.05	1.78
17	BACK TO	10,129	0.03	1.27

Table 3.8 3S OF bigrams that freely collocate

R	3S 2w OF	% OF
2	OF A	4.740
3	OF HIS	4.486
4	OF HER	3.475
8	OF MY	1.550
9	OF THEM	1.510
10	OF THAT	1.040
11	OF THIS	1.033
12	OF THEIR	1.015
17	OF HIM	0.767
20	OF AN	0.716
26	OF YOUR	0.705

3.2.3 Trigrams and clusters

Remaining with the 3S corpus data, I shall look and see how the bigrams described above fit into longer clusters of words or whether *of* and *to* have clusters that do not necessarily incorporate the most frequent bigrams. The nature of these longer chunks means that, away from a purely collocational investigation, colligations and pragmatic functions (the semantic associations) become more relevant.

3.2.4 OF Trigrams and clusters

We have seen that *of the* is clearly a dominant use of the item and we shall see that *of* with *the* plays a prominent role in *of* usage. Overall, moving from bigrams to longer clusters, there are two distinct categories: those bigrams that, relatively, freely collocate with a large number of other items and those that form a constituent part of longer clusters. Table 3.8 shows the former and Table 3.9 the latter.

It is interesting to see that Table 3.8 mostly mirrors Table 3.3 – it indicates the *of* and determiner collocate with a wider range of other items. *Of the*, however, possibly because it is such a predominant usage form, can be found as an integral part of a number of fixed longer chunks, as the selection shown in Table 3.9 demonstrates. The form here found extends the findings presented by Renouf and Sinclair (1991) who

Table 3.9   OF prominent 2w–4w clusters

R	3S 2w OF	% OF	R	3S 3w OF	% OF	R	3S 4w OF	% OF
1	OF THE	22.69	26	REST OF THE	0.23	3	THE REST OF THE	0.23
5	OUT OF	3.38	1	OUT OF THE	1.26	15	OUT OF THE WINDOW	0.09
6	ONE OF	2.68	2	ONE OF THE	1.26	28	IN ONE OF THE	0.07
16	END OF	0.79	3	THE END OF	0.53	1	THE END OF THE	0.27
18	SIDE OF	0.74	30	THE SIDE OF	0.22	11	THE OTHER SIDE OF	0.13

Table 3.10   OF with THE predominant usage formats

	Format	Concordance lines	Example
1)	*Of the*	165,163	out *of the* window
2)	*The X of*	217,058	*the* middle *of*
3)	*The X of the*	64,638	*the* end *of the*
4)	*The X of the X of*	2,022	*the* tombstone *of the* Countess *of* (Malfi)
5)	*The X of the X of the*	510	*the* brother *of the* Queen *of the* (English)

looked, amongst other things, at "**a + ? + of**" and "**an + ? + of**". These were named by them as *collocational frameworks*. As the *? + of* has been investigated above, this section focusses on the fact that this particular framework appears to existed in a form that can be extended where *of the* is concerned. In fact, there are large number of *of* bigrams that are highly frequent are, in fact, appearing because they appear in conjunction with *the*. It must be highlighted that the format *of X the*,[5] in sharp contrast to both *of the* and *the X of* is infrequent: it only occurs 12,675 times and the most frequent constructions are **out *of X the*** (255 concordance lines), **instead *of X the*** (188), **though *of X* the** (170), **and of X the other** (117).

By contrast, the dominant colligational formats, tying the two items in a number of ways, are shown in Table 3.10. What stands out is shown in line 2: **the X of** appears nearly one-third more often than the most frequent *of* bigram. This indicates a very interesting colligational quality of the item. Just under one third (29.8 per cent) of all uses of **the X of** (2) includes the bigram *of the* (3); while the further duplication within a complex clause, as in (4) and (5) are rare and most concordance lines seem to describe either a person or a place.

Looking at recurring clusters, **the X of** is more frequent than *of the, one of,* or *of a,* as a comparison of Table 3.11 with Table 3.12 demonstrates.

Table 3.11 THE X OF most frequent clusters

the X *of* cluster	Freq
THE X OF THE	64,638
IN THE X OF	21,178
THE X OF A	15,023
THE X OF HIS	13,369
TO THE X OF	12,148
AT THE X OF	12,128
ON THE X OF	9,688
OF THE X OF	9,410
THE X OF HER	8,879
AND THE X OF	7,886

Table 3.12 Comparison OF THE, ONE OF and OF A most frequent clusters

of the cluster	Freq	*one of* cluster	Freq	*of a* cluster	Freq
OUT OF THE	9,193	ONE OF THE	9,150	OF A MAN	1,083
ONE OF THE	9,150	ONE OF THEM	1,864	OUT OF A	811
END OF THE	3,152	WAS ONE OF	1,561	BIT OF A	560
PART OF THE	2,815	ONE OF THOSE	1,534	THAT OF A	405
SOME OF THE	2,448	ONE OF HIS	1,330	END OF A	393
OF THE HOUSE	2,390	IN ONE OF	1,061	MUCH OF A	380
OF THE ROOM	2,012	OF ONE OF	823	PART OF A	359
REST OF THE	1,690	ONE OF HER	717	OF A WOMAN	337
OF THE WORLD	1,680	ONE OF THESE	707	OF A VERY	311
OF THE DAY	1,303	TO ONE OF	636	OF A FEW	293

Table 3.11 highlights another issue. Feminist literary critics can feel vindicated, as there is a clear preference for reference to *man/him/his* compared to *woman/her*. Most of the clusters thus discussed are purely descriptive – as a reader of a novel would expect.

With reference to Table 3.12 it must be noted that *the* appears as 5.05 per cent of the whole corpus and *a* as 2.12 per cent, *one* is a far less frequent 0.30 per cent. Amongst bigrams *of a* is far more frequent than *one of*; yet amongst trigrams *one* shows far stronger attachment to the item *of*.

The first row of Table 3.12 shows that *of* with *the* combines with the other highly frequent words found to form longer clusters with *of the*, *of* with the definite article, indefinite article and numeral *one* appear to be employed for different uses. We can see, for example, that there is a strong preference for *x of the* in uses like *part of a/part of the*.

Where it is *of the x* it is specific – *of the house/world/day* – clusters with *of the* give direct indication of the place of action: rooms, houses as well as relevant frameworks: *of the day, of the world*. Another observation is that *of a* repeated trigrams are far less frequent, which is to be expected with an indefinite article. There is a certain overlap: *out of the/out of a, part of the/part of a* and *end of the/end of a* are within the top ten most frequent trigrams. As with *of the*, a post-positioned item means something more definite than when it is pre-positioned: *of a man, that of a* and *of a woman*. In direct comparison it is notable that the words and word-position used with the indefinite article are different from the definite article: *bit of a, much of a, of a very, of a few*.

The strongest contrast, however, is to be found with *one of* – which is almost exclusively followed by determiners, with other highly frequent trigrams being *one of my, one of your, one of our*. *One of a*, however, is rather less frequent (occurring only 182 times). Yet there are only few trigrams where this is incorporated, all of which fitting into discursive format: *of course I, and of course, of course he/it/you, of course not, but of course*.

Of course I occurs 1,217 times (0.16 per cent of all occurrences of *of*), all the others are occurring between 450 and 670 times, making these chunks as well as the phrase *out of the question* (278 occurrences) far less prominent examples of *of*-usage. The only other long cluster forms that employ *of* is also discursive rather than descriptive: *as a matter of fact* is ranked the 13th most frequent 5-word cluster (286 concordance lines – 0.04 per cent of all uses of *of*) and the 19th-ranked question *what do you think of* (219 occurrences), when all the other long clusters appear to refer to place or time.

Shorter clusters re-combine into longer ones. A typical example is *the rest of* (3,011 occurrences) and *of the world* (1,680). Intuitively, the resulting *the rest of the world* would not be typical of *of* usage. However, it appears within the 50 most used 5w clusters. As we shall see, its use is not restricted to works of fiction either.

Looking at the long clusters, we can find, however, the most repeated uses and the most salient semantic forms. *Of* appears in these clusters predominantly in the function of a preposition. Table 3.13 highlights this clearly – *of* in its longest, formulaic clusters tends to refer to a place: the *end/middle/centre/back/front/top/edge/other side* of. *The end of the* neatly splits into a description of place (followed by *world, street, room, road*) or time (*day, month, year*).

While the collocations and colligational structure here remain the same, it is interesting to note that in the corpus, indications of more

Table 3.13 Long OF clusters

R	OF 4w cluster	Freq.	% OF	R	OF 5w cluster	Freq.	% OF
1	THE END OF THE	1,916	0.263	1	AT THE END OF THE	875	0.120
2	AT THE END OF	1,716	0.235	2	IN THE MIDDLE OF THE	812	0.112
3	THE REST OF THE	1,684	0.231	3	THE OTHER SIDE OF THE	791	0.109
4	IN THE MIDDLE OF	1,400	0.192	4	ON THE OTHER SIDE OF	631	0.087
5	THE TOP OF THE	1,141	0.157	5	AT THE TOP OF THE	398	0.055
6	THE EDGE OF THE	1,115	0.153	6	ON THE EDGE OF THE	364	0.050
7	THE MIDDLE OF THE	1,085	0.150	7	AT THE BACK OF THE	358	0.049
8	THE BACK OF THE	1,063	0.146	8	IN THE DIRECTION OF THE	355	0.049
9	IN FRONT OF THE	985	0.135	9	AT THE BOTTOM OF THE	344	0.047
10	THE SIDE OF THE	985	0.135	10	IN THE CENTRE OF THE	322	0.044
11	THE OTHER SIDE OF	965	0.131	11	THE OTHER END OF THE	319	0.044
12	OTHER SIDE OF THE	797	0.110	12	AT THE FOOT OF THE	312	0.043

distant places (*other side of* rather than *side of; the end of* rather than *the front of*) are more frequent. Yet references to time (*at the end of the day* compared to *at the end of the month*) are more frequent for smaller units. It is also interesting to note that there are far fewer *the start/beginning of the*. In fact, the trigram *beginning of the* occurs a mere 221 times. Also notable are the two ground-level descriptions of place: *at the bottom of the* and *at the foot of the* examples that, with 5-word clusters, we find the colligational and semantic structure *at the [place] of the* with increased frequency, also *in the [place] of the* and, to a lesser degree, *on the [place] of the*. There is, indeed, a clear attraction between items like *end, middle*, etc. and *of*. With the exception of *back of*, most of such terms, roughly half of the time, are followed by *of* – to be precise, between 35.6 per cent (*side of*) and 64.8 per cent (*edge of*).[6] See Note 6 for full details how these descriptors occur. This does explain why they are so very prominent in the most frequent 4w and 5w clusters, as shown in Table 3.14.

There is no visible automatic link between this type of word and the frequency it occurs with *of*. We can see that the most frequent long *of* clusters with *back, other* and *side* are the most frequent key terms but these have the least attraction to *of* amongst long clusters. By contrast, *middle, edge, bottom, centre, rest, top,* and *end* are occurring with a strong preference in *of* 4-word clusters: they appear to have a predisposition to be located here. In particular, we find that *middle* mostly comes in a construction including *middle of* (62.8 per cent of all uses of *middle*). In comparison to all other terms *middle* stands out as being the only place-reference which, in almost half of all its uses, appears in a 4-word *of* construction. When we look at 5-word clusters, this is true for *edge, bottom* and *centre*.

While *back to* is the most frequent bigram for back (occurring in over 20 per cent of all uses), *back of* is not (5.5 per cent) it can also be used as a noun or an adjective. Though *side* is also found in different word categories, *side of* represents over one-third of its uses. For all this, there is no apparent reason why *edge* and *middle* should show a stronger preference for such a collocation and colligation than *top* or *front*. Neither can we determine why *at the top of the* occurs 398 times but *to the top of the* only 186 times, when *to* is an item four times as frequent in the corpus as *at*. One explanation for these unexpected attractions can be given through Hoey's theory of Lexical Priming (2005), stipulating that frequently repeated patterns determine one form of usage over another. Another claim can be made, namely that *of* in longer clusters, displays an extremely strong tendency (in other words, is primed to) to be part of a longer noun phrase which uses a place descriptor. This, in fact,

Table 3.14 Key place terms and occurrence in the most frequent S3 long clusters

Key term	N	4w cluster	% of keyterm	5w cluster	% of keyterm
BACK	50,003	THE BACK OF THE	2.12	AT THE BACK OF THE	0.07
OTHER	36,417	THE OTHER SIDE OF	2.60	THE OTHER SIDE OF THE	2.17
SIDE	15,208	THE SIDE OF THE	6.48	THE OTHER SIDE OF THE	5.20
END	12,430	THE END OF THE	15.40	AT THE END OF THE	7.04
FRONT	8,220	IN FRONT OF THE	11.98	IN FRONT OF THE FIRE	0.79
REST	7,682	THE REST OF THE	21.92	FOR THE REST OF THE	2.98
TOP	5,291	THE TOP OF THE	21.56	AT THE TOP OF THE	7.52
FOOT	3,898	AT THE FOOT OF	10.75	AT THE FOOT OF THE	8.00
EDGE	3,009	THE EDGE OF THE	37.10	ON THE EDGE OF THE	12.10
MIDDLE	2,958	IN THE MIDDLE OF	47.32	IN THE MIDDLE OF THE	27.45
BOTTOM	2,319	THE BOTTOM OF THE	29.02	AT THE BOTTOM OF THE	14.83
CENTRE	2,208	THE CENTRE OF THE	28.90	IN THE CENTRE OF THE	14.58

holds true even where the head-noun describes time: *at the end of the month* refers to a specific time; however, it could also be described as a specific place within the month. In a calendar, for example, time, the fourth dimension, is displayed on a two-dimensional sheet: the end of a month or a year being on the bottom right.

3.2.5   TO usage in trigrams and long clusters

Compared to *of* usage, there are a number of parallels when considering *to*, yet the differences appear even more striking.

Both *of* and *to* have *the* as the most frequent right collocate, yet this is far more pronounced in *of* usage and, as can be seen in the following, this produces the key differences. Crucially, the combination **to X the** appears in only 46,561 concordance lines – around half the frequency of the bigram *to the* – and therefore in stark contrast with the usage found for *of* with *the*. Nor does this combination appear as a constituent part of frequent longer clusters, as the most frequent, *began to X the* occurs only 692 times. When looking at the distribution of collocates in *to* trigrams, a relatively clear split into two major and a third, discourse-specific, groups can be seen. These *to* collocates clearly delineate word functions. Group 1 are the place-indicators (prepositions) which use the bigram *to the*. Group 2 are the *to*-Infinitives: these split into prime-verb use and other-verb use. Group 3 are also *to* with *verb* – yet these are specifically to indicate ability (*able to*) or intent (*going to, want to*) or subjective evaluation (*seemed to*). As Table 3.15 shows, *to the* is the colligation format for *to* in a preposition function, collocating with items like *back, on, up down* on the left-hand side. This is supplemented by the form indicating directionality (*to the door*). Broadly speaking, Cappelle's (2004: 25) claim that a "directional particle may, for reasons of terminological economy, be called 'intransitive prepositions', they have different distributional properties from directional PPs, ought not to be analyzed as reduced directional PPs, and do not always have the same meaning as formally related directional PPs" has been supported by the findings here. Indeed, "calling them a sort of prepositions blinds us to these facts". The one issue here is the sequence of those collocates, as they appear in the following order of frequency (percentages within the whole corpus): *on* (0.65 per cent), *up* (0.28 per cent), *about* (0.21 per cent), *back* (0.16 per cent), *down* (0.16 per cent), *over* (0.15 per cent).

It must also be noted that neither **from to the* nor **by to the* does appear, and there are only six lines of *out to the*. Instead, it can be seen that the four most frequent prepositions with *to* are clearly dominant in

31

Table 3.15 TO THE clustering ("prepositions" Group 1)

R	2w TO	Freq.	% TO	R	3w TO	Freq	% TO	R	5w TO cluster	Freq	% TO
1	TO THE	80,579	10.14	2	BACK TO THE	3,321	0.420	3	TO THE TOP OF THE	186	0.024
				6	ON TO THE	2,665	0.335	4	TO THE END OF THE	184	0.024
				9	UP TO THE	2,151	0.276	6	FROM ONE TO THE OTHER	172	0.022
				14	DOWN TO THE	1,801	0.227	8	TO THE EDGE OF THE	155	0.020
				54	OVER TO THE	908	0.114	11	ON THE TOP OF THE	145	0.019
				50+	ABOUT TO THE	579	0.074	12	TO THE BACK OF THE	139	0.018
				34	TO THE DOOR	1,337	0.167				
				33	WENT TO THE	1,332	0.164				

the fiction sub-corpus. In this, it becomes obvious that the word *back* is a key collocate for both *of* and *to*. Figure 3.1 demonstrates how the two most frequent *to the* clusters appear.

It is also important to note that the long *to*-Prep clusters are incorporating key place markers with *of*. They are naturally less frequent than what we have encountered in section 3.2.2. It must be noted that the most frequent long clusters incorporating *to the* refer to endpoints: *top of the, end of the*. There is no reference to the middle.

Table 3.16 shows that *to*-Infinitive constructions are pervasive for *to* constructions. They appear in the majority of the highly frequent bigrams and trigrams. Furthermore, dominant use of the prime verbs – be (was), do, have (had) – can be seen. It must be noted that *to have* constructions are more frequent than *have to* constructions. Also, there is a strong tendency to use "human" abilities: *see, go, get, make, take, say* are all within the most frequent verbs associated with the *to*-Infinitive constructions. It can also be seen that clusters incorporating *to be* clearly

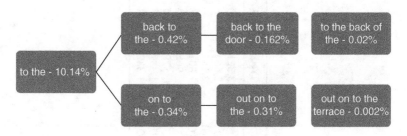

Figure 3.1   TO THE most frequent clusters (Group 1)

Table 3.16   TO with prime and other verbs clustering ("*to*-Infinitive" Group 2)

N	3Sources 2w TO	Freq.	% tot	% TO	N	3w TO cluster	Freq	% TO
2	TO BE	52,463	0.17	6.60	1	TO BE A	3,519	0.440
4	TO DO	15,910	0.05	2.01	8	TO DO WITH	2,555	0.322
5	TO SEE	15,533	0.05	1.96	13	TO HAVE A	1,802	0.227
9	TO HAVE	13,983	0.05	1.76	15	TO LOOK AT	1,790	0.225
12	TO GO	11,555	0.04	1.45	16	TO SEE THE	1,750	0.220
13	TO GET	10,957	0.04	1.38	17	NOT TO BE	1,743	0.218
14	TO MAKE	10,928	0.04	1.37	18	WAS TO BE	1,732	0.217
15	HAVE TO	10,475	0.03	1.31	20	TO BE THE	1,673	0.204
18	TO SAY	9,926	0.03	1.25	21	I HAVE TO	1,584	0.199
20	HAD TO	9,377	0.03	1.22	23	TO THINK OF	1,545	0.194
23	BEGAN TO	8,438	0.03	1.11	24	TO MAKE A	1,470	0.185
25	TO TAKE	8,207	0.03	1.03	25	I HAD TO	1,442	0.182

dominate, with the indefinite article use (*to be a*) appearing twice as frequent as the definite article use. This is contrasted by *I have to* (present tense) which is about as frequent as *I had to* (past perfect). Pragmatic uses of these frequent verbs also become discoverable: *to look at* is an active act: *he turned to look at her*; *she turned her head to look at*; *continued to look at her*. *To see the* is different, referring to accidental use: *turned in time to see the*; *to see the back of the*; *was surprised to see the*.

Yet, there is one common collocate – *want*. This leads us to find both *want to look at you/the stuff/the pictures/Alice* and (*want* being twice as frequent as *wanted*), *I want to see the world/damage/Tiber* and (*want to* being twice as frequent as *wanted to*), where *look at* seems to indicate something more direct, defined or personal.

There are also three sets of words, similar in their frequencies, which reflect narrative voice: *not to be, was to be, to be the*; similarly, *to think of*. It can be seen that these key verbs form *to*-Infinitive constructions that form a large proportion of the trigrams in this fiction corpus. Biber (2000: 208) highlights that *to* constructions with *think* are amongst the most frequent such forms found in conversations, and fiction writers seem to try to mirror that. He does not mention, however, that the (also very frequent) *to know* tends to appear in a negative sense (see below).

When we turn to the discourse markers (*to*-Infinitive constructions with a specific purpose) we do encounter the strongest evidence of formulaicity as is shown in Table 3.17. Apart from the reference to vision (*seemed to be*), all these clusters seem to refer to something to be done in the future: *I am not going to be able to do it*; *you ought to be able to see her*. It must be observed how frequently these utterances use a negation.

It appears to show that there is not just simply the *going to* future tense form – something similar can also be expressed with *should like to* or *ought to*. Also, *going to* is often found in combination with *able to*. *Should like to* appears to contemporary readers as an odd expression – it occurs in 686 lines but only in 143 texts out of the 543 in the corpus (there is a similar amount of concordance lines for *to be able to*, yet it appears in nearly 300 texts). *Want to* appears to be employed mostly in its negative form. Even where there is no direct use of *not*, there is clear negative prosody: *it was too intense for me, if you do want to know*; *and I want to know who gave the orders*; *why do you always want to be bosomy blondes*, etc. In this context, I use the term "utterance" for a purpose: these "discourse markers" do, indeed, exclusively appear in the spoken exchanges found in novels. This does also explain why a larger number of long clusters can be found with *going to*, *want to* etc., as spoken text tends to be far more formulaic – and authors clearly try to reflect this. In fact, the

Table 3.17 3S – TO discourse-marker clusters (Group 3)

R	2w TO	N	%TO	R	3w TO cluster	N	%TO	R	4w TO cluster	N	%TO	R	5w Word TO	N	%TO
8	GOING TO	14153	1.78	3	BE ABLE TO	2976	0.37	1	I DON'T WANT TO	1091	0.14	1	WHAT ARE YOU GOING TO	214	0.03
13	SEEMED TO	11466	1.41	4	WAS GOING TO	2913	0.37	2	DIDN'T WANT TO	1012	0.13	2	ARE YOU GOING TO DO	187	0.02
17	WANT TO	10262	1.29	5	I WANT TO	2703	0.34	3	HE WAS GOING TO	814	0.1	7	DO YOU WANT ME TO	166	0.02
	ABLE TO	6416	0.81	7	SEEMED TO BE	2591	0.33	5	TO BE ABLE TO	631	0.79	9	DON'T KNOW WHAT TO DO	151	0.02
				12	GOING TO BE	1960	0.25	6	I SHOULD LIKE TO	630	0.79	10	IT SEEMS TO ME THAT	146	0.02
				19	YOU WANT TO	1732	0.22	7	I WANT YOU TO	616	0.77	16	I SHOULD LIKE TO KNOW	121	0.02
				22	DON'T WANT TO	1556		9	ARE YOU GOING TO	592	0.75	17	SHE DID NOT WANT TO	121	0.02
								10	I'M NOT GOING TO	301	0.04	18	TO TELL YOU THE TRUTH	114	0.02
								12	SHE DIDN'T WANT TO	287	0.36	22	IT WAS GOING TO BE	109	0.01
								13	I DIDN'T WANT TO	261	0.34	24	WANT TO TALK TO YOU	108	0.01
								14	YOU DON'T WANT TO	243	0.31	25	I AM SORRY TO SAY	106	0.01
								15	DON'T WANT TO BE	185	0.02				
								16	HE DIDN'T WANT TO	184	0.02				
								18	YOU'RE NOT GOING TO	144	0.02				
								19	DON'T WANT TO GO	139	0.02				
								20	IT'S GOING TO BE	135	0.02				
								22	WON'T BE ABLE TO	126	0.02				
								23	I'M GOING TO BE	120	0.02				
								24	DON'T WANT YOU TO	118	0.02				

5w clusters in Table 3.16 have a number of set phrases: *don't know what to do; to tell the truth; I am sorry to say.* One more point of interest is that the key verbs are followed by *to be – seemed to be, going to be, have to be.* It is the second most frequent collocate for *want to.* This is different only for *able to* where it is pre-positioned and where a variety of lemmas are the most prevalent: *to be able to* (2,976), *been able to* (1,029), *was able to* (667), *being able to* (377). It can be seen that the majority usage of *to* falls into three distinct categories. *Going to, seemed to* and *want to* are used in around half of all their respective occurrences, *able to* appears in 93 per cent, as the total amount of occurrences for *able* is 6,857.

This is in clear contrast to the five top bigrams in Group 1, where *to have* and *have to* combined appear in less than 20 per cent of all uses of *have.* This is similar with *to do. To be, to see* and *to go* all appear in one-third of all uses of the verbs. This can be seen as collocational preference hinting at semantic function.

The one construction that reflects narrative flow as well as discourse is *to do,* as Figure 3.2 demonstrates. "I have no idea *what TO DO with* him" is an example of using the two most frequent collocates on either side. That *to* appears most prominently in longer clusters seems to be

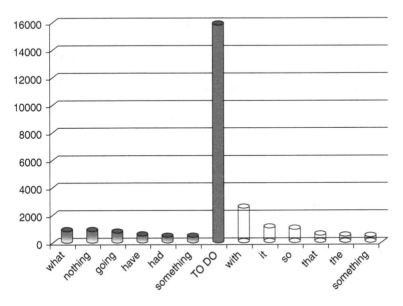

Figure 3.2 Most frequent collocates to the *left* and to the *right* of TO DO

mainly due to formulaic discourse-driven sets of words and, to a lesser extent, because of prepositional phrases, which make strong reference to end points.

The next step is to look at and compare the three sub-corpora to see if there are any particular differences in use. A full discussion of all findings will follow at a later stage, once material from the other sets of corpora has been analysed.

3.3   Differences between sub-corpora

While all three sets of texts fit into the same genre – novel-based fiction – there are obvious differences. The BNC-F covers 20th-century fiction, but uses no full texts. The ANC-F and 19C corpora are based on full texts, the former of the first dozen or so years of the 20th century, the latter covering published novels of the full preceding century. Crucially though, we compare British with American English data. For this comparison, the focus will be on trigrams and longer clusters.

3.3.1   OF usage compared

The bigrams show that within the three sub-corpora *of the* accounts for over 25 per cent of all *of* uses. *Of a* is a distant next-frequent bigram with under 6 per cent. The top five bigrams are also the same. The main difference appears to be *of course*, identified as a discourse marker, which only ranks 13th in 19C (1.22 per cent), ninth in the ANC-F (1.90 per cent) but is prominent in the BNC-F, where it ranks seventh (2.94 per cent). Trigrams, similarly, stand out by their uniformity. The four highest occurring trigrams are the same. Apart from the single instance of *in front of*, which in 19C is ranked 26th. Within the 12 most used trigrams, the same wordings can found throughout. With the 40 most used ones, there seems to be slightly more overlap between 19C and ANC-F, though amongst the most frequent of these, the ranking and percentage of use is closer for BNC-F and ANC-F. Table 3.18 shows that there is a lot of space-descriptive use of *of* in 19C. *Part of the* appears with similar frequencies in the other sub-corpora, yet is ranked sixth in ANC-F and 12th in BNC-F. *Of the house* is, relatively, slightly more frequent in BNC-F but is only ranked 18th, while it is markedly less frequent in ANC-F, where it ranks 15th. *Of the room* can be described in the same way. What does stand out is the "general-purpose preposition of concession" (Quirk et al., 1985: 705) *in spite of*. Ranked 25th in ANC-F where it appears in 0.24 per cent of all *of* uses. It is ranked even lower in BNC-F, with 0.21 per cent. *The name of* occurs in less than 0.16 per cent of uses in ANC-F, 0.17 per cent in the BNC-F.

Table 3.18 OF top divergent trigrams

R	19C	%	R	BNC-F	%	R	ANC-F	%
3	PART OF THE	0.460	5	A COUPLE OF	0.728	9	OF THE WORLD	0.385
6	OF THE HOUSE	0.355	6	A LOT OF	0.709	11	OF ALL THE	0.358
10	IN SPITE OF	0.310	7	SIDE OF THE	0.661	13	WAS ONE OF	0.329
14	THE NAME OF	0.267	10	THE BACK OF	0.618	16	OF THE PEOPLE	0.270
15	OF THE ROOM	0.258	13	A BIT OF	0.401			

Table 3.19 OF top common 4w

R	19C	Freq	BNC-F	Freq	ANC-F	Freq
1	AT THE END OF	641	THE END OF THE	1,317	THE REST OF THE	56
2	THE END OF THE	593	THE REST OF THE	1,166	AT THE END OF	55
3	THE REST OF THE	553	AT THE END OF	1,068	WAS ONE OF THE	44
4	IN THE MIDST OF	532	IN THE MIDDLE OF	1,018	IN FRONT OF THE[7]	42

This clearly marks the usage of its time, as 19C records *in the name of god* and even oaths like *in the name of your Christianity, go* or the interesting phrase *in the name of wonder* which appears several times in different texts. This stands in marked contrast with the BNC-F, where we can find vague, not to say, colloquial itemisers: *a couple /a lot /a bit of*. None of these are found in the 40 most frequent 19C trigrams, while *a lot of* is ranked 8th (0.42 per cent) in ANC-F.[8]

Table 3.19 shows a high degree of agreement between the corpora.[9] While the proportional percentages differ, the same 4w clusters appear in the top slots. The 11 texts of the ANC-F present an intriguing vista, fitting between 19th- and 20th-century British usage: the word "midst" has fallen out of usage. In the BNC-F *in the midst* of occurs only 95 times. In 19C, *in the middle of* ranks ninth and occurs 395 times. In the ANC-F *in the middle of* ranks sixth (31 occurrences) followed by *in the midst of* (N=30). Further investigation shows that these two items are used very differently. *The midst of* has a very restricted number of L1 prepositions: *in, into, from* (BNC-F and C19) also, *through* and *of* (C19). R1 are determiners, R2 conjunctions, determiners or modifiers, where *the midst of* has nouns in R1 and R2 positions.

The end of the (ranked fifth, N=38, in the ANC-F) and *at the end* stand out as prominent uses. This would mean that the most frequently found clusters refer to the end (*at the end of the day, at the end of the week, reached the end of the bridge*) to the middle (*in the middle of the night/ room/floor, along in the middle of it came an old woman*) while "rest of" appears also for time – *for the rest of the day/time/her life* – and secondly for part-of descriptions – *the rest of the family, the rest of her house*. All the examples are from the BNC-F.

Interestingly, there are also key clusters that are found to be used to describe parts of a house – *the back of the (room), the side of the (house), the other side of, the door of the, out of the room, out of the window* or *the top of the (stairs)*. All of these appear in the 20 most frequent 4w clusters in the three sub-corpora. In the 19C there is, however, a clear preference for *out of the room* and *the door of the* compared to the BNC-F: in the BNC-F *out of the window*, however, appear proportionally three times more often. That difference is starker still when it comes to *the edge of the*, ranked fifth in the BNC-F and occurring 867 times – proportionally over four times more often than in 19C. *The edge of the* is typically followed by items like *bed, table, wood, cliff* or *desk*, meaning that they are frequently referring to items found in a house.

Yet, while the BNC-F is using *of* in a strongly descriptive way, both 19C and ANC-F also have 4w clusters that indicate description of action or dialogue: *in the course of* (ranked fifth in 19C and 11th in ANC-F) and *for the sake of* (sixth in 19C and 17th in ANC-F). These are far rarer in the BNC-F and occur, proportionally, three times less often there than in 19C. The ANC-F stands out with the usage of the 4w cluster *as a matter of (fact, course)* which is ranked 8th (29 occurrences), but occurs with far less prominence in either 19C or BNC-F.

Looking at the longest (i.e. 5w–6w) clusters, Table 3.20, the level of convergence amongst the most frequent clusters is almost absolute. When considering the frequencies, it has to be kept in mind that the longest meaningful 5-word string found in BNC-F, *I don't want to*, occurs only 859 times. It can also be said that the first and third most frequent string in 19C and BNC-F are also the two most common long clusters in the LOB corpus. It can be noted that the absolute and relative frequencies are higher for the most frequent clusters in the BNC-F: this is probably due to the fact that the BNC-F uses sections, rather than whole texts, unlike the other two corpora. There are comparatively few strings that are unique to any corpus: *a quarter of an hour* and *in the course of the* are in 19C (ranked fourth and sixth, respectively) but rare in BNC-F.

The same can be said of the phrases *at the head of* and *what do you think of* – both being amongst the twelve most frequent long OF clusters in 19C but infrequent in their use in BNC-F. By contrast, the BNC-F shows usage of *out of the corner of (the eye), the far end of* and *there was no sign of* (ranked 9th to 11th in BNC-F), yet these are infrequent in 19C. *On the edge of the* and *as a matter of fact* are prominent in BNC-F and

Table 3.20 OF most frequent long clusters

OF long cluster	R 19C	Frq	%	R BNC-F	Frq	%	R ANC-F	Frq	%
AT THE END OF THE	1	254	0.069	1	605	0.179	6	16	0.069
IN THE MIDDLE OF THE	2	245	0.066	2	547	0.163	2	20	0.089
THE OTHER SIDE OF THE	3	228	0.062	3	541	0.161	1	24	0.106
ON THE OTHER SIDE OF THE	7	152	0.041	5	357	0.106	7	15	0.064
IN THE DIRECTION OF THE	8	145	0.039	16	197	0.059	8	13	0.058
AT THE HEAD OF THE	9	130	0.035	43	90	0.033	9	12	0.058
THE OTHER END OF THE	10	123	0.033	18	189	0.056	13	8	0.035
AT THE BOTTOM OF THE	10	123	0.033	13	218	0.065			
WHAT DO YOU THINK OF	11	120	0.032	40	92	0.034	12	9	0.041
AT THE FOOT OF THE	13	118	0.032	17	190	0.056			
AT THE BACK OF THE	15	112	0.030	8	242	0.072			
IN THE CENTRE OF THE	17	99	0.027	14	213	0.061	11	10	0.045
AT THE TOP OF THE	18	94	0.025	7	294	0.088	11	10	0.045
AS A MATTER OF COURSE	22	87	0.023	7	26	0.007			
ON THE EDGE OF THE	38	60	0.016	6	298	0.089	15	6	0.029
AS A MATTER OF FACT	60	47	0.013	12	220	0.066	3	19	0.084

ANC-F respectively, while there is a strong preference for *as a matter of course* in 19th-century literature.

Overall, *of* usage in long strings of words is almost exclusively used for spatial descriptors. In all three corpora, *end* comes before *middle*, and *middle* comes before *other side* (*at the side of* only appears in BNC-F – ranked 26th). *Middle* is preferred to *centre* (note the use in ANC-F) and the metaphorical terms *bottom, foot, edge*, etc. are less frequent, especially in the dozen books of the ANC-F. Despite these differences, however, what stands out is the high level of conformity amongst the long *of* clusters across all the corpora, despite being sourced from texts resulting from creative works from different periods and countries. This fits very well with Hoey's claim that

> ...what we are now contemplating, (...), is the possibility of finding bonding across texts written between three and fourteen years apart, solely because of the mental concordances of the authors retained records of the texts they had read, which in turn were written in the light of *their* author's mental concordances, which (perhaps) included sentences drawn from a common primary source (author's highlights). (Hoey, 1995: 90)

This was part of Hoey's investigation into the concept of *bonding* which, using corpus linguistic techniques and a wealth of data, was later developed into his Lexical Priming Theory (Hoey, 2003, and after). Novels in particular hark back to earlier works by previous novelists, and not just through the use of pastiche. In fact, at times, similarities are deemed so great that there have been accusations of plagiarism.

3.3.2   TO usage compared

When we look at differences between strings of words with *to* in the three corpora, the three most commonly used bigrams, *to the, to be* and *to her* are the same, apart from 19C which has *to me* ranked third (19th in BNC-F, 13th in ANC-F). Fifty per cent of the top 19C bigrams are found in BNC-F (100 per cent within the top 22), 80 per cent are also occurring in the ANC-F (100 per cent within the top 21). Clear divergence can be found, however, when longer sets of *to* clusters are looked at, indicating that the overall findings presented above hide concrete differences. Table 3.21 shows that only within the six most frequent clusters appear with roughly similar rankings and frequencies. Applying statistical testing, comparing 19C and BNC-F reveals that there is no significant difference only for *to see the* while *be able to* is

Table 3.21 TO comparable trigrams

TO 3w	R 19C	%	R BNC-F	%	R ANC-F	%
TO GO TO	1	0.434	4	0.582	1	0.730
TO BE A	2	0.429	6	0.521	3	0.538
BE ABLE TO	3	0.341	3	0.597	6	0.400
TO SEE THE	15	0.248	32	0.226	30	0.259

Table 3.22 TO diverging trigrams

TO 3w	R 19C	%	R BNC-F	%	R ANC-F	%
WAS TO BE	4	0.340	83	0.151	12	0.329
TO SPEAK TO	5	0.336	38	0.211	40	0.213
NOT TO BE	6	0.319	59	0.174	23	0.271
SEEMED TO BE	8	0.278	11	0.418	4	0.431
TO BE THE	12	0.258	42	0.203	66	0.178
TO THINK OF	13	0.250	63	0.173	26	0.262
I WANT TO	14	0.240	7	0.516	2	0.649
WAS GOING TO	37	0.180	2	0.602	8	0.380
TO TALK TO	73	0.128	8	0.452	13	0.322
GOING TO BE	144	0.095	10	0.419	44	0.209

very significantly less used in 19C. Statistical testing supports what their raw data presents in Table 3.22. Rather strong divergence highlights the specific uses of *to* in the different corpora: *was to be, not to be* and *to think of* are relatively infrequent in BNC-F compared to ANC-F and, in particular, 19C. *Was going to, to talk to* and *going to be* are rare in 19C, highlighting that BNC-F favours a style that makes a lot of use of *going to* constructions – see Table 3.23. This indicates that it is the BNC-F that creates such a subsection of *to* usage, with 11,892 occurrences of *going to* in BNC-F compared to only 3,907 in 19C and ANC-F combined.

The other striking difference concerns the 19C preference for *to speak to* as opposed to *to talk to*. While the former is not used that much less in ANC-F compared to BNC-F, the latter is dispreferred in 19C. While both tables show that *to be* is integrated strongly, the variations in use ("was to be" vs "was going to" or "to speak" vs "to talk") create visible divergence. When we look at the case of *I'm going to* (Table 3.23) we can see a change over time. The phrase is rather rare in 19C, yet can be seen as the standard in ANC and clearly as the one acceptable form in BNC-F. The non-contracted form, *I am going to*, however, clearly was the accepted standard in 19th-century British fiction and is still

Table 3.23   The case of *I'm going to/I am going to*

TO 3w	F 19C	%	F BNC-F	%	F ANC-F	%
I'M GOING TO	92	0.028	1,325	0.319	40	0.180
I AM GOING TO	290	0.090	139	0.032	18	0.081
combined	*382*	*0.11*	*1,464*	*0.35*	*58*	*0.29*

Table 3.24   TO 4w clusters

TO 4w	N 19C	%	N BNC-F	%	N ANC-F	%
TO BE ABLE TO	2	0.127	2	0.191	1	0.186
TO GO TO THE	6	0.075	5	0.148	3	0.152
I DON'T WANT TO	9	0.058	1	0.207	6	0.120
I WANT YOU TO	10	0.055	12	0.105	2	0.155
NOTHING TO DO WITH	14	0.053	6	0.117	28	0.072
HE WAS GOING TO	17	0.050	4	0.156	4	0.152
TO GO BACK TO	20	0.048	9	0.109	5	0.127

comparatively frequent in its use in ANC. The full form is, however, only marginal in its use in 20th-century British fiction.

Table 3.24 shows the clusters which are broadly comparable by proportional frequency or ranking or both. However, statistical testing shows that all the listed clusters are significantly less frequent in 19C compared to BNC-F. 19C has lower occurrences compared to ANC-F as well, though these are significant to a lesser extent. The divergence between BNC-F and ANC-F is, however, marginal. Table 3.24 shows a significant preference for negation markers in BNC-F that is not mirrored in 19C or (to a lesser level of significance) ANC-F. Overall, only *to be able to* can be seen as used equally. A further phrase shows a difference between BE and AE: *from time to time*. This is ranked 4th in 19C, 17th in BNC-F and occurs in both around 75 times in every 100,000 *to* uses. It is, however, less than half as frequent in the ANC-F.[10] It must be seen as highly context specific. In all the prepared speech podcasts the phrase occurs only 26 times: in all the casual spoken data, it occurs 13 times. This idea appears to be confirmed by Rice (1999: 271), who looked at patterns of acquisition for *to* and *for* amongst children: "... there were essentially no temporal usages of *to* beyond a few examples by one child sampled at age 5."

I am sorry to (in BNC-F combined with *I'm sorry to*) are ranked 16th (19C) and 20th (BNC-F) and occur around 50 times in 100,000 uses. It occurs, however, only twice in the entire ANC-F. *To speak to you*, on the other hand, ranks seventh in both 19C and ANC-F but is substantially less used in BNC-F. It is these 4w clusters that show the largest difference in language use between the 19th and 20th centuries, however. The majority of the 20-most frequent 19C clusters are very infrequent in BNC-F (with the ANC-F lying somewhere in-between). We find that phrase like *I should like to, was not to be, it seemed to me, that is to say* and *I am sorry to* have not fully disappeared after 1900, but stopped being used frequently.

When it comes to 5–6w clusters, total numbers are too low to give any reliable assessment. The only string found to be shared in common is *do you want me to*, within the five most frequent long clusters and occurring between 0.03 and 0.04 per cent of all *to* uses. More important, though, is the difference between *I want to speak to (you)* which is found to be very frequent in 19C and ANC-F but barely occurs in BNC-F. By comparison, *I want to talk to (you)* is the form usually found in BNC-F. The latter phrase is slightly less frequent than the alternative in ANC-F, and much less frequent in 19C. These are style features peculiar to the three sets of text. Nevertheless, the low absolute count here can only provide rough indications.

Pragmatically, however, the majority of the 100 most frequent *to* long clusters across all three sub-corpora are forms of speech – statements, questions.

3.4   Summing up

This chapter has demonstrated some clear changes that have taken place over time. More contemporary literature appears to be using more informal forms like *a couple of, a lot of, I'm going to*. There is also a shift from writing *in the midst of* to *in the middle of*. In most cases, the early 20th-century US material takes in the middle-ground between 19C and BNC-F. Looking at *of* and *to* use in general, we have seen that both *of* and *to* are followed by articles and personal pronouns in the most frequent bigrams. There is strong *of the* usage patterns are mirrored by the pattern employing *the x of*. *Of* appears predominantly in prepositional use, usually as spatial descriptors within a house or compound. In its most frequent uses, *of* is not employed for the possessive. *To* usage occurs, amongst the most frequent clusters, in three groups: as preposition, as *to*-Infinitive constructions and for discourse markers. The last group prominently employs *going to* to express movement, intention and future events.

The following chapters will demonstrate in how far *of* and *to* usage are similar or differ in other text forms. A more detailed overall analysis can then be found in Chapter 6.

4
OF and TO in Semi-Prepared Speech

4.1 Introduction

The focus of this chapter will be on prepared and semi-prepared spoken texts: material written to be delivered in spoken form to a larger informed, yet non-specialist audience as well as material prepared prior to speaking to the public (but not necessarily taking full recourse to consecutive written notes).

This chapter aims is to provide a fully corpus-driven investigation into the occurrence patterns of the items *of* and *to* within the context of public speeches. There have been in-depth investigations into the structure of spoken English (for example, Carter & McCarthy: 2001). Similarly, instances of corpus-based research into prepared speeches are numerous (Partington: 2003, to name just one). Similarly, a string of corpus-based investigations into academic speech (that is, lectures presented) is to be found. Yet amongst spoken language produced, there is a further sub-category that appears to be close to some of the above: that of public speeches. It must be assumed that these are texts that have been carefully prepared. Amongst such texts, there are two areas where further sub-division can be found:

1. speeches that have been written-to-be-spoken
2. speeches that have been prepared but are freely presented.

Furthermore:

a. speeches that are presented by a single speaker
b. speeches that are presented by multiple speakers in a panel discussion or are part of a question-and-answer session.

In this chapter, the focus will be on how the two highly frequent items are employed in such presentations that are free to be listened to/ viewed by the interested public. The aim will be to answer two key questions. First, in what way are the items *of* and *to* employed in their most frequent forms of usage? That is, are there set structural and pragmatic preferences and what do these indicate about usage patterns for the two items? Second, are there qualitatively measurable differences between the single-speaker and the multiple-speaker material? In the context of this investigation I shall also, albeit briefly, compare the results from my corpora with academic English as found in BASE and BAWE.

The research is based on three main corpora: the BBC Reith Lectures from 1948 to 2011, the LSE Public Lectures from 2006 to 2013 and Public Lectures on artworks held by National Museums Liverpool (NML) between 2006 and 2011. Furthermore, a variety of transcripts from a number of public events and presentations held by a variety of organisations over the last decade have been added, to have a further, less heterogeneous sub-corpus. The total number of tokens across all corpora is 1,449,718 items. Apart from the sources, the corpora are further divided into sub-corpora along the following criteria:

1. Sources: BBC, LSE, NML and VAR
2. Type of speech: (a) single-speaker lecture; (b) multiple-speaker lecture plus Q&A sessions after a lecture.

Further subdivisions will be described below. This section will look at the usage patterns found for *of* and *to* in the target corpora, moving from the very general to specific and characteristic details.

4.2 The sources

This section describes the three main sources – BBC, LSE and NML – and gives details where to find the originals and describes the sets of text involved. Details can be found in Appendix 4.i–4.v.

4.2.1 Sub-corpus: BBC Radio

The BBC Reith Lectures, in honour of the founder of the Corporation, were started in 1948 and initially broadcast on the Home Service and later moved to its current home, BBC Radio 4. It was transmitted every year since, though both 1977 and 1992 lectures are not available. The latest transcript ready for download is from the year 2011. Each year, a chosen speaker – usually a public figure, a philosopher, historian or scientist – delivers a series of speeches over a period of several weeks.

The number of lectures vary – there are only two by Aung San Suu Kyi (in 2011), while John Zachary Young delivered eight lectures in 1950. In order to have a fair distribution, two lectures were chosen, at random, by each of the speakers for each year. The majority of the speakers are British, a number are from the USA and a minority come from overseas with English not necessarily being their first language. Speeches usually lasted 30–45 minutes. One thing that could not be randomised, however, is the distribution of speakers by gender: early transcripts reflect a clear bias towards male speakers, while more recent recordings show that the BBC is striving to invite women as well as men to give a Reith Lecture.

Starting with the year 2006, there is a transcriptions of the introduction and, more importantly, a full transcription of the ensuing Question-and-Answer (Q&A) sessions.

4.2.2   Sub-corpus: London School of Economics: LSE Public Lectures and Events

These are the transcripts of speeches delivered to staff, students and anybody interested, as arranged by the LSE, covering a period from October 2006 up to March 2013. The subject matter shows a clear bias towards economics, though there are also a large number of speeches concerned with national and international politics as well as some that look at the area of arts and humanities. Given the kind of background under which these lectures have been arranged, the vast majority (in fact, there are very few exceptions) of the presenters are male. There are a large number of politicians – either British or international – economists and heads of central banks. Even if English is not their native language, they are well versed in using the language proficiently as their language of business. Prepared speeches, furthermore, will have been worked on by adept specialists. Speeches vary in length. No times are advertised, but the transcripts can be as short as five and as long as 20+ pages. There is also clear evidence that a large number of the lectures delivered are *not* transcripts but the written text of prepared speeches. Some of the downloads have a note warning "check against delivery" and a very small number even say "embargoed until" – showing that public figures (usually politicians) use the LSE event as a forum to announce policies with the probable aim to make headlines. It must be noted that, unlike in Reith, NML or VAR, there is no multiple-speaker sub-corpus in LSE and the Q&A sessions are available for only four of the lectures.

4.2.3   Sub-corpus: National Museums Liverpool

In the time between May 2006 and February 2011, National Museums Liverpool recorded their regularly held talks on pieces from their collection. The podcasts vary in length considerably: the shortest is just over ten minutes, the longest nearly 70 minutes long. The majority last between 30 and 45 minutes.

The majority of the lectures were given by senior employees (curators, head of education) of NML, though a sizable number has been given by guest speakers. The selection ensures that there is only one transcript per speaker.

4.2.4   Sub-corpus: Various Sources (VAR)

This is a random collection of material rendered through a basic trawl through websites with the search "podcast transcripts UK" and "presentation transcripts UK", which resulted in wide-ranging sources, including a podcast from a cancer research foundation and a transcript of a presentation given to web developers.

The VAR corpus is also unevenly split: There are 122,225 words in the multiple-speaker and 75,637 words in the single-speaker corpus. This sub-corpus therefore acts very much as a control group. All transcripts come from events staged between 2009 and 2013.

4.2.5   Corpus sizes and distribution

The files used here have been split into two parts: One which has only the lectures itself and another, which has only the Panel or Q&A section. The discussion of results will show in what way this division is necessary and relevant (Table 4.1).

One section – SSM – therefore represents single-speaker prepared speeches; the other – MSM – material is semi-prepared, but reflects that it reacts to other speakers.

4.3   The "normal" distribution patterns

The corpora investigated here fall into three categories: one set are fully prepared speeches. While the writers will have had the audience of listeners in mind, the presented text will be a revised and edited, prepared speech of the form where people read off the page and only make

Table 4.1   OF and TO distribution in SSM and MSM

	Total tokens	OF	TO
SSM – single-speaker material (286 files)	1,181,521	46,858 3.966%	33,636 2.846%
MSM – multiple-speaker material (48 files)	246,845	7,068 2.863%	7.097 2.875%

minor, if any, adjustments in their delivery. The LSE and Reith Lectures fall into this category.

A second set are speeches and expositions that have been prepared and might have been delivered several times before to similar groups of listeners. The key feature here is that the speaker does not read off a script. Rather, gestures and externalities (slides, artworks) are part of the delivery. Most of the NML corpus falls into this category.

The third set is a hybrid collection, the main feature of which is a degree of interactive exchange between a number of speakers. There is a degree of preparedness in all of these, and it can be expected that all speakers use a tone and register appropriate for the occasion while their utterances also display a certain amount of reference to the previous speakers. The NML and VAR sub-corpora, which have several speakers as well as the Q&A section of the 2006–2011 Reith Lectures, fall into this category.

The corpus, being largely based on transcripts of what has been heard, does belong into the category of *spoken* English. However, seen from a different perspective, the material has been edited prior to delivery.[1] The text to be read out has been written first. Consequently, it could be said that the material should really be classed as *written* English. A first step, therefore, is to compare the *podcast transcript* data both with written data (fiction) and casually spoken (British) English to give a first impression of whether the broad usage pattern found is closer to the written or the spoken form.

Figure 4.1 compares the overall frequencies of use for *of* and *to* The first set of bars gives the combined percentage use of the two items for all single-speaker podcasts (SSM). The second set is the combined figures for multiple-speaker presentations and Q&A sessions (MSM).

We see that *to* is fairly level in the two types of corpora. However, in the in the single-speaker podcast corpus, we do find *of* being significantly more frequently used than *to*.

As public lectures, the closest related spoken form could be said to be that of academic lectures. Yet when we look at the numbers presented in Figure 4.2, we can see that the percentages found in academic lectures broadly agree with what we have in the Q&A and multiple-speaker (plenary) sessions. It is academic writing that structurally resembles the *of* and *to* use most: here and in the single-speaker public lectures do we find a significantly stronger use of the item *of*. The difference is minimal in the proportional use in all other corpora; in academic writing, however, it is even stronger than in the single-speaker podcasts:

This particular distribution of the two items appears to be, therefore, particular to two specific types of text. The next step will be to see how

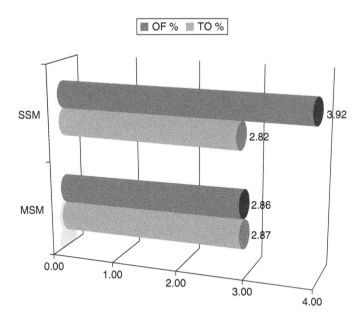

Figure 4.1 TO and OF proportional frequencies in podcasts, comparing single-speaker (SSM) to multiple-speaker (MSM) material

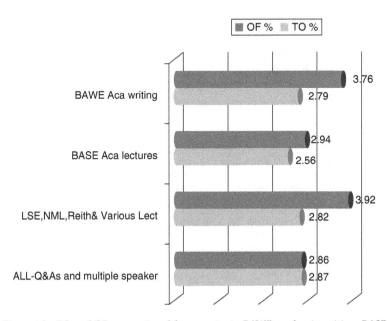

Figure 4.2 TO and OF proportional frequencies in BAWE academic writing, BASE academic lectures and podcast corpora

both *of* and *to* are being used in the podcast sub-corpora to deliver an explanation as to why *of* is found to be so much more prominent. The BASE and BAWE corpora of academic spoken and written texts (covering the period 2004–2007) presented here are providing figures that are broadly similar to those found in the (larger but older) BNC.

4.4   The distribution patterns of OF and TO within corpora

One of the key issues discussed throughout this book the relevance *of* and *to* have as building blocks in the English language. A detailed account of the distribution patterns of these items in the podcast corpora will follow. When we look at the distribution of the items, we recognise that *of* and *to* are not simply highly frequent as single items; they are also part of the most frequent clusters found in any given corpus, as Pace-Sigge (2013: 191) has highlighted with reference to the 5 million-word corpus of casual conversation, CANCODE. Table 4.2 highlights that both *of* and *to* are prominently used words.

In particular, we find that *of* appears the more frequent the longer the cluster, while *to* usage decreases in frequency the longer the cluster. So there seems to be a preference for *to* occurring in shorter chunks. When the podcast sub-corpora clusters are viewed, a similar distribution pattern becomes apparent. If anything, the *of* and *to* usage is more prominent, with both *of* and *to* appearing within the five highest occurring 2w clusters in almost all sub-corpora. In the light of this, these small items cannot simply be understood as highly frequent, yet semantically empty units; they also appear to be elementary parts of formulaic multi-word units.[2] Table 4.3 demonstrates how deeply *of* and, to a lesser degree, *to*

Table 4.2   OF and TO distribution in CanCode chunks. (Adapted from O'Keeffe / McCarthy and Carter (2007: 65ff).)

length of chunk	2-word	3-word	4-word	5-word	6-word
ranks in top 20 for: OF *cluster*	7th, 9th	2nd, 7th 14th, 18th	4th, 5th 6th, 7th 11th, 19th	2nd, 10th, 11th, 13th 14th, 16th, 19th	2nd 3rd 4th 6th, 8th, 9th, 10th, 12th, 14th, 15th
ranks in top 20 for: TO *cluster*	14th, 17th, 19th	8th, 11th	6th, 18th	5th, 17th	11th, 13th, 17th

Table 4.3 OF and TO (bold) occurrence scheme in Reith Sub-corpus most frequent clusters

Rank	Reith bigram	Freq.	%	R	Reith trigram	F	%	R	Reith 4-word-cluster	F	R	Reith 5-word-cluster	F
1	OF THE	4,740	0.947	2	ONE OF THE	187	0.037	4	IN THE CASE OF	42	1	# PER CENT OF THE	19
4	TO THE	1,402	0.280	3	OF THE WORLD	158	0.032	5	# PER CENT OF	41	3	AT THE END OF THE	14
6	TO BE	1,250	0.250	9	PART OF THE	118	0.024	8	OF THE UNITED STATES	33	3	THE FREEDOM OF THE WILL	14
9	OF A	910	0.182	10	SOME OF THE	114	0.023	11	ONE OF THE MOST	32	4	IN THE MIDDLE OF THE	13
28	OF OUR	433	0.087	12	IN TERMS OF	109	0.022	12	THE REST OF THE	30	5	LOSS OF THE STABLE STATE	12
				18	IN ORDER TO	84	0.017	13	IT SEEMS TO ME	29	6	THE LOSS OF THE STABLE	11
				22	HAVE TO BE	77	0.015	14	THE END OF THE	29	6	THE LOSS OF THE STABLE STATE	11
				29	BE ABLE TO	69	0.014	15	AT THE END OF	27	7	IT SEEMS TO ME THAT	10
								15	IS ONE OF THE	25	8	IN THE CASE OF THE	9
								15	ON THE BASIS OF	25	9	ABOUT # PER CENT OF	8
								17	PARTS OF THE WORLD	23	9	IN SUCH A WAY AS TO	8

are permeating the language of podcasts – the occurrence in just one sub-corpus, the Reith single-speaker corpus, is used here by way of demonstration. Amongst the 2w and 5w clusters, *of* appears as an integral part of the most used clusters; apart from 2w clusters, it appears in the majority of the ten most frequent clusters. *To* is less prominent in this sub-corpus, this reflects what we have shown in Figures 4.1 and 4.2. Apart from this, Table 4.3 highlights a key characteristic of these items in the Reith corpus: both *of* and *to* are being used to be highly descriptive; *of* often for something specific (*of the world, of the United States, per cent of*) while *to* is either abstract (*have to be, be able to*), or tends to be vague and mainly functions as a discourse element: *it seems to me, in such a way as to.*

4.5   The use of TO in podcasts

This section will focus on the use of *to* in the target corpora. As we have seen in Appendix 1.1, with the exception of the spoken conversation corpora, *to* occurs in the span of 2.6–2.9 per cent in every corpus. The proportional occurrence amount of this item can therefore be deemed as fairly stable. Below, we shall investigate if the actual occurrence patterns of this item can be said to be equally stable in the different sets of podcasts, or whether there a clear difference between either single- and multiple-speaker texts or a difference between the sets of texts found in each sub-corpus.

4.5.1   The use of *to* compared in the two types of podcast

We have seen (in Figures 4.1 and 4.2) that, overall, there appears to be no difference in the percentages of use of *to* in the multiple-speaker set of corpora when compared to the single-speaker set. However, a closer look indicates that there are purely numerical differences when the different sub-corpora are shown in detail.

Figure 4.3 shows some degree of difference when we look at the amount of *to* occurring in the spoken material. LSE is the only group where the procentual use of *to* is lower in the multiple-speaker section. However, the LSE Q&A consists of only four files and is discounted below. There is very little difference between the single-speaker and the multiple-speaker presentation in the NML. The greatest divergence is seen in Reith and in the selection of sources collected as VAR, where *to* occurs slightly more often in group presentations than in single-speaker presentations.

However, overall, none of these differences appear to be more than marginal, nor does it seem to matter that there are only very few Q&As

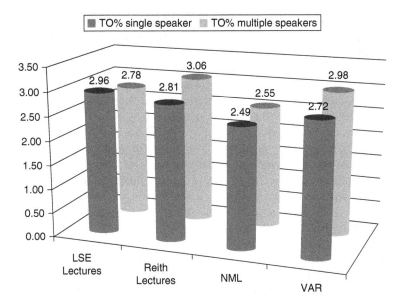

Figure 4.3 Direct comparison of TO occurrence frequency of single- and multiple-speaker parts of the podcasts

for the LSE lectures or that there are larger multiple- than single-speaker VAR sub-corpora. Furthermore, Figure 4.3 shows that there are the overall differences between the sets of podcasts. While not very strong, it is still noteworthy that *to* appears, proportionally, over 20 per cent more often in the BBC data (3.17 per cent) than in the Liverpool data (2.49 per cent) amongst the single speaker data, and falls to 2.55 and 3.06 per cent, respectively, in the multiple-speaker data.

4.5.2 The use of *to* compared in single-speaker podcast sub-corpora

In this section, a particular subset of spoken language will be examined in detail for its usage-pattern of the item *to*. A traditional view of language would maintain that, while genre-specific (minor) variations can be expected, the structural role of *to* is to remain stable and unvaried.

While all the material neatly fits into the same category – public lectures – there are a number of points that can be deemed to explain differences: foremost, that different audiences are being addressed; secondly, that the Reith Lectures are the one subset that covers the whole post-WWII era.

Initially, one would expect the LSE and Reith corpora to be the most similar, given that their main point of distinction is the time-frame of the data. The NML data is close in being a public lecture but also has strong elements of description. The VAR corpus, lastly, is rather small and primarily functions as a control corpus. For this comparison, we shall focus on trigrams – the best source of meaningful chunks that appear with reasonably high frequencies (cf. O'Keeffe et al., 2007). Table 4.4 demonstrates how the item *to* occurs – usually as the *to*-Infinitive (mostly with *able*), with prime verbs (*be* and *have*). Furthermore, as a link to the speech functions of public presentations and podcasts, there is a clear predominance of personal pronouns (*I*, *we*) and imperative forms (*in order to, have to be, try to, need to*).[3] *Be able to* is in all cases the preferred choice in comparison with *to be able*. The latter is always found as part of the 4w cluster *to be able to*.

Able appears to be always used to express a facility or ability: "Will you be able to filter...", "I would like to be able to keep", etc. At the same time, the level of divergence present is noteworthy. *Be able to* is the most frequent trigram cluster overall, yet it is not the most frequently occurring *to* cluster, by a wide margin, in the LSE sub-corpus. We find *to be a* ranked as the third or fourth most frequent *to* trigram cluster in all sub-corpora bar LSE. Conversely, *have to be* is far more preferred in the Reith sub-corpus and *we need to* in the LSE. Likewise, we can find *to try to* and *seems to be* as relatively frequent in only the

Table 4.4 Comparisons of rank, occurrence and proportional percentage of TO trigram clusters in the single-speaker sub-corpora

Cluster	Reith R	N	%	LSE R	N	%	NML R	N	%	VAR. R	N	%
BE ABLE TO	1	91	0.64	2	128	0.92	1	37	0.93	1	19	1.33
IN ORDER TO	2	86	0.61	4	120	0.87	5	30	0.76	2	14	0.98
HAVE TO BE	3	82	0.60	22	34	0.25	22	11	0.26		<5	
TO BE A	4	78	0.55	8	58	0.42	3	33	0.83	4	12	0.83
TO TRY TO	5	75	0.53	12	50	0.36	14	20	*0.50*	7	8	0.56
WE HAVE TO	6	72	0.51	5	77	0.55	21	12	0.27		<5	
I WANT TO	8	62	0.45	3	121	0.87	17	17	0.41	3	13	0.91
WE NEED TO	9	51	0.36	1	183	*1.32*	23	10	0.25	7	8	0.56
SEEMS TO ME	9	51	*0.36*	>30	14	0.10		<5		8	7	0.49
TO BE ABLE	16	36	0.26	7	64	0.45	8	27	0.68	5	11	0.77
WOULD LIKE TO	19	32	0.23	10	54	0.40	12	23	0.58	8	7	0.49
GOING TO BE	21	29	0.21	14	44	0.32	4	32	*0.82*	8	7	0.49
NEED TO BE	26	23	0.16	6	71	0.51	27	6	0.14		<5	
YOU HAVE TO	24	25	0.14	23	33	0.23	21	12	0.27	4	12	0.83
TO TALK ABOUT	30	19	0.12	19	38	0.27	25	8	*0.20*	4	12	0.83
TO DO WITH	17	37	0.24	>30	18	0.13	2	37	0.93		<5	

Reith and VAR corpora, yet it is rare in the other two. In Biber (2000: 298), *try to* is recorded as occurring fairly frequently in academic prose (100 in a million times) and in spoken conversation (300 in a million times). The prepared speeches seem to reflect this usage pattern, in this case, to some extent.

As pointed out earlier, *to* usage seems to reflect a discourse function, where the speaker wants to link two clauses and connect something existing with a state to be reached (all examples from Reith):

> Another danger is that, **in order to** leave room for teaching and research buildings to expand...
> ... taking advantage of regular refresher courses **in order to** keep in touch with new developments.
> ... today a doctor must pass strict examinations **in order to** be allowed to practise.
> ... the emotional sustenance which they need **in order to** develop into well-balanced beings.

A similar motion from a here-state to a there-state is expressed with *have to be* use:

> If power supplies **have to be** reduced in an emergency...
> Both oil and gas **have to be** landed in the United Kingdom...
>
> If it's really a computer, its operations **have to be** defined syntactically...

However, *have to be* can also occur as a form of directive:

> But now, once again, we **have to be** very careful in how we interpret the question.
> And there's an obvious reason why they **have to be** inadequate, since the argument rests on a truth.

In that, *have to be* mirrors the also fairly frequent *we need to* – the most frequent trigram *to* cluster in the LSE sub-corpus. However, the latter is less abstract and looks at concrete issues:

> Student interaction is one thing we **need to** work on...
> We **need to** make sure we facilitate that mixing...
> Ministers **need to** be informed of such decisions in advance...

Moving the focus to the key sub-corpora, we can see that each corpus has one or a set of trigram clusters that are particularly frequent, whereas the level of infrequent use is similar in the other two.[4] Table 4.5 shows that each individual corpus has three key clusters within their six highest occurring trigram *to* clusters. Still more notable is the fact that the four Reith clusters are in no relation to each other, while LSE has a clear preference for *need to* and NML for *going to* constructions. Also, in LSE, we see authorship through the use of personal pronouns: *I want to* and (the audience-inclusive) *we need to*. The NML sub-corpus has the vague and imprecise marker *to do with*.

In relation to what has been pointed out above, the Reith corpus seems to be more abstract in linking from the here to another stage; the LSE speakers, by contrast, ask for concrete action. Indeed, the cluster *need to be* tends to come after *we* or *we + AUX*: "We will **need to be** able to", "We would **need to be** fleet of foot", etc. Otherwise, *need to be* linked to a concrete group of actors: "Banks/Europeans/politicians/ students/they **need to be...**"

By contrast, the NML usage of *to* in many cases sounds rather less formal and closer to spoken than written English: this may reflect that, rather than reading from a lectern, the speaker stands in front of a group and may or may not have notes to assist her or him, rather than reading out a text. We see the phrase *to do with* as rather vague. It often follows *anything, mainly* or *mostly*. Indeed, the only time it occurs as part of a longer cluster appears in *something to do with* (six occurrences).

Table 4.5 Comparisons of the most prominent trigram TO clusters in the Reith, LSE and NML sub-corpora

Cluster REITH	Rank	Freq.	%
IN ORDER TO	2	86	0.61
HAVE TO BE	3	82	0.60
TO TRY TO	5	75	0.53
Cluster LSE	**Rank**	**Freq.**	**%**
WE NEED TO	1	183	1.32
I WANT TO	3	121	0.87
NEED TO BE	6	71	0.53
Cluster VAR	**Rank**	**Freq.**	**%**
TO DO WITH	2	37	0.93
GOING TO BE	4	32	0.82
WAS GOING TO	6	29	0.75

Was going to, found to be highly frequent in the NML sub-corpus, is usually preceded by *I*, and is in company of other clusters – *I'm going to, I am going to* and *I am not going to*. Quite often the cluster *is going to be*, even if not part of the phrase *I'm going to be*, refers back to the speaker or is used to bring in a personal connection:

> This, let me move on, **is going to be** flats and offices, I don't know who owns...
> So everybody's idea of Heaven surely **is going to be** something very personal. In my painting it **was going to be** a personal thing and I also felt that should one actually enter Heaven...
> My talk today **is going to be** an invitation to come along on a journey...

Notably, some connection between "going to" and the idea of "movement" can be found – despite the fact that, in all cases, "going to" is meant to describe a future state. This stands in contradiction to Bybee's claim that "the form *gonna* [going to] is associated with the intention / future meaning and not with the movement-in-space or purpose meaning" (Bybee, 2006: 724). Bybee makes the claim sound as if it is true at all times. While the "intention and future meaning" are detectable, the prosodic features – in this case, close collocates like the verbs *move*, *enter*, and the noun *journey* – still provide a clear link to the feature of "movement-in-space."

This, to conclude, highlights the key connection found in all three public corpora (and VAR corroborates this view): the most prominent *to* constructions are being employed to guide the listener from a real or perceived "here" to a different state or sphere. These may be expressed in different forms (more formal when more prepared, more casual when spoken more freely). Analysed pragmatically, this makes sense: lectures and, in particular, public lectures, are *persuasive texts*. The speakers, as we have shown, use *to* constructions to move the listener from a real or imagined situation to a state that the speaker wants them to picture.

4.5.3 The use of *to* compared in multiple-speaker podcast sub-corpora

This discussion will be relatively short, the focus being on Reith Q&A, NML and VAR multiple-speaker sub-corpora, as the LSE data is not sufficiently large enough for this comparison. All three sub-corpora reflect *to* use in a restricted linguistic environment. However, the Reith Q&A reflects questions put by an educated audience and the moderation of the host, Sue Lawley. Both the NML and VAR data reflect the talk of a panel of speakers and the questions put to this panel by an audience that is clearly interested yet is, unlike the Reid Q&A, not composed solely of subject specialists.

Table 4.6 varies from Table 4.4, which indicates usage in the single-speaker sub-corpora, in a number of ways. We notice, first of all, that the relative stratification and uniformity present in Table 4.4 is largely absent. There is no single trigram *to* cluster that is the most frequent across all corpora. Nor do we find that all the clusters are the same or used to the same extent. Looking at the two tables in parallel underlines the fact that Table 4.6 shows evidence of more freely spoken English: it is far more formulaic. This can be seen by the fact that all the most frequent clusters in all of the sub-corpora are appearing, proportionately, more than twice as often.

It can also be seen by restricted variety: in the Reith Q&A in particular we see a large number of clusters which appear with the same frequency. There are, however, also a number of clear parallels: The same *to* trigram clusters are found to be employed amongst the most frequent 25 clusters in both collections. For example, both use *be able to* more frequently than *to be able*.[5] The latter is always found as part of the 4w cluster *to be able to*. This shows the colligational structure: in *be able to*, the *be* can take any lemma (*am able to, are able to*) while the *to-Infinitive* rules that *to be able* cannot use a different form of the

Table 4.6 Comparisons of rank, occurrence and proportional percentage of TO-trigram clusters in the multiple-speaker sub-corpora

Cluster	R	N Reith Q&A	%	R	N NML-m	%	R	N VAR-m	%
WE HAVE TO	1	30	2.01	8	11	0.68	11	25	0.69
I'M GOING TO	1	30	2.01	6	13	0.80	n/a	5	0.01
TO TRY TO	2	20	1.38	11	8	0.49	20	16	0.44
TO GO TO	3	19	1.36	5	14	0.86	12	24	0.66
GOING TO BE	6	14	0.97	2	19	1.17	1	77	2.11
WE NEED TO	8	12	0.83	7	12	0.74	3	62	1.70
YOU HAVE TO	9	11	0.76	9	10	0.62	5	49	1.34
BE ABLE TO	9	11	0.76	8	13	0.80	2	76	2.11
IN ORDER TO	9	11	0.76	9	10	0.62	12	24	0.66
TO DO THAT	9	11	0.76	14	5	0.31	13	23	0.63
IS GOING TO	10	10	0.69	12	7	0.43	14	22	0.60
WE'RE GOING TO	11	9	0.62	10	9	0.56	16	20	0.55
I WANT TO	11	9	0.62	1	23	1.42	7	40	1.10
TO BE ABLE	12	8	0.55	13	6	0.37	4	53	1.45
YOU WANT TO	13	7	0.48	14	5	0.31	9	30	0.82

prime verb *be*. What stands out in the multiple-speaker sub-corpora is the strong use of personal pronouns – both the inclusive *we* and, to a lesser extent, the use of *I* to introduce a concept or idea: *I'm going to*, *I want to*. Furthermore, we can see that the use of movement and progression in the wording used is reflected by the very frequent use of *going to* clusters. *I'm going to* and *going to be* are amongst the most frequent trigram clusters here.

The other obvious difference lies in the use of simple infinitive phrases. *To try to* appears in both sets of corpora. However, it is both ranked higher and clearly more frequent in the multiple speaker corpora. The difference is even more stark when we look at *to go to*. This cluster appears just nine times in the Reith, ten times in the LSE single-speaker material; only within the NML corpora the differences are minimal.[6] *To go to* is also fairly descriptive: "to go to the Science Museum", "He very much wants to go to China"; with *to go to* typically following after *want* are typical examples. The use of *to do that* appears to be corpus-specific. It is fairly rare (0.1 per cent or less of all uses of *to* in single-speaker sub-corpora) in all sub-corpora bar NML – this mirrors what has been found with regards to *to go to*. The prosody of the cluster indicates far more uncertainty and a negative assessment being reflected: "We tried **to do that**", "We are unable **to do that** because" and "It is very difficult **to do that**" are recurring usage patterns of this trigram cluster in all three multiple-speaker sub-corpora.[7] If we are looking at the overall most used trigram *to* cluster amongst the multiple-speaker sub-corpora, we see that *going to be* usually follows a form of *be* – *am, are, is, were*. The distribution of these are uneven, however; while Reith and NML roughly have equal usage of *is/I'm/we're* **going to be**, the VAR corpus predominantly has *is* **going to be** (13 out of 71 concordance lines) and *we're* **going to be** (eight out of 71). There is not a single occurrence of *I'm* **going to be**.

The prosody of this cluster would have to be classed as neutral. "**Going to be** happy" and "is **going to be** invested" are positive, yet there are also uses of "countries that are **going to be** exploited" and "He's **going to be** railing against". Indeed, the discourse function of the cluster is different for each of the sub-corpora. In the Reith Q&A, it is used to refer to a future state. In the NML multiple-speaker corpus, it is often a topic outline. In the VAR, which has the majority of the negative connotations, it is often used as a turn of phrase – "If you were **going to be** honest", "That's **going to be** misleading" – where the future reference seems to be used to tone down the content.

To sum up, focussing on the most frequent trigram clusters incorporating *to*, these can be found to be the same for both single- and multiple-speaker sub-corpora. The prepared speeches in the single-speaker set show a large amount of agreement, with clusters like *be able to* and *in order to* being within the five most frequent such clusters in all four sub-corpora.

While the multiple-speaker corpora can be shown to employ the same set of trigram highly frequent clusters, usage tends to be more formulaic (which indicates a lower level of pre-editing) and far less uniform. Not one of the three sub-corpora investigated uses the same trigram *to* cluster to the same degree (rank and proportional percentage) as another. One key difference has become apparent in the use of *going to be*, which appears differently in the way that it forms parts of larger clusters in VAR compared to Reith or NML. Looking at the discourse functions of some of the clusters, we can see that even apparently innocuous clusters like *to do that* carry a specific, negative prosody in their spoken use.

4.6   OF usage compared in the two types of podcast

We have previously seen that *of* appears more frequently than *to*. Below, the available data for each sub-corpus will be analysed, moving from the general to the specific.

Figure 4.4 shows how the percentages can be found in the relevant sub-corpora. It shows strong *of* use displayed in the Reith single-speaker sub-corpus is characteristic for this set of podcasts. While all four

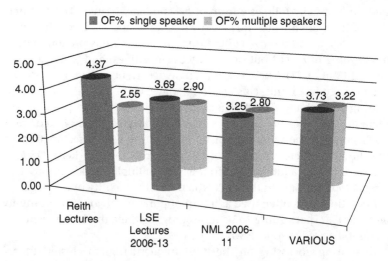

Figure 4.4   Percentage occurrence for OF in the sub-corpora

sub-corpora use *of* more frequently than *to* and this is more pronounced in the single- than in the multiple-speaker corpora, the variations seem to be rooted in the history of the material: it must not be forgotten that, while all sub-corpora reflect use of the last ten years, the Reith Lectures single-speaker sub-corpus covers the period from 1948 to 2011. That the percentages found for NML are comparatively lower might be down to the fact that, while these are also prepared speeches, they were freely delivered, not off a lectern. How this influences *of* usage patterns will be described in the following two sections.

4.6.1 OF usage compared in single-speaker podcast sub-corpora

The item *of* appears in a role that is clearly delineated from the role *to* has. Where we have seen *to* in a temporal or directional context, *of* is descriptive and, a lot of the time, it is descriptive in a vague way. It is also closely linked to numbers and counting in the podcast corpora.

Table 4.7 shows that *of* usage, in contrast to *to*, is far more stable and fixed in its use amongst single speakers. The most frequent trigram *to* clusters in the three largest sub-corpora all amount to less than 1 per cent of all *to* uses; *one of the*, by contrast, is more prominent, ranging in its use between 1.16 per cent (Reith) and 3.64 per cent (NML) of all uses of *of*. Furthermore, with the exception of NML, there is a clear drop between the most frequently occurring cluster and the rest. In NML, this pattern occurs between the two most frequent clusters and the rest. Another key difference is the link to other word categories. Whereas *to* appears with verbs and pronouns, the most frequent occurrences of *of*

Table 4.7 Comparisons of rank, occurrence and proportional percentage OF-trigram clusters in the single-speaker sub-corpora

Cluster	R	N Reith	%	R	N LSE	%	R	N NML	%	R	N VAR	%
ONE OF THE	1	254	1.16	1	228	1.32	2	187	3.64	1	97	3.43
OF THE WORLD	2	170	0.77	4	139	0.81	31	10	0.19	13	9	0.32
PART OF THE	3	152	0.69	2	155	0.90	4	65	1.26	2	26	0.92
SOME OF THE	4	142	0.65	3	144	0.83	5	64	1.25	3	21	0.74
IN TERMS OF	5	123	0.56	5	108	0.63	3	76	1.47	17	8	0.28
A SENSE OF	7	73	0.33	44	21	0.12	33	8	0.15	18	7	0.25
OUT OF THE	8	70	0.32	12	62	0.36	11	34	0.66	12	13	0.46
THE IDEA OF	9	69	0.32	31	34	0.20	12	33	0.64	16	9	0.32
A KIND OF	10	67	0.31	16	53	0.31	12	33	0.64	11	14	0.50
THE REST OF	11	66	0.31	19	48	0.28	31	10	0.19	13	12	0.43
A LOT OF	34	36	0.16	8	82	0.48	1	189	3.65	8	15	0.53

are here all linked to a noun. This also highlights a key characteristic for the item *of*: "one *of* the", "part *of* the", "some *of* the" or "out *of* the" see *of* used to pinpoint a part of a larger whole. For this, the relative rankings and even frequencies across all sub-corpora are similar. That *of* in these corpora is typically used as a way to refer to a part of a given entity is fairly obvious when looking at Table 4.7. Indeed, the phrase *a number of* appears between 0.27 per cent and 0.64 per cent of all *of* uses. More importantly, it is the 10th, 11th or 14th most frequent trigram *of*-phrase in the collections. Linked to this, Table 4.7 also highlights that *of* appears clearly with a preference for a specific number element: the vagueness markers – *some of the, a kind of, a lot of* [8] – are clearly lower in their frequency and overall presence. It must be noted that "a kind of" is a post-modifying phrase indicating *quality*, while "a lot of" indicates *quantity* (cf. Quirk et al., 1985: 702).

Of, however, can also appear to indicate a corpus-specific use of words: *of the world*, therefore, is highly frequent in the Reith and LSE corpora (which cover a lot of similar subjects); they are notably less frequent in the other two sub-corpora, though. This is even more pronounced when we look at *a sense of* which appears to be a phrase which is rather particular to the Reith sub-corpus. It can be noted in the VAR corpus, where it is ranked within the top 20, but is seldom used, comparatively, in the other two corpora.

We can also see that the sub-corpus which is closest in representing unscripted, free recitation and speech, the NML recordings, show a strong tendency to formulaicity: the seven highest occurring trigram clusters range between 0.95 per cent and 3.65 per cent of all *of* uses; in fact, the three highest occurring *of* trigram clusters are amongst the five most frequent trigram clusters in NML overall.

Overall, viewing the most frequent *of* trigram clusters, we can see that the majority of these appear across the board in all sub-corpora. They are either not far removed in their proportional frequency or in their ranking of use from each other, underlining the idea that the usage of the item *of* is relatively stable – at least within one fairly narrowly defined genre.

4.6.2   "One of the" and "in terms of"

The segment *one of the* is a great linking part, usually introducing a more elaborate description. The use of *one* serves to capture the audience's attention. Preceded by *it is, it was, this is, there was*, etc., *one of the* is used to draw out the point where the listeners curiosity will be rewarded, as it is often followed by terms like *best, big, most, first, things, great, reasons, earliest, main.* It must be noted that the majority of these actually mirror the term *one* directly. It also appears fairly frequently in connection with a name – as in "Nicholas Stern, **one of the** intellectual leaders", "Plato was **one of the** earliest believers in eugenics" or "Goethe, who was **one of the** first Germans to be genuinely interested in other cultures." Throughout all four sub-corpora, we find this trigram cluster as part of the longer *[that/it][is] one of the things.* The difference here is the issue of prominence. In NML, it is within a larger, complex, clause: ... *that is one of the* things ... In the other corpora, it starts a new clause: *One of the things...*

This stands in clear contrast to the usage of *in terms of* which is employed with a high degree of flexibility across the sub-corpora.[9] The only time it can be part of a longer cluster is *in terms of the*, which may be preceded by a connector like *and* or *but*. *In terms of* is amongst the 13 most frequent 3w clusters overall in the three main sub-corpora, the exception being the VAR sub-corpus. Subsequently, we find *in terms of* is one of the most frequently occurring trigram phrases in the podcast transcripts viewed, and its very flexibility appears to make it ideal for a wide range of topics. This same flexibility allows it to appear in complex clauses, for example, "the deal goes far beyond what any other multilateral round has ever achieved **in terms of** reduction of obstacles to trade" (LSE), "Indeed, when considering these initial conditions, Jean spoke **in terms of** 'the finger of God agitating the ether'" (Reith), or "...and it seems to have made a big impact **in terms of** their awareness of what was happening and could happen to the country" (NML). All these uses appear to confirm the function of the subjunct of the phrase.

This seems to indicate that both *one of the things* as well as *in terms of* act as signals for the listener. It seems to be a stylistic device that prepares the listener to pay attention as a key piece of information will follow directly after. A lexical item of a type that can be expected in a pervasive speech.

As such, these sets of words fulfil a key requirement set out by Hoey with regards to lexical priming: the listener expects a key concept to follow either of these phrases. Likewise, a skilled orator would be found to employ such a device. There is no evidence that any conscious process in either the production or the reception is involved. However, both speaker and listener seem to be primed to meet such an expectation.

As will be seen in section 4.6.4, these two clusters are even more dominant when multiple-speaker podcasts' *of* use is considered.

4.6.3   OF usage compared in multiple-speaker podcast sub-corpora

Above, we have highlighted that *of* usage appears to be less varied than *to* usage. This section will look at whether the greater amount of variation found amongst multiple-speaker use mirrors the findings presented in this sub-section. Data for LSE is left out, as only four transcripts are available, which is deemed insufficient for this analysis.

In direct comparison of the most frequent trigram clusters occurring, we see further evidence that *of* use is remarkably stable for this type of genre: a lot of the same cluster can be found in both, single- and multiple-speaker sets: Table 4.8 has *one of the* as the most frequent clusters for Reith and NML. This indicates broadly similar usage in both the single and the multiple-speaker sub-corpora. This table gives an overview of clusters ranked amongst the top 20. Overall, one in five uses of *one of the* is part of the 4-gram *one of the things*. This reflects the predominant use of the phrase: it provides a specific description as in "... **one of the things** that China keeps repeating...."

By contrast, only a few occurrences of *some of the things, many of the things* or *a lot of the things* exist. Likewise, other phrases that use *of* tend to be fairly specific – *in terms of, of the world* and *the idea of* appear both higher in their overall ranking and with a higher procentual proportion of *of* usage in the multiple-speaker set of corpora. Both in Reith and VAR, and to a lesser degree in NML, we find *part of the* as having a preference for places "part of the world", "part of the city" and "part of the community".

This leads to two key differences being observed. Firstly, *of* usage amongst multiple speakers shows a slightly higher degree of vagueness

Table 4.8 Comparisons of rank, occurrence and proportional percentage OF-trigram clusters in the multiple-speaker sub-corpora

Cluster	R	N Reith Q&A	%	R	N NML-m	%	R	N VAR-m	%
ONE OF THE	1	48	3.98	1	72	3.52	3	120	3.51
IN TERMS OF	2	16	1.33	2	57	2.79	2	125	3.66
A LOT OF	3	16	1.33	4	37	1.81	1	198	5.79
OF THE THINGS	4	11	0.91	6	25	1.22	6	36	1.05
MANY OF THE	5	10	0.83	17	7	0.34	28	6	0.18
SOME OF THE	6	9	0.83	3	54	2.64	4	98	2.87
PART OF THE	6	9	0.83	7	21	1.03	5	42	1.23
OF THE WORLD	6	9	0.83	11	13	0.64	19	15	0.44
THE SORT OF	8	7	0.58	12	12	0.59	12	22	0.64
ONE OF THE THINGS	8	7	0.58	8	19	0.93	9	25	0.73

than amongst single speakers. While the ranking seen in Table 4.8 is not widely different from those shown in Table 4.7, the proportional frequency of usage is far higher. *A lot of, many of the, some of the, a/the sort of, the kind of* all use vagueness markers. *A lot of* is the one trigram that is clearly more prominent throughout all multiple-speaker sub-corpora, compared to the single-speaker data. This may reflect that we are looking at an exchange by different participants in a discourse here. Options are being left open for other panel speakers, or audience members, to disagree with what has been expressed. This is in clear divergence to what we have seen amongst single-speaker delivery, which appears to be more focussed and self-assured.[10]

Secondly, and more importantly, it can be seen that relatively unscripted, free recitation and speech is reflected by a strong tendency to formulaicity. The three highest occurring trigram clusters cover between 6.64 per cent (Reith) and 12.96 per cent (VAR) of all *of* uses; this is broadly comparable to what has been pointed out with regards to the NML single-speaker occurrence pattern (see 4.6.3). Furthermore, amongst the 3w clusters listed above, a number recombine into larger *of* clusters.

4.7 Single-speaker vs multiple-speaker material

4.7.1 Situating the genre of public lectures

In this chapter, we see the importance of the items *to* and *of* as a key element inside the most common clusters in English corpora. Both items are employed by single presenters or by a panel of multiple presenters and in Question-and-Answer sessions. Figure 4.2 seems to indicate that the preferred use of *of* makes the single-speaker podcast material resemble the patterns found in academic writing.

In the podcasts, *to* makes up 2.82 per cent of all words; in academic writing it is 2.63 per cent. *Of* is far more frequent, appearing in 3.92 per cent of all words in the single-speaker podcast corpus, and in 4.26 per cent of academic writing. Statistical testing, however, appears to tell a different story: All values are well above the threshold indicating significant difference (cf. Rayson: n.d.). There is a tendency, however, for *of* and *to* usage frequencies being closer to what can be found in academic writing than to what can be found in academic lectures. Yet the difference of frequency is clearly more marked for *of* than for *to*. Table 4.9 shows that public lectures are significantly different to the academic corpora material: something that may indicate genre-specificity. Statistical testing in Table 4.10 shows no difference in use of *to* where the two types of sub-corpora are compared, *of* appears significantly

Table 4.9   Log-likelihood values podcasts and academic material

	Observed frequencies		Expected frequencies		*Log – likelihood*
	Academic lectures	Single speaker	Academic lectures	Single speaker	
TO	27,770	33,967	29,076	32,661	*111*
OF	28,088	47,160	35,440	39,808	*2,924*
	Academic writing	Single speaker	Academic writing	Single speaker	
TO	425,400	33,967	427,623	31,744	*164*
OF	690,263	47,160	686,465	50,958	*311*

Table 4.10   Log-likelihood values comparing single- and multiple-speaker sub-corpora

	Observed frequencies		Expected frequencies		*Log – likelihood*
	Multiple speaker	Single speaker	Multiple speaker	Single speaker	
TO	7,097	33,967	6992.01	34071.99	*1.89*
OF	7,069	47,160	9233.63	44995.37	*655.03*
TOTAL	246,845	1202,873			

more frequent in the single speaker set when compared to the panel and Q&A set of texts.

4.7.2   The case of *to*

Statistical testing confirms that Table 4.4 gives a fairly accurate picture when we look at the usage frequencies for *be able to* and *to be able* in the Reith, LSE and *NML* corpora. There is virtually no difference between the LSE and *NML* corpora. The strongest difference is found for the use of *to be able* which is less preferred in the Reith sub-corpus.[11] While there is, therefore, some variation amongst the most frequently occurring corpora with regards to their collocates, the colligation aspect indicates a stable structure being employed in all sub-corpora: *to*-Infinitive is the dominant grammatical form. Amongst the podcasts, we do not find the *love to/like* to construction described by de Smet and Cuyckens (2005), although there is a preference for verbs, just as Sinclair ([1970] 2004) described. Biber (2000) highlighted that the key collocates in academic prose are *like*, *tend* and *appear*. While none of these are preferred options here, *try* and *want*, described as frequent verb-collocates of *to* in spoken discourse, are amongst the top ten and top 20 trigrams with *to*. As for the pragmatics of use, the key connection found in all three public corpora (and the VAR sub-corpus corroborates this view): this seems to indicate that *to* constructions are being employed to guide the listener from a real or perceived "here" to a different state or sphere. This would make perfect sense: lectures and, in particular, public lectures, are *pervasive texts*. The speakers use, as shown in section 4.5.4, *to* constructions to move the listener from a real or imagined situation to a state that the speaker wants them to picture.

The clearest difference becomes visible when statistical tests are run. Looking at the highly frequent clusters *be able to, in order to, have to be, to be a, to try to* and also *to be able*, no strongly significant differences between the respective percentages of usage can be found. What can be seen, however, is that certain clusters differ (see also Tables 4.4 and 4.5) to the point of significance in the Reith corpus in direct comparison. Table 4.5 highlights corpus-specific divergence of the most frequently used *to* trigrams. There is no significant difference in the proportional use of *in order to* within the three sub-corpora. This is in contrast to *have to be* which is clearly preferred in Reith – very significantly more so than in LSE and with a degree of significance compared to NML.[12] One possible explanation lies in the time-frame covered. While all sub-corpora have fairly recent material, only the Reith corpus includes material from as early as 1948. Based on this, we can assume that the formula *have to be* has become less frequent in use over time.

All the other clusters in Table 4.5 have been statistically checked, and the higher rank and percentage in an individual sub-corpus is mirrored by the strongly significant divergence: the respective trigrams are always markedly more prominent in this one sub-corpus, and not in the other two. For *to* usage in multiple-speaker podcast material, the Reith Q&A, NML and VAR panel and Q&A material has been compared. It has to be noted that the most frequent clusters – in particular, longer clusters – are different from the ones found amongst the single-speaker sub-corpora. *Going to be* appears only 114 times in the single-speaker corpus, around the same amount as the 105 occurrences in the far smaller selection of multiple-speaker files. Table 4.6 seems to indicate that the 20 most frequently occurring clusters appear with different rankings and percentages, a log-likelihood test of *to go to, going to be, in order to, be able to* and *we need to* has shown that there is zero to little divergence in use – the exception being *be able to* which are significantly more used in VAR than the other two corpora (99.9th percentile; 0.1 per cent level; p < 0.001; critical value ~12.5). There is some stronger use of *going to be* and *we need to* as well, but not to a high degree. The same formulaic phrases keep coming up within the same band of frequency and the key to most of them is the lemma *go to*. This is either expressed as *have-forms+to go to* or *want+to go to*, giving a sense of obligation. We see that the same sets of *to* trigram clusters are employed amongst the most frequent 25 clusters in both *to* single- and multiple-speaker sub-corpora. Both use *be able to* more frequently than *to be able*, too. *Going to* is an indicator of (near) future events; it also carries negative prosody at times: *never going to be, not going to*. The item *to* is not only occurring less frequently than *of*; its spread is also notably thinner. Even the most frequently occurring clusters are used by fewer speakers (i.e. they occur in fewer files). Table 4.11 highlights that the issue of *formulaicity* is far more prominent in the multiple-speaker sub-corpora compared to the single-speaker sessions. This is most probably explained by their more informal and less-prepared nature. At the same time, it must be noted that around half of the speakers in the multiple-speaker use the same trigrams, and around one-third the same 4-grams independent of content or the speaker's background. It must be noted that the phrase *going to be* stands out in MSM – this has been discussed in detail in section 4.5.4.

By contrast, *I would like to* seems rather formal and pre-edited: it is only found in a small number of files. With regards to the fairly low usage of *to be able to*, this seems to reflect casual spoken usages (see Chapter 5).

4.7.3   OF usage patterns

Of amongst the single and multiple-speaker sessions appear mostly to refer to a wider place: either as a section (*part of*) or very specific (*of the world*). These example appear in just over half of all the transcripts (163

Table 4.11   Core n-grams spread in single- and multiple-speaker sub-corpora[13]

	N SSM/ FILES	% of files in sub-corpus	N MSM/ FILES	% of files in sub-corpus
IN ORDER TO	118/286	41.4	21/48	43.8
WE NEED TO	86/286	30.2	24/48	50.0
I WANT TO	105/286	36.8	22/48	45.8
BE ABLE TO	101/286	35.4	25/48	52.1
GOING TO BE	64/286	22.4	29/48	60.4
I WOULD LIKE TO	45/286	15.8	13/48	27.1
TO BE ABLE TO	44/286	15.4	16/48	33.3

out of 286 files for *part of*) and just under half for *of the world* (128 out of 286 files) in the single-speaker sub-corpora, and these proportions are fully mirrored in the multiple-speaker sub-corpora.

Of occurs with a high frequency in all sub-corpora, though the level of divergence is significant. Amongst the single-speaker Reith Lectures, 4.37/100 words are *of*, yet it is only 3.25 per cent of all words in the NML sub-corpus. The use of the item, however, is far more stable: *one of the*, *part of the*, *some of the* and *in terms of*[14] are all found amongst the top five trigrams in all four sub-corpora. This notion of referring to a "part of a whole" can even be extended to the abstract descriptions – where we get *a sense of*, *the idea of* and *a kind of*. The usage pattern found here reflects to a high degree what both Sinclair and Sebastian Hoffmann have said. Furthermore, one unique noun stands out: *world (of the world)* which is fairly frequent in both Reith and LSE and is also recorded fairly often fiction and casual spoken corpora. Table 4.7 gives some idea that there is a level of divergence in both the rankings and percentages of particular phrases; this difference is seemingly connected to the material in each of the sub-corpora.

Thus, Reith and the LSE sub-corpora represent the most formal use of language; NML and VAR are more informal. Reith represents some older use of English; NML has elements of conversational English. When the log-likelihood statistical test is applied to the highly frequent clusters given in Table 4.7, however, this explanation is insufficient. What stands out here are the NML data, in particular in comparison to Reith single-speakers: ten of the 13 clusters differ significantly; most of them through being proportionally far more frequent. Comparing NML to the LSE sub-corpus, we still find six significant differences in frequency of use. Overall, the Reith sub-corpus shows a significant comparative underuse of *a lot of*. The other difference that the statistical test reveals is also clear from the raw percentages: *one of the* is rather less strongly used in Reith and LSE, whereas *of the world* appears more in these two sub-corpora than in NML and VAR.

Looking at the multiple-speaker material, few of the differences seen above remain. *In terms of*, *a lot*, *some of the* and *many of the* are significantly more frequently used in VAR than in Reith; *a lot of* is also significantly more used in VAR compared to NML. The largest divergence between and NML, however, is only *some of the*, which is significantly more frequent in NML. This shows strong overuse of *a lot of* in VAR and strong underuse of *some of the* in Reith, yet no clear reasons for this are apparent. The use of the item *of* single-speaker corpora is demonstrated through the predominant usage of the phrase *one of the* – the most frequent trigram in all the sub-corpora. *A lot of*, by contrast, is less than half as frequent and is only heard in around one-third of the texts. However, when we focus on the multiple-speaker corpus, these two phrases are similar in frequency: 258 for *a lot of*; 223 for *one of the*; and they both appear in almost every podcast. Table 4.12 demonstrates a higher degree of formulaicity in the multiple-speaker podcasts, as can be expected.

However, *a lot* of is used almost universally in the multiple-speaker sub-corpora. This is in sharp contrast to the single-speaker corpora. Naturally, as clusters become longer, they occur in fewer instances and therefore in fewer files.

Yet *of* very clearly is key to locate items: on a scale, like a time scale, for example. We see that these three n-grams can be seen as stock-phrases within less carefully planned speech.

It can be also seen that there is a clear tendency by the speakers to avoid the personal referrer *I* – this is avoided almost fully amongst the prepared speeches by single-speakers.

While the chunk *one of* is fairly neutral, Table 4.13 also highlights that the longer phrase *one of the things* appears in almost half of the multiple-speaker files but is avoided by over 90 per cent of the single-speaker presentations. This can be seen as an indication that the use of *things* is deemed too vague and therefore too colloquial, too.

Table 4.12   *One of the* and *a lot of* occurrence spread in single- and multiple-speaker sub-corpora

	N SSM/ FILES	*% of files in sub-corpus*	N MSM/ FILES	*% of files in sub-corpus*
ONE OF THE	219/286	75.8	40/48	83.3
A LOT OF	86/286	30.1	45/48	93.8

Table 4.13   Spread of the most frequent multiple-speaker long cluster phrases

	N MSM/ FILES	*% of files in sub-corpus*	N SSM/ FILES	*% of files in sub-corpus*
ONE OF THE THINGS	22/48	41.7	28/286	9.8
ONE OF THE THINGS THAT	16/48	33.3	16/286	5.6
I THINK ONE OF THE	8/48	16.7	5/286	1.8

Table 4.14 Spread of highly frequent referrer-of phrases within the sub-corpora

	N SSM/ FILES	% of files in sub-corpus	N MSM/ FILES	% of files in sub-corpus
THE END OF THE	67/286	23.5	10/48	20.8
AT THE END OF THE	42/286	14.7	6/48	12.5
THE BEGINNING OF	58/286	20.3	12/48	25.0
AT THE BEGINNING OF	25/286	8.8	8/48	16.7
IN THE MIDDLE OF	41/286	14.4	5/48	10.4
IN THE MIDDLE OF THE	25/286	8.8	2/48	4.1

Table 4.14 shows that references to *beginning, middle* and *end* occur in similar proportions in the single- and multiple-speaker sub-corpora. The most frequent long 4- and 5-grams with *of* are the following: *the end of the* (110 occurrences) and *at the end of the* (49). This is matched by *the beginning of* (70 occurrences) and *at the beginning of* (28). The centre is referred to slightly less often, however: *in the middle of* (55 occurrences) and *in the middle of the* (33).

This does, to a large extent, demonstrate how stable the usage pattern of *of* is: colligational and collocational lexical items are highly frequent throughout with little divergence created by different groups of speakers. The clearest divergences are only found within long *of* clusters. The right-hand entries of Table 4.13 demonstrate that the most frequent 4- and 5-grams for *of* are rather rare (they tend to occur about once per speaker in around 2–10 per cent of all files). The left-hand side of Table 4.13 shows that the same clusters are strongly predominant, by contrast, in the multiple-speaker sub-corpora.

4.8 Summing up

The earlier discussion has highlighted the fact that *to*, whilst used generally for similar purposes (guiding the listener from a perceived *here* to an intended *there*), shows significant corpus-dependent levels of variation; and the level of variation is markedly higher where multiple-speaker sub-corpora are compared.

Within the narrow genre of podcasts, the majority of highly frequent clusters incorporating *of* can be found across the board. There is pervasive evidence showing a high degree of stability and conformity in *of* usage in all sub-corpora. Multiple-speaker usage tends to use a greater amount of vagueness markers. both *of* and *to* display strong evidence that there is a greater use of formulaic language in multiple-speaker corpora. This reflects the free and not very pre-edited nature of the panel and Q&A discussions, where speakers are forced to react to what has been previously said and have had fewer chances of pre-construction.

To usage does, in the corpora investigated, support earlier research. The use of *to* is far more subject- and speaker-specific than the use of *of*. Consequently, there are far fewer instances of salient long clusters in the corpus. We also see a very clear divergence of the phrases used (and their respective frequency of use) where single- and multiple-speaker sub-corpora are compared. Consequently, *in order to, we need to* and *I would like to* are the most frequent 3-/4-grams in the single-speaker sub-corpora – none of which appear in half of the files. By contrast, we hear *going to be, we need to, you have to* and *to make sure that* in the multiple-speaker sub-corpora.

To sum up, in the subset of "podcasts", clear semantic and pragmatic functions can be seen – and these are restricted within the genre. On the surface of it, the levels of frequency as well as the usage of some key features show that the language of podcasts is closer to *academic writing* than the obvious comparator, academic lectures. Viewing the usage in detail, corpus-specificity becomes apparent.

When focussing on colligational properties rather than collocations, we can identify that *to* mostly appears in the form of *to*-Infinitive constructions and *of* as descriptive constructions, specifying parts of a larger whole. Pragmatically, the majority of the highly frequent clusters with *of* and *to* in this corpus function as the speaker's lead-ins. This means that they are clear signalling points which are introducing passages or ideas and therefore play a role as speech acts.

The users of these items do not produce *of* or *to* at random; nor do they use them with a conscious purpose. A possible explanation is that they have been primed, being listeners and experienced speakers, into using set constructions and phrases – collocation and colligations that make up lexical items incorporating *of* or *to* – that have been accepted through a high degree of usage. That we find the same phrases and grammatical constructions time and again – used by different speakers, in different eras, talking about different subjects – indicates that neither *of* nor *to* are simply slotted in at random: their use appears to be in a narrow, fairly restricted frame. In a long speech, levels of concentration and full comprehension cannot be expected to be kept up throughout for any given audience. Therefore, a skilled speaker has to indicate the sections of his speech he or she deems important enough to be focussed upon by the listeners. The targeted use of these *of* and *to* phrases fulfil this speech act function.

5
OF and TO Usage in Spoken Texts

5.1 Introduction

> If you have occasion to write a conversation down,
> you are very likely to find it disjointed, stumbling and
> inarticulate. If you do react like this, that is because
> what you expect to find in speech follows your expec-
> tation of written language, particularly prose. It is
> difficult not to regard speech as an imperfect version
> of the written language.
>
> (Knowles, 1987: 5)

Knowles highlights two crucial points with regards to spoken language
here: first, our common expectations, driven by years of schooling, to
expect language to be *the written word*; and second, that spoken language appears to follow a pattern quite different to what we have in
written text, giving rise to the impression that the spoken is "disjointed
and inarticulate".

For this chapter, the focus will be on the occurrence patterns found
in *casually spoken British English*. For this the BNC Spoken Conversation
(BNC-C) sub-corpus will be used as well as a collection based on more
recent recordings collected in Hackney, London; Havering, Essex (now
an outer East London Borough); Lancaster; Liverpool; and Tyneside.
This will be supplemented by a selection taken from the COLT corpus.[1] A selection was made of the London and Tyneside material to
be closer in size to the other corpora. It is hoped that the variety of
sources, coming from different parts of England, speakers of different
age groups and recorded in a number of different decades creates a fair
representation of contemporary spoken British English. The combined

Table 5.1   Sub-corpora used

Name	Files (no.)	Tokens	OF	OF %	TO	TO %
COLT	91	152,418	1,754	1.12	2,371	1.51
Hackney	44	217,980	2,906	1.33	4,166	1.90
Havering	18	247,866	3,045	1.22	5,068	2.04
Lancaster	119	180,830	2,748	1.48	4,170	2.24
Liverpool	62	207,821	2,831	1.28	3,573	1.51
Tyneside	17	222,821	3,163	1.20	4,989	1.90
Total (4CC)	*357*	*1,229,793*	*16,447*	*1.27*	*24,337*	*1.88*
BNC-C	153	4,217,072	42,310	1.00	73,492	1.74

assortment will be referred to as the Four Corners (Lancaster, Liverpool, London and Newcastle) Corpus – 4CC.[2] Details of the sub-corpora are listed in Table 5.1.

The table shows that *of* and *to* are considerably less frequent in spoken than in fiction texts. More crucially, *to* appears far more frequent in all of the sub-corpora. It is well documented that spoken English displays a number of marked differences to written English, one of them being the higher degree of formulaicity (Carter and McCarthy, 1995; Bieber et al., 1998; Wray, 2002; etc.). Another feature of casually spoken language is that production is online and spontaneous. This means that a speaker cannot edit what is produced unless it has been considered carefully before speaking starts. Therefore, false starts, repetition and non-lexical markers (mmh, erm, etc.) occur, as do pauses and non-verbal actions, laughter amongst them. A speaker will also be a partner in a dialogue with one or more other people, meaning that utterances must often be created in direct response. The corpora in question do not record gestures, tone of voice or activities in the background which may influence what is said. Most of the corpora used have been transcribed specifically for the purposes of corpus research. The Lancaster and Tyneside material, however, is based on oral history records and can be expected to have a higher degree of editing of the words actually said (this would include normalisation). As far as I am aware, only the SCO part of the Liverpool corpus has large sections of transcripts purely based on exchanges that were not specifically elicited by a researcher. Overall, spoken corpora are a less precise collection of data than corpora based on written texts. Still, they are, in general, deemed as a sufficient reflection of naturally occurring language use. Statistical testing shows that both *of* and *to* are significantly less used in the BNC-C compared to 4CC, which is also reflected in the raw percentages.

In this chapter it will be investigated in what way *of* and *to* appear in the two collections of spoken data – 4CC and BNC-C. The focus will be to see in what MWUs these items tend to occur and whether there are general trends which may appear concurrent with the results presented on *of* and *to* usage in fiction and semi-prepared spoken texts. A question raised by Pace-Sigge (2009) will be revisited in this chapter: are there obvious differences in spoken language use *of* and *to* in different speech corpora.

5.2 Usage patterns in spoken corpora

5.2.1 Usage patterns for both items

Starting with a broad overview of the most frequent clusters found in all spoken corpora, Table 5.2, reveals a familiar pattern. It has to be noted that these 512 files are representing the BNC-C mostly, being 3.5 times larger than the 4CC component. Still: *of* with determiner features strongly, whereas, by contrast, only *to the* occurs amongst the most frequent *to* bigrams. *Of* is used for counting (*one of*) and this, as the trigrams make clear, means counting mostly of vague rather than precise quantities. *To* bigrams show predominance of *to*-Infinitive prime verbs (ranked fifth is *to be*) whereas the 3w and 4w clusters feature *used to*, *go to*, *want to*, etc.,[3] strongly reflecting narratives and interaction, as highlighted by the predominance of interrogative forms.

In contrast to this, 4w *of* clusters show the strong occurrence of nouns, it is the actual nouns that are of note. Speakers refer to *a lot of people* – the context of which will be investigated further below.

Table 5.2 OF and TO most frequent clusters in BNC-C and 4CC combined

R	2w OF	Freq.	%	3w OF	Freq.	%	4w OF	F	%
1	OF THE	8,298	14.12	A LOT OF	2,982	5.08	A BIT OF A	378	0.64
2	SORT OF	6,091	10.37	A BIT OF	1,359	2.31	THE END OF THE	368	0.63
3	ONE OF	3,487	5.93	ONE OF THE	1,096	1.87	A LOT OF PEOPLE	358	0.62
4	OF THEM	3,187	5.42	A COUPLE OF	1,043	1.78	A CUP OF TEA	312	0.56

R	2w TO	Freq.	%	3w TO	Freq.	%	4w TO	F	%
1	USED TO	7,101	7.26	TO GO TO	1,799	1.84	TO GO TO THE	452	0.46
2	HAVE TO	6,578	6.72	YOU HAVE TO	1,245	1.27	DO YOU WANT TO	371	0.38
3	TO GO	6,291	6.43	I USED TO	1,179	1.21	ARE YOU GOING TO	293	0.30
4	TO THE	6,142	6.31	YOU WANT TO	1,073	1.10	TO BE ABLE TO	270	0.28

An observer will also realise that a British obsession is not just prover-
bial: *a cup of tea* is offered so often in the conversations recorded that
the actual set of words appears amongst the most used here.

There are only few highly frequent long clusters of *to* – most likely
due to the preference for *to*-Infinitive constructions – yet we can
see constructions incorporating *go to, going to, used to* and *want to*
throughout. The interesting finding here is, again, when we look at
of, where the most frequent long clusters are given in Figure 5.1. This
mirrors exactly the long clusters found in fiction and prepared-speech
corpora analysed earlier – down to the point that "end of" (935 occurrences) is markedly more frequent than "middle of" (271). "Beginning
of" is rare (100 occurrences). The one alternative which is fairly
frequently found is the 4w cluster *the rest of the* (129 occurrences –
0.2 per cent of all *of* uses). Similarly, *the other side of* is noteworthy, as
it appears to be an *of* string, which regularly occurs regardless of the
genre of text.

It might be said that there is little validity in looking at long clusters
of the items *of* and *to* as the total figures are low. It must be said, however, that the most frequent, consistent 5w cluster for these sub-corpora
is *you know what I mean* which occurs 608 times (0,11 per cent within
the combined BNC-C and 4CC corpus).

Below, the usage occurrence – and the pattern of these and other uses
of *of* and *to* – will be shown and analysed in more detail.

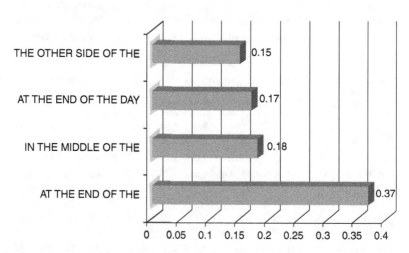

Figure 5.1 End of the relative occurrence pattern (combined percentages for
BNC-C and 4CC)

5.3 Overall usage patterns for OF

5.3.1 OF bigrams

Looking at the occurrence pattern for *of* bigrams we find a high level of agreement within the top ten. *Of the* and *of a* are ranked first (around 15 per cent of all *of* uses) and eighth (just below 4 per cent) respectively. Likewise, *of them* is ranked fourth (over 5 per cent). The majority of the top 15 bigrams appear in both sub-corpora. Both BNC-C and 4CC show little use of *of an* – 0.51 and 0.26 per cent of all uses of *of*. This makes sense: overall, the item *a* occurs 15 times more frequently than the item *an*. The discourse marker *of course* is also noticeable, being ranked tenth (3.1 per cent) in BNC-C and seventh (4.0 per cent) in 4CC. What appears to be specific to the spoken usage is, however, the strong use of vagueness markers. So we have *sort of, one of, lot of, bit of, some of, couple of* and *kind of* – see details in Table 5.3. It must be noted that, apart from the two most frequent bigrams (*of the, sort of*), the divergence between the two corpora is significant. Similarly, *some of* appears statistically stronger use than expected in BNC-C. All the other ones listed in Table 5.3 appear (to a lesser or stronger degree) significantly less used in 4CC than in BNC-C with the exception of *lot of* (see endnote 4) and *kind of*, which displays a preference in 4CC. This requires a more detailed investigation. *That kind of* appears proportionally as often in both. There seems to be a slight preference of *that kind of thing* in 4CC and a lot of these lines come from the Havering and Hackney sub-corpora. In the BNC-C, *a kind of* and *what kind of* seem to be more often used for rhetorical questions (the latter is used by the recorder to elicit information in around ten cases in 4CC). It is noticeable, however, that *kind of like, kind of stuff* and *like kind of* are by far more prominent in 4CC. The first is almost exclusively used by Liverpool speakers and two Havering

Table 5.3 OF bigrams with vagueness markers

OF 2w	Rank BNC-C	Freq.	%	Rank 4CC	Freq.	%
SORT OF	2	4,517	10.675	2	1,822	11.070
ONE OF	3	2,878	6.802	5	811	4.930
LOT OF[4]	6	2,065	4.880	3	1,184	7.199
BIT OF	9	1,585	3.746	13	376	2.297
SOME OF	11	1,222	2.888	11	405	2.462
COUPLE OF	13	1,047	2.474	14	322	1.958
KIND OF	23	504	1.192	9	584	3.574

speakers, the latter by London speakers. *Like kind of* is only recorded coming from Liverpool or London speakers. This can indicate that differences between the spoken sub-corpora show a change of use over time (the BNC-C is older and records only a few instances) or reflects a regional preference (see Pace-Sigge: 2013). When, by contrast, we look at *lot of*, the most frequent collocates to the left and to the right are the same, with no marked difference in percentages.

The bigram 'bit of' is most significantly underrepresented in 4CC when compared to BNC-C. Whole phrases that incorporate this bigram may only occur in BNC-C: *nice bit of* (12) or *bit of paper* (34) occur only in BNC-C, and *bit of it* (38) is far rarer (four occurrences in fact) in 4CC. Just outside the top 20 ranked bigrams is also *part of*, which occurs in 1.25 per cent of all uses of *of* in 4CC, yet only 0.84 per cent – significantly lower – in BNC-C. Overall, the differences reflect specific usage by sub-sections of informants but do not alter decisively which clusters with *of* are used with high frequency in spoken corpora. We find three main uses of *of* amongst the bigrams:

1.   *of* with determiner (*of the, of them, of it, of a, of that, of those*);
2a. *of* with vague countables (*one of, lot of, bit of, some of, couple of, kind of, end of*);
2b. vagueness marker (*sort of*);
3   *of* + discourse marker (*of course, think of*).

For (2), it must be noted that *one of* is nearly five times as frequent as *end of* in BNC-C and 4CC and both are far less vague than *kind of*.

5.3.2   OF trigrams

As has been pointed out before, trigrams provide an insight into the salient use of single items within MWUs while occurring with sufficiently high frequencies.

While there are clear differences between the sets of corpora,[5] as we have already highlighted above, it is fairly clear that *of* in spoken utterances shows a pervasive usage of "part of" – usually in a vague way, as Table 5.4 demonstrates. There is no strongly significant divergence between the corpora for *one of the, sort of thing, some of the, bit of a* and *that sort of*. *A lot of, a bit of* and *a couple of* are more key in 4CC. By contrast, only *some of them* is significantly more frequent in BNC-C. These trigrams need further investigation.

Though there are no difference in the trigrams, *that sort of* appears, most commonly, as *and that sort of* and *all that sort of* which are both, proportionally, far more frequent in 4CC.

Table 5.4   OF trigrams with count markers

3w OF	BNC-C	Freq.	%	4CC	Freq.	%
A LOT OF	1	1,833	4.332	1	1,085	6.597
A BIT OF	2	1,081	2.489	3	258	1.551
A COUPLE OF	3	796	1.881	4	241	1.465
ONE OF THE	4	738	1.744	2	328	1.963
ONE OF THEM	5	649	1.533	11	138	0.839
ONE OF THOSE	8	481	4.144	27	73	0.450
SORT OF THING	9	410	0.969	6	196	1.200
BIT OF A	11	369	0.872	15	115	0.699
ONE OF THESE	12	339	0.822	60	54	0.337
SOME OF THE	14	295	0.690	16	114	0.697
SOME OF THEM	15	292	0.689	9	170	1.037
THAT SORT OF	16	288	0.685	10	146	0.888

Looking at the divergent trigrams, *a lot of* seems to have acquired a stronger use of the modifier "quite" which is proportionally far more frequent in 4CC, whereas *got a lot of* is far more frequent, proportionally, in BNC-C. In the infrequent case where "got" is L2, both sub-corpora usually list *got quite a lot of*. *In a couple* of is clearly more frequent in BNC-C. However, while the proportional differences of *In a couple of days/weeks/ years* are not very different, *a couple of times* is clearly preferred by 4CC compared to BNC-C. There seems to be no obvious differences in the use of *a bit of*. As for *one of*-with-*DET*, the BNC-C shows again a strong preference to preface this with got – mostly *got one of them, got one of those*; these are mirrored by *have one of them, have one of these*. These are, however, rare in 4CC, and five of the six *have one of* uses are in the COLT sub-corpus. That *one of these* is more frequent in BNC-C seems to be only explained by the (near-) absence of the clusters *have one of these, want one of these* in 4CC.[6]

Far less frequent are, in the spoken corpora, *of* in prepositional use and *of* with discourse markers. While *out of the* and *the back of the* are, to a degree, less prominently used in 4CC, the differences are not as stark amongst prepositional use as they are amongst the countables described above.

Table 5.5 also shows four prominent forms where *of* is used with a discourse marker and, in the case of *what sort of*, as an interrogative. In utterances, these are seen as highly context-dependent. For the majority of trigrams the statistical differences are minor. Still, *what sort of* and *and of course* occur more often than expected in 4CC; *a couple of, out of the, the back of* and *sort of like* occur more often in BNC-C. Looking at the concordance lines in detail, 4CC shows a preferred use for *and of course* (N=153). This is found as constituent part in the longer cluster *and of course there was/were* – most of which come from the Lancaster

Table 5.5   OF trigrams with prepositions and discourse markers

3w OF	R BNC-C	Freq.	%	R 4CC	Freq.	%
OUT OF THE	7	486	1.148	12	130	0.790
END OF THE	13	337	0.820	18	101	0.614
THE BACK OF	19	250	0.591	28	66	0.401
IN FRONT OF	20	241	0.570	17	109	0.663
SORT OF THING	*9*	*410*	*0.969*	*6*	*196*	*1.200*
SORT OF LIKE	*22*	*221*	*0.522*	*>50*	*49*	*0.308*
AND OF COURSE	*26*	*200*	*0.480*	*8*	*171*	*1.039*
WHAT SORT OF	*>50*	*124*	*0.029*	*7*	*183*	*1.111*

data. In BNC-C only *and of course there's* can be found (N=5). In BNC-C, it is mostly preceded by *yeah*; in the 4CC, it is *er*. *And of course I* appears as often in both corpora; *as of course you* is, in raw figures, even more frequent in 4CC, indicating a preference in 4CC. That *what sort of* is so prominent in 4CC is based on the fact that the interviewer, in the London and Tyneside data, uses these to elicit information ("What sort of things do you like", etc.). Once these are taken out, the figures are, if anything, lower than found in BNC-C. Otherwise, there are no structural or collocation differences that are of note.

To sum up, the majority of the *of* trigrams investigated are employed for vague count markers and the more specific descriptions using *one of* or *couple of* (meaning: two). The most frequent prepositional uses are *out of*, *end of*, *back of front of* – in this order of frequency in both corpora. The main discourse markers employ *sort of* and *of course*.

5.3.4   OF long clusters

One salient feature is that the convergence between BNC-C and 4CC is greater the longer the clusters are. This is exemplified by the 4w cluster *a cup of tea* – ranked fourth in BNC-C and 11th in 4CC.[7] However, the longer forms, *have a cup of tea* and *want a cup of tea*, occur with frequencies that display no statistically significant difference. Looking at the rankings however, *want a cup of tea* is preferred in BNC-C and *have a cup of tea* in 4CC.[8] More convergent still are *the end of the* and *at the end of the* which are both, proportionally, slightly more frequent and rank higher in BNC-C. The phrase *at the end of the day*, however, is one of the most frequent long *of* clusters uttered – 0.17 and 0.16 per cent of all *of* uses in BNC-C and 4CC. The majority of the long phrases relate to vague counting descriptors and have been discussed in 5.3.4. Amongst the longer clusters we find that the number of expressions seems to be, amongst the 30 most frequently occurring ones, reduced to three. The most frequent 4w cluster is *a **bit** of a* – occurring in 0.7 and 0.6 per cent of all uses of *of*. The other 4w cluster is *a little **bit** of* which occurs only around half as frequently.

There is also *the **rest** of the* –used in just under 0.2 per cent in BNC-C and just under 0.3 per cent in 4CC (there is no statistical significant difference), and ranked around 20th in both.

In the middle of (the) is, however, significantly more frequent in BNC-C, occurring only 33 times in 4CC, yet 162 times in the 3.5-times larger BNC-C. However, the raw numbers here appear to be the only reason to give space for a more varied set of collocates. *Sort of thing* is only marginally more used in 4CC; *that sort of thing* is slightly less marginal but *and that sort of thing* is significantly more used than in BNC-C. There are not enough instances in either sub-corpus to see any clear trends. What can be said, however, is that nine of the 24 concordance lines come from Lancaster material and four are idiosyncratic to a single Havering source.

Table 5.6 focusses on the usage of clusters incorporating *a **lot** of*. Overall, there are few differences. We find here that *a lot of money* is something frequently talked about by all sources. *A lot of people* is significantly more frequent in 4CC. Searching for yet more detail, this explained by the fact that there is a preference for *quite a lot of people* and *I mean a lot of people* spoken by London sources and *and a lot of people* said by the Liverpool sources. There are far fewer instances of these MWUs in BNC-C. *A lot of the* is a chunk that is also significantly higher in frequency in 4CC than in BNC-C. The main collocates to the left and the right are different as well and this is almost exclusively due to the Liverpool speakers who say *I think a lot of the...* and *a lot of the people/girls/teachers/parents* as well as *a lot of the places*. In sharp contrast, the two most frequent R-collocates in BNC-C are *time* and *stuff*. So 4CC (mainly Liverpool and some London speakers) show a preference for

Table 5.6 Long clusters with *a lot of* that are significantly divergent in frequency

4–6w OF	R BNC-C	N	%	R 4CC	N	%
A LOT OF MONEY	6	178	0.420	9	63	0.383
A LOT OF PEOPLE	7	175	0.416	1	189	1.150
A LOT OF THE	17	97	0.229	6	79	0.480
QUITE A LOT OF	21	85	0.200	4	84	0.510

person – and place references. *A lot of the time*, however, is used in equal proportion in both sub-corpora. *Quite a lot of people* again, seems to be mainly a Liverpool usage, while both 4CC and BNC-C use the *quite a lot of money* strongly.

Otherwise, there are no strong trends that would explain why *quite a lot of* is significantly more used in 4CC.

To sum up, we see that some clear stock phrases – *a cup of tea, a lot of money, that sort of thing, at the end of the day* are common in spoken British English and re-occur fairly frequently regardless of the sources. This is even true for a fairly low-frequency phrase relating to time: *three quarters of an hour* is marginal (25 occurrences in BNC-C) yet the proportional equivalent occurs also in 4CC. The other fact revealed here is how long clusters can reveal characteristic speech community use – to a point where proportional frequencies become statistically significantly higher. We have shown instances where London, Liverpool or Lancaster speakers preferred a certain long *of* construction more than other UK speakers.

5.4 Usage patterns for TO

5.4.1 TO bigrams

While *to* usage in fiction and prepared-speech texts has been found to be fairly consistent regardless of source, this cannot be said of *to* use found in these two collections of transcripts. Looking at the top 20 bigrams, we find both consistency (i.e. minimal differences in proportional use and ranking) and also clear outliers (i.e. which have statistically very significant differences in frequency), which mark the particular use within each sub-corpus.

Focussing on Table 5.7 first, it can be seen that the same key bigrams as described in Chapters 3 and 4 are prominent here, too. *To the* and *to* with *be, have, do* and *go*. If we just look at rankings, *to get* also fits into

Table 5.7 Most frequent similar TO bigrams in BNC-C and 4CC

2 w TO	R BNC-C	N	%	R 4CC	N	%
TO GO	2	4,916	6.690	3	1,660	6.880
TO THE	3	4,861	6.614	2	1,677	6.890
TO DO[9]	4	4,759	6.475	5	1,247	5.124
TO BE	5	4,474	6.088	4	1,619	6.652
TO HAVE	12	2,483	3.379	12	758	3.115

Table 5.8   Most frequent divergent TO bigrams in BNC-C and 4CC

2 w TO	R BNC-C	N	%	R 4CC	N	%
HAVE TO	1	6,015	8.185	7	1,013	4.162
GOING TO	6	4,327	5.887	11	780	3.205
TO GET	7	4,304	5.810	8	981	4.030
GOT TO	8	3,541	4.818	18	465	1.911
WANT TO	9	3,496	4.757	22	432	1.775
USED TO	10	2,813	3.812	1	3,808	15.647
GO TO	11	2,800	3.810	6	1,242	5.110
TO ME	13	1,915	2.607	15	506	2.079
HAD TO	14	1,808	2.460	10	924	3.797
WENT TO	24	1,341	1.824	9	979	4.029

this category. It has to be highlighted that these are similar in use, with only really *to do* being markedly lower in frequency in 4CC.

Far more interesting, however, are the bigrams shown in Table 5.8, all of which diverge in frequency to a highly significant degree. This is reflected in *have to* – the most frequent BNC-C bigram but only ranked seventh in 4CC, or *used to* where this relation is inversed. In fact, the bigrams show, like a microcosm, what multi-unit forms will dominate the longer clusters: *have to, going to, to get, got to* and *want to* for BNC-C and *used to, go to, had to* and *went to* for 4CC.

Note how these forms reflect what Fischer said about *to*-Infinitive grammaticalisation and, quoting Plank, its occurrence in informal speech:

> Plank (1984: 338–339) notes that these verbs are unlike auxiliaries in that they occur with *to*, but notes at the same time that these same auxiliaries "allow the conjunction [i.e. *to*] to be reduced and contracted in informal speech", even when this is not fast speech, and before pauses, indicating that this *to* has grammaticalised and become as it were affixed to the matrix verb.
>
> (Fischer, 2000: 161)

Here, I shall concentrate on the two most frequent bigrams of each sub-corpus as all other bigrams are playing a clear role as essential components of the longer clusters discussed below. *Have to* appears in BNC-C at a significantly higher frequency. It is a combination of two highly frequent items (*have* makes up 0.47 per cent of the whole 4CC, 0.69 per cent of the whole BNC-C).[10] The way we find *have to* so much more frequent in BNC-C mirrors exactly how much more frequent *have to* is in relation to 4CC, which indicates that *have to* is a fixed colligational form for the item *have* regardless of sources: *have to* appears in both at around 10 per cent of all uses of *have*. When looking at the concordance lines, both sub-corpora have *you have to* as the most frequent use. However, this is followed by the personal self-reference *I have to* in 4CC, where it is mainly used by Liverpool speakers, and then by younger London speakers but only very rarely by speakers of other regions (or the other age groups of London speakers). While in BNC-C *you have to* occurs 968 times, *I have to* has 425 lines; in 4CC it is 235 to 110 lines – a difference that is significant but only marginally so. There is a significant difference for the third-most frequent R1 collocate, as *don't have to* occurs 93 times in 4CC, yet 545 times in the 3.5-times larger BNC-C. The largest difference can be found for *I (will) have to* which is the preferred BNC-C form, occurring 1,349 times, but only 68 times in 4CC. This represents the strongest divergence for sets like *you'll/I'll/we'll/he'll have to*. Furthermore, BNC-C records 100 instances of *gonna have to* – more than twice as many, proportionally, as the 14 instances in 4CC.

Used to is a very special lexical item as the combination reflects something I like to term **mono-collocational**: *used* almost always appears in the form of *used to*. This is largely true for BNC-C, where 84.4 per cent of *used* concordance-lines are *used to* and there is an even stronger bind in 4CC, where 93.9 per cent of all concordance lines are *used to*.[11] Therefore, I propose to call a term mono-collocational if a single word is bound to another either eight (or more) out of ten times. Alternatively, a single item can be deemed mono-collocational if other collocates are of low relative frequencies. *Use* is only very rarely employed for "usage": *of course the boys and girls used the gymnasium*. Instead, *used to* is as part of the narrative flow: Well, Mike used to do it like that" or "I used to live in, eh, Penny Lane." Thus retelling things of the past: "One side used to vote Conservative"; "boys used to chalk stumps". This reflects the material that makes up most of 4CC – researchers who try to elicit information through interview techniques – either for oral history archives (Tyneside, Lancaster) or to record patterns of speech (London). This impression is supported by the fact that my own Liverpool material, which is based on a lot of casual conversation (rather than historical fact finding) where *used to* occurs comparatively less frequently than the other parts of 4CC. This, therefore, is the most likely reason why *used to* forms are so dominant as an instrumental part of *to* MWUs in 4CC.

I used to is the most frequent form in both sub-corpora. *The-NP-used to* and *used to-VP-the* appear in both to a similar extent, too. However, *and I used to* is significantly more frequent in 4CC. Furthermore, 4CC appears more community-orientated in its outlook: *we used to* occurs nearly 700 times, but fewer than 300 times in the much larger BNC-C.

5.4.2 TO trigrams

As hinted above, unlike what we have seen with the usage of *of*, *to*-clusters longer than bigrams diverge sharply between the two sub-corpora. While the same trigrams occur across the 50 most frequent sets, both the proportional frequencies and rank of trigrams are different. This appears to be a particular feature of spoken English, as highlighted by Pace-Sigge (2009, 2013). Looking at the data at hand, two issues are very apparent: firstly, the most frequent BNC-C cluster is ranked 23rd in 4CC; the most frequent 4CC cluster is not even within the 50 most frequent BNC-C trigrams; and secondly, the sixth-most frequent cluster in 4CC is the last one to have more occurrences (398) than there are files (357). As there are only 155 BNC-C files, this issue does not arise. There is only one trigram which is fully similar in use: *to go to*. *To do it* is, proportionally, less than half as frequent in 4CC and is ranked only 30th.

Table 5.9 demonstrates what has been highlighted for *to* bigrams already: *have to* and *got to* are more frequent in BNC-C. An explanation for the prominent use of *I went to* in 4CC (more than twice as frequent, proportionally, as in BNC-C) is that it answers interviewers questions: *I went to school*, etc. Above, the preference for the use of *will* ('ll) in BNC-C has been shown.

Be able to is very strongly used in the Spoken-Conversation part of the BNC but rather rare in the Liverpool Spoken English as has been discussed in Pace-Sigge (2013: 167, and 176). When a direct comparison is made, *be able to* displays a curiously low usage in North-West England,

Table 5.9 Top 10 TO trigrams in BNC-C and 4CC

R	3w TO BNC-C	Freq.	%	R	3w TO 4CC	Freq.	%
1	I'VE GOT TO	1,890	2.571	1	WE USED TO	692	2.843
2	I'LL HAVE TO	1,457	1.983	2	I USED TO	625	2.568
3	TO GO TO	1,275	1.734	3	TO GO TO	569	2.338
4	YOU HAVE TO	1,087	1.479	4	USED TO GO	485	1.992
5	YOU WANT TO	1,057	1.421	5	THEY USED TO	439	1.800
6	BE ABLE TO	928	1.262	6	USED TO BE	398	1.635
7	YOU'VE GOT TO	870	1.184	7	USED TO HAVE	348	1.422
8	TO DO IT	809	1.101	8	I WENT TO	334	1.372
9	I SAID TO	806	1.100	9	HE USED TO	307	1.311
10	I WANT TO	724	0.985	10	YOU USED TO	300	1.232

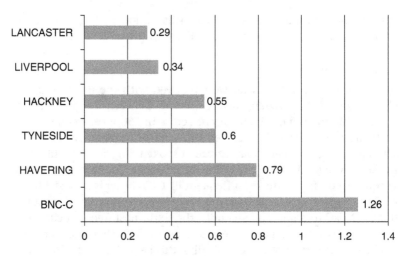

Figure 5.2   Be able to usage per speech community

as Figure 5.2 shows. There is no obvious explanation, however, why this should be found to be so much more frequently used in the BNC-C or why the speakers in the North-East of England seem to employ it nearly twice as often as in the North-West.

BNC-C shows a prevalence of employing patterns like **I-VP-to** or **You-VP-to** and the key verbs are *got*, *have* and *want*, as well as *said*. By contrast, almost all highly frequent 4CC trigrams incorporate *used to*. Therefore, 4CC records *used to* with *I* and *you*, and other personal pronouns like *we*, *they* and *he*. Amongst the Lancaster and London speakers, the phrases incorporating either *used to* or *we used to* are also the most frequent bigrams/trigrams for the by a considerable margin (usually more than 1:2) compared to the next-most frequent such cluster. Amongst Liverpool speakers, the two most frequent bigrams are the same and *I went to/I used to* are the most frequent trigrams.[12] Amongst speakers from Tyneside, the most frequent bigrams and trigrams are closer in frequency, with a margin of only 4:3. Furthermore, the preference for *used to* in 4CC is also the reason why *to go to* is proportionally far more frequent as 180 concordance lines of these are *used to go to*.

By contrast, *to*-trigrams with the verbs *said* and *want* are significantly more prominent in their use in BNC-C. With regards to *said to*, said occurs in 0.46 per cent of all words in BNC-C, but only in 0.22 per cent in 4CC. Both 4CC and BNC-C show *said to her/him*, while *and I said to* is slightly preferred by speakers in 4CC. Otherwise, apart from being proportionally over three times more frequent in BNC-C, there seem to be no structural differences in usage. *Want*, also, is far more frequent in BNC-C, where it occurs in 0.24 per cent of all tokens, when its frequency in 4CC is a mere 0.08 per cent. This appears to correlate with the fact that *you want to* occurs in 1.42 per cent of all *to* uses in BNC-C but only in 0.44 per cent in 4CC. This gap is far narrower for *don't want to*, which, proportionally, occurs about twice as frequent in BNC-C. It must be noted that there is a clear parallelism of usage when we look at *want to go*, which is, proportionally, four times as frequent in BNC-C than it is in 4CC. Consequently, we find this cluster in relative equivalence to the preferred *used to go* in 4CC.

Compared to bigrams, it is noticeable that trigrams incorporating *going to* – *you're going to* and *I'm going to* – are not within the ten most frequent. They can be found, however, amongst the 11–20 most frequent *to*-trigrams in BNC-C and the 11–30 most frequent trigrams in 4CC. Less frequent still are the chunks *you going to* ("are you going to", mostly) and *going to be*. All of these can be found proportionally less in 4CC than BNC-C, highlighting how informal the material at hand is. We see here, again, that *going* is more frequent overall in BNC-C, where it makes up 0.25 per cent of all words, but only 0.16 per cent in 4CC. At the same time, the proportion of *going to* usage as a total of all uses of *going* is slightly higher – 41.7 per cent in BNC-C compared to 36.6 per cent in 4CC. This stands in marked contrast to what we have seen occurring in semi-prepared speech.

As far as colligations are concerned, these are extremely delineated for spoken English. To show this, the 50 most frequent trigrams are viewed. These comprise 2.6 per cent to 0.39 per cent of all BNC-C *to* trigrams and 2.6 per cent to 0.72 per cent in 4CC. The majority are infinitive forms: **V-*to*-V** (*want to go, used to play*). The second most common form found are those of prepositional use: the most prominent one is ranked third most frequent in both sub-corpora: *to go to*. This is mostly followed by *the* in both sub-corpora, followed by *a, that, it* or other nouns (bed, work, sleep, school etc. in BNC-C; school, church, work in 4CC). The strong use of *bed* and *sleep* indicates that parents talk about children.

Prepositional use, however, appear in only six of these 50 trigrams in BNC-C and 11 in 4CC. Essentially, amongst the most used spoken 3w clusters, speakers only use prepositions for the lemma go (*going, went*) and say (*said*). *We went to* is used with similar frequencies (around 0.4 per cent of all *to* uses).

While the majority of all cases of *going to* appear as a tense marker, *going to* is far less often employed with *to* as a preposition (as in *going to school, going to the pub, are you going to Holly Cottage*). *I went to* is significantly more frequent in 4CC (1.3 per cent of all *to* uses) than BNC-C

Table 5.10 *To*-Infinitive and obligation usage

	Rank occurring	Trigrams
BNC-C *I+obligation*	1st, 2nd, 19th, 23rd	I'll have to, I've got to, I had to, I have to
4CC *I+obligation*	4th, 7th, 21st, 59th	I had to, I've got to, I have to, I'll have to
BNC-C *YOU+obligation*	13th, 22nd, 36th	you have to, you've got to, you'll have to
4CC *YOU+obligation*	12th, 16th, 129th	you have to, you had to, you got to

(0.49 per cent); this is even more true for *you went to*, which is rare in BNC-C. There is also the verb *talk*, which is found more often in 4CC, it appears, as the recorders in the Tyneside corpus repeatedly seem to say *I want to talk to you about* and such like.

When we look at the functions in discourse these trigrams indicate, the BNC-C has a preference for recounting, as indicated by the strong use of **used to-V**.

While both 4CC and BNC-C have *You're going to* and *I'm going to* as an indicator of a future event (*Yeah, we are going to next Friday*), these are significantly more used in BNC-C than 4CC.[13] A clearly marked use of *to*-trigrams is the desire to talk about obligation, employing forms of *have to (had to)*, *got to* and, also making use of *want to*. The usage pattern, again, is differing between the two sub-corpora. This can be demonstrated by looking at the divergent rankings and trigrams that occur when **I+obligation** or **YOU+obligation** are compared, as in Table 5.10.

Amongst the less frequent trigrams, two stand out: *supposed to be* does not vary too much in relative percentage of usage: 0.55 per cent of all *to* uses in BNC-C, 0.72 per cent in 4CC. The most common form is *it's supposed to be a* followed by *supposed to be* V-ing. This is contrasted by the use of *to be honest*. In 4CC, this is the 48th most frequent *to* trigram, appearing in 0.23 per cent of all uses of *to* in 4CC. Contrast this to the marginal usage in BNC-C where it appears in a mere 0.163 per cent of all uses. The reason for this is simple: 65 per cent of all such concordance lines are utterances by Liverpool speakers (see also Pace-Sigge, 2013: 169–170), the other 35 per cent are Havering or Hackney speakers, yet no other group of speakers appears to use this phrase.

Trigrams are seen as a standard way of viewing MWUs and items with their close collocates. Looking at *to* in spoken usage, we see that it is bigrams that form the essential backbone: a formulaic structure that sets out what is to be found in longer clusters. This may be an indication of how set and repetitive usage forms are in spoken English.

5.4.3 TO long clusters

There is a relatively low figures for longer clusters, and therefore a large amount of *to*-Infinitive uses with a large variety of verbs. Consequently, this sub-section concentrates on 4-word clusters and here only on the most frequent ones in order to be relevant.

Again, we can see that the core *to* bigrams and trigrams are key elements for longer clusters, too. Consequently, there are only two *to*-Inf clusters that are fairly frequent. First, *to be able to* (followed by V-Inf.) is fairly consistent in the way it is used. It ranks ninth (0.31 per cent) in BNC-C and 16th (0.23 per cent) amongst *to* 4w clusters. Second, the question *do you want to (go/do)* appears as the most frequent 4w *to* cluster in BNC-C (0.48 per cent of all *to* uses), yet is far less frequent in 4CC (0.16 per cent). In the BNC-C, *do you want me to* occurs in 0.24 per cent of all *to* uses. There is a relative equivalent to this in 4CC: *do you like to (hear, hear people, watch)*. The most common 4w cluster is the prepositional use *to go to the* ranked second in BNC-C (third in 4CC), occurring in 0.45 per cent and 0.52 per cent of all *to* uses, respectively. Within the 20 most frequent 4w clusters, the only other prepositions involve speech directed at another person: *I said to him* (0.24 per cent) and *I said to her* (0.20 per cent) in BNC-C; *to talk to you* (0.27 per cent) in 4CC.

It must be briefly noted that the construction **want to-V-it** occurs (proportionally) five times more frequently in BNC-C and the form **if-pronoun-want to** three times more frequently in BNC-C than in 4CC.

Overall, as we have seen amongst trigrams, BNC-C has a preference for clusters with *going to* or *want to* while *used to* constructions are predominant in 4CC. In spoken British English, there is a marked prevalence to use *to* for *to*-Infinitive usage, while the prepositions are few and reduced to usage with *go-lemmas* or "speech" verbs. While usage for interrogation purposes is still found in one long fixed phrase, the use for obligational intent is found in only fairly low frequencies amongst longer *to* clusters.

5.5 Summing up

What can be seen when looking at the usage of the items *of* and *to* in spoken English is that, compared to prepared English, the majority of MWUs are fairly restricted in their use. Amongst the uses of *of*, the genitive is not found present amongst the most frequent uses. Prepositional use is most clearly found amongst longer clusters, and similar to what has been shown in other genres, the link to *end, middle* and *other side* appears consistently enough to be called a salient feature. Most of the bigrams and a marked portion of trigrams do fit into the impression that spoken language tends to be vague (cf. McCarthy, 1998: 118; Bieber et al., 1999; Carter, 2004; Carter and McCarthy, 2006: 202–203). There is a predominant use of non-specific countables (*sort of, bit of*) and vague referrers (*a lot of people*) and these seem to be standard formulaic phrases in spoken British English, culminating in the overall pervasive use of *at the end of the day* or *have a cup of tea.*

As far as *to* is concerned, it has been shown that the majority of the uses occur with *to*+Verb. As highlighted in Pace-Sigge (2009, 2013), the resultant (longer) clusters are different even for corpora deemed to be highly comparable. We saw how restricted, amongst the most frequently used short clusters with *to*, spoken English use is; that prepositions are only found with respect to these two types of direction. It was shown that a lot of specific *to* MWUs reflect a very specific type of use in spoken discourse. This may be due to phrases that are very salient in their use for one specific speech community (*to be honest* for Liverpool speakers) or a particular way of addressing informants that uses a fairly frequent phrase but makes it noticeable through overuse (*I want to talk to you about*). Where there appears to be the most consistent use of *to* MWUs is in the area of prepositional use. These are far less frequently found amongst the most used clusters. These also reveal two of the key forms of human interaction in discourse (at least for the material cited here) – to move (*go to, went to*) and to speak (*said to, talk to*) There is a given salience here, too; the act of moving is usually preceded by a personal pronoun like I, *you, we* or *they;* while speech is directed to the another person: *said/talk to you/him/her.*

Finally, this chapter has uncovered how the different ways of understanding *going to* are employed in utterances. While there is always the application of a literal "going from A to B", *going to* here is most often used to indicate something to happen in the (near) future: *I'm going to get those trainers.*

6
Discussion: Usage Patterns for OF and TO in British English

6.1 Introduction

I call this "British English" because the element of US-American fiction texts is rather small. So are the differences highlighted (see Chapter 3). This may be partly due to the size of the material – and also partly due to the fact that US literature, for a long time, modelled itself on British writings. The process of creating a distinctive, "American" voice did not start until the later 19th century (see, amongst others, Weisbuch, 1986).

This chapter will be concerned with summing up the findings of the previous three chapters and, in a way, to compare notes: in how far are there salient collocational as well as colligational trends in the uses of the items *of* and *to* that go beyond genre boundaries? What, on the other hand, are the characteristic uses which define *of* and *to* usage in fiction, in prepared spoken texts, in casual, conversational speech? Lastly – where can overlap between the genres be found and in how far can differences be defined?

A further task for this chapter will be to see in what way the research undertaken is useful. What does it tell us about the nature of these small words and MWUs? Should there be further research into those items that are so overwhelmingly bound to another item so that we can speak of mono-collocationalism?

Attempting to answer this requires looking at the corpora data in both a horizontal and vertical way. A horizontal review of the research presented in chapters 3–5 is undertaken by comparing data of the same genre but from different sources. This will be covered in Section 6.2. This is followed by comparing corpora vertically – that is, across genre boundaries. This approach will be the particular focus of this chapter, intended to answer the question in how far *of* and *to* fulfil the same or very much similar functions in British English usage in general. At the same time, clear divergence in use highlights both the genre- and context-dependant employment of the items, as Section 6.3 shall uncover.

6.2   OF and TO – compared horizontally

6.2.1   OF MWUs

When concentrating on the top 12 uses of the item *of* as it appears in bigrams, trigrams and longer clusters for each of the three genres – fiction, prepared/semi-prepared speeches and casual spoken – a great deal of consistency can be found (see Appendix 6.i–6.iv). *Of the* is the most frequent bigram for all sub-corpora, being employed in around 25 per cent of all uses of *of* throughout apart from the spoken sub-corpora, where the figure is around 15 per cent. I shall start with the fiction corpora, where the next most frequent bigram *of a* fulfils a similar function, while *of*-with-pronoun is the other strongly used form. The third function is that of vague discourse particle use: *one of, sort of, kind of.* Trigrams and longer clusters are dominated by spatial descriptors, for example, *out of the.* Tyler and Evans (2003: 212) describe the relation of *out* and *out of* as such:

> Many of the senses associated with *out* also apply to *out of.* A key difference, however, is that in such senses out of overtly codes the LM. For instance, in the Not In Situ Sense, *out* functions as an adprep:
> (7.59) A: Is it possible to see the doctor this afternoon?
> B: I'm afraid she's *out* all day.
> In contrast, out of functions as a preposition, specifically requiring an overtly articulated LM which surfaces as a noun:
> (7.60) The doctor is *out of* the office
> (cf. *The doctor is out the office today).

This makes sense in the light of the findings presented here, in particular the strong occurrence for the chunk *out of the.* In trigrams and longer clusters with *of*, a clear hierarchy of descriptors emerges. First, there is *(at) the end of (the)*, followed by *in the middle of / in the midst of* – though amongst the 5w clusters, both BNC-F and 19C employ *in the middle of the.* The third longest cluster, for both, is *(on) the other side of (the)*. Finally, other extreme spatial pointers are employed – *at the edge of the, at the top of the, the far end of the* (BNC-F) or *at the head of the, at the other end of the* (19C). While there is reference to *the end*, "the start" or "the beginning" is far less frequent in use. Likewise, a reference to "the side of" can be expected to be found far less frequently than *the other side of*. The clear line of division can be found by the greater use of colloquial-sounding discourse markers in the (20th-century) BNC-F: *of course, kind of, a couple of* or *a lot of*. *Some of the* is, however, similar in ranking and – roughly – frequency in both.

It is amongst the mono-collocational items that a number of crucial differences can be made out. *Sort of* is (close to) mono-collocational, 81.3 per cent in BNC-F and 76.4 per cent of all uses of *sort* are followed by *of*. However, the difference is with the left-collocate. In BNC-C, *the* is preferred (914/5,020 times): *he was the sort of man*. In 19C, *a* is preferred (1,271/3,719 times): *and I took a sort of misliking to him*. Furthermore, both *that sort of* and *some sort of* are fairly commonly used in BNC-F. By ranking and frequency, only *that sort of* is equivalent in 19C, while *some sort of* occurs, proportionally, twice as often in BNC-F. A look at the concordance lines seem to indicate a less impersonal and formal style in BNC-F. A far stronger tendency of a change over time can be found with the word *kind*. *Kind* is more frequent than *sort* in 19C, while *sort* and *kind* appear with about the same frequency in the BNC-C. In both 19C and BNC-F, *a* precedes *sort* in about one-fifth of all cases, *the* in about one-sixth of all cases. However, in BNC-F, *kind of* is nearly mono-collocational, as *of* follows *kind* in 3,544 of 5,385 instances (65.8 per cent). In 19C, by contrast, this happens only in 1,387 of 4,701 concordance lines (29.5 per cent). *Kind of* (the vagueness marker) is clearly the dominant usage found in 20th-century literature, as *kind to* (the sentiment) occurs only 212 times. In 19C, *kind of* is the most frequent form, yet *kind to*, occurring 356 times, is a notable form in 19th-century literary works.

Looking next at *of* usage in public speeches, it can be seen that the single-speaker material is to a high degree prepared and written-to-be-spoken by the fact that the single-speaker data shares some features with the written fiction data, while the multiple speaker data bears some resemblance with the spoken data. Overall, however, both single and multiple-speaker podcast transcripts highlight the use of *of* as a tool fitting its discourse purpose. Dominant amongst the bigrams are, therefore, count procedures, all of which fit into the "part of" category: *one of, lot of, some of, part of*. These are linked to the vague *kind of* and *sort of* and the more specific use with a concrete determiner: *of this, of that*. So we have *at the end of this series; the result of this situation* as well as *the expansion of that city; what are the consequences of that?* It must be noted that ***the/a -N-of – this/that*** is the preferred structure here and that *of* *this* appears to be used in more abstract contexts – hence the preference to find these amongst the single-speaker material.

Countables also found amongst the trigrams: *some of the, part of the, the sort of, the kind of* and the very specific *in terms of* (mostly followed by *the/a*-NP). These can be preceded by connectors: *in terms of heating and in terms of water management; but, in terms of the current budget,* or to create a new phrase: *think in terms of.* None of these collocates do take a dominant role, however. While there is a lot of overlap on the surface, amongst the longer clusters there are instances in the single speaker material appear to be more formal; the Q&As and panel discussions are more informal. The former has *in the case of, on the basis of, as a result of* – all phrases that are deemed to be more academic in use (see LDOCE, 2006) whereas in the latter the 4w cluster *a lot of the people* is ranked fifth and *a little bit of* ninth. Looking at the usage in detail, *a lot of the* is strongly used in the casual spoken data. Eight out of 38 concordance lines introducing a new clause with "that", for example: *it is true that a lot of the writers of the Simpsons* ... . Likewise, there are 17 concordance lines of *a bit of* where the speaker avoids giving specific information, as in *the way prize works is actually a bit of a stitch up*; or, alternatively, to fit with the *part of* constructions which are found to permeate these types of texts: *I'm going to read you a bit of a letter I had from a reader.*

Both sub-corpora have *at the end of the* as amongst the most frequent long clusters and these are mostly employed as a time marker (*at the end of the day* or *at the end of the 19th century*). The former is fully idiomatic and not meant to be taken literally and this brings about a qualitative difference. *At the end of the day* occurs 5/17 times (just under one-third) in the single-speaker concordance lines, but only 7/49 times (one in seven) amongst the single-speaker presentations. By contrast, in order to refer to a time-frame, the multiple-speaker data highlights strongly the phrase *a lot of the time.*

A similar situation is presented by the use of *one of the things that* which appears in 0.37 per cent of all *of* uses amongst the multiple speakers but only in 0.05 per cent in the single-speaker transcripts. In the latter, it often starts a sentence (shown by following a full stop in the transcript). In the discussion part, it often follows *and, I think* or *that was* while *that's one of the things that* occurs only in the single-speaker sub-corpus.

Finally, the spatial reference *the other side of* occurs in both sub-corpora – in the multiple speaker section nearly three times as frequently. However, the patterns do not differ, though there are only very few concordance lines in either collection. The phrases in the speeches are used metaphorically: of *the other side of the coin* and *the other side of the fence.*

Usage forms for *of* amongst the spoken data reveal a great deal of uniformity, highlighting the amount of formulaic acts performed when spontaneous utterances leave little space for prepared or edited production. Thus, nine out of the top ten most frequent bigrams are found in both sub-corpora with slight variation in frequency and rank. Amongst the trigrams this is seven out of ten and it becomes clear that the focus for speakers is on using *of* for vague numerical descriptors like *a lot/bit/couple of*. There are also discourse markers: *and of course* or *that sort of (thing)* – which in 4CC reflect interviewer questions, too: *what sort of/kind of*. The use of *of* as a preposition appears in only one spatial (*out of the*) and one time (*end of the*) reference.

Amongst longer clusters the reduction in phrases for certain functions becomes ever more prominent. Amongst the 12 most frequent phrases, *that sort of thing* appears to be the only discourse-marker phrase. For prepositions there is only *at the end of (the)* and, less frequently, *the middle of the*. Amongst the vague countables, there is *(it's) a bit of (a)*, yet forms with *lot of* are dominant, and *a lot of people* and *a lot of money* is a clear topic of conversation that keeps appearing amongst different groups of speakers. Similarly, the offer *want a cup of tea* [?] makes a mark – in British spoken conversation, this appears in well over one of a thousand uses of *of*.

The phrase *at the end of* appears in half of all cases as *at the end of the day* – the metaphorical form which is, in a few cases, substituted by *at the end of it* – *I'll be expecting a big pay rise at the end of it; there is a job at the end of it*. The other function is a reference to a clear time-frame or a space marker, and, in both sub-corpora, *at the end of term* and *at the end of the road* occur.

6.2.2   TO MWUs

As has been pointed out before, unlike *of the*, *to the* has a far less prominent role across all sub-corpora. It appears with the almost exact same frequency in the two main fiction corpora – 11.5 per cent. Beyond that, collocates and clusters with *to*, in detail, show a far greater amount of variation than do any MWUs with *of*. Consequently, the top three bigrams in BNC-F, *to the*, *to be* and *to her*, appear in the four top ranks of 19C (with broadly similar proportional frequencies). In the 12 most frequent bigrams, only *to see* (just over 2 per cent of all uses of *to*) and *to do* (2.5 per cent in BNC-F and just under 2 per cent in 19C) are shared. Overall, however, apart from *to the* and *to be*, there is a strong use of *to* followed by a pronoun. In the longer 19C MWUs, it can be seen that where the same clusters occur, they are proportionally less frequent (though they may rank higher). One possible explanation for that could be found in that 19C has full texts rather than excerpts only as found in BNC-F.[1] In direct comparison, there are four 3w and three 4w clusters amongst the top 12 ranks that are shared in the sub-corpora. These are *to be a, to go to (the)* and *(to) be able to:* these are all *to*-Infinitive phrases, as is the lesser-used *seemed to be*.

The clear dividing line between the two sub-corpora lies in the way that discourse markers are employed. In particular, *to* with *going* is fairly dominant throughout *to* clusters of any length in BNC-F. Similar is the use of *I want to*: both are mostly employed to refer to future actions. *I want to*, in 19C, is ranked clearly lower (14th instead of seventh trigram) and has, proportionally, around half as many occurrences (0.22 instead of 0.51 per cent). The request *I want you to* fits in this usage pattern (it appears in 0.1 instead of 0.05 per cent of all uses in BNC-F). While this phrase is followed by the same words, the emphasis has shifted from the 19th to the 20th century, it seems, from *I want you to come/be/tell/give* to *want you to know/go/meet take* while *(what) I want you to do* appears very much in the same way in both sub-corpora. The other key difference appears to be a strong indicator of change over time: while the 19C corpus records *(I want) to speak to (you)*, the BNC-F equivalent (ranked lower but with higher proportional percentage of all *to* use) is *(I want) to talk to (you)*. Occurring only marginally in BNC-F is the collocate "somebody" – *somebody to talk to* as well as *to talk to somebody*: none of these MWUs occur with *to speak to* or *to talk to* in 19C. It must be kept in mind, though, that repeat *to* clusters 4w and 5w clusters are not very frequent.

All in all, the predominant uses of *to* in fictional British texts are found to be the *to*-Infinitive, with *to* as a preposition the far lesser used pattern. See Tyler and Evans (2003: 145) for an in-depth discussion and prototypical behaviour *to* as a preposition, in particular in contrast with the use of *for*. This seems to mirror the results here fairly well.

Looking at the podcasts, there are eight out of 12 bigrams that single- and multiple-speakers have in common. This figure halves for trigrams and there are only four common 4w clusters. Amongst the bigrams, only two are ranked the same: *to do* and *have to*, ranked fourth and fifth respectively, though only being half as frequent, proportionally, in the SSM. *To the* (10.7 per cent of all uses of to) is used substantially more frequently than *to be* (7.9 per cent) in the single-speaker material. Amongst MSM data, however, *to be* (8.1 per cent) and *to the* (7.4 per cent) are far closer together. In this respect, the latter is more like casual speech, the former more like the (carefully written) fiction texts. *To the* is employed in the same way in both corpora. So we find *you can go back to the 90s* (multiple speakers) and *history goes back to the year 1740* (single speaker). *To be* is also largely similar. Nevertheless, in the MSM material the phrase *needs to be* is far more prominent than in the single speaker corpus (and slightly more frequent than *need to be*). Amongst single speakers, *need to be* occurs 50 per cent more often than *needs to be*. So we have *need to be aware of* (prominent in MSM) and *need to be able to* (SSM) – slightly divergent use; *needs to be addressed/organised/completes* (SSM) and *needs to be addressed/complemented/subsidised* (MSM) which, on the level of colligation is the same.

Both sub-corpora show a preference for *have to* compared to *to have* though the difference is far stronger in MSM: 4.1 compared to 2.9 per cent (0.3 per cent difference in SSM). The usage of *going to* is significant: ranked third in MSM (7.1 per cent of all uses of *to*) but only ranked 11th in SSM (1.6 per cent). The same is to be found for *going to be*: ranked first with 1.5 per cent in MSM and ranked 12th with 0.3 per cent in SSM. However, *is going to be* is broadly similar in usage by rank (fourth and sixth) and percentage (0.3 and 0.1).

Amongst the trigrams there is fairly strong agreement in the use of three key phrases: *be able to* (*they might be able to bring stability, let us hope we will be able to make further offers*), *I want to* (*because I want to be a good public servant, because I want to come onto that a bit later on*) and *we have to* (*and we have to be willing to make this investment, so we have to find money, foods, ideas*) – all these phrases reflect the style and topics of public speeches.

Amongst the 4w MWUs, phrases with *going to* are found throughout. *To be able to* is ranked first in both sub-corpora (0.9 per cent in MSM and 0.4 per cent in SSM). What stands out as specific in this material is the hedging phrase *it seems to me* – ranked third in SSM and seventh in MSM. However, on closer inspection, the latter appears proportionally twice as often, with *it seems to be that*, and *and it seems to me* being five times more frequent amongst the Q&A and plenary material. Looking at the colligational structures, however, there is no difference to be found.

Lastly, the casually spoken data: amongst the 12 most frequent trigrams, eight can be found in both BNC-C and 4CC. But the difference in rank and proportional usage can be stark. *To the, to go, to be* and *to have* are very similar in rank and percentage of use. By contrast, *have to* is ranked first in BNC-F with 8.2 per cent of all *to* uses, while it is ranked seventh with half that frequency in 4CC. *Used to* is ranked first in 4CC occurring in 17 per cent of all *to* uses. It is ranked tenth with around a quarter of this frequency in BNC-F. This strong employment of *used to* means that, amongst trigrams and 4w-clusters, observers only find a single common MWU within the top 12: the third ranked *to go to (the)* is slightly more frequent in 4CC.

It must be stressed that all the most frequent forms found in 4CC and BNC-C – *going to, want to, have to, something to, talk to* – are listed by Rice (1999: 272) as the earliest constructions learned (children around age 3):

> Generally, infinitival uses of *to* outpaced spatial uses in both onset and frequency. To be sure, uses of *to* in constructions involving the catenative or phrasal modal, want to, only marginally preceded spatial usages; however, nearly all the children produced this use of *to* during the sampling period, but less than half ever used to spatially.

It goes without saying that people of that age do not make speeches or write novels. This also does explain the absence of *used to*: aged three, there is simply no historical background that could be back-referenced. It is acquired later and is then (almost exclusively) said to recall past experiences. Nevertheless, it is highly relevant that the most frequent *to* constructions are acquired, it seems, as an MWU, and then widely employed in a formulaic way.

The colligations show few differences: the predominant use is *to*-Infinitive, or rather, **v-*to*-v-Inf.** There is a strong pragmatic use for *to* as a discourse-maker: *going to, used to* is employed in a clearly defined form of *to* as a preposition: often with the direction to another person, indicated through the use of personal pronouns. Thus, "I said to him", "to talk to you". The impression that *"to* is a weird word" (Pace-Sigge, 2009) is most justified when the focus is on spoken English when we look at the proportional use of collocations only, which diverge most widely, even in corpora that can be assumed to be fairly similar.

6.3   OF and TO – compared vertically

6.3.1   Introduction

So far this book has concentrated on detailed use of the items *of* and *to* in three different genres and different sub-corpora within each genre. Furthermore, there has been more prominence on collocations than on structures. Quirk et al., referring to a single function say that "complex prepositions [a sequence that is indivisible both in terms of syntax and in terms of meaning] may be subdivided into two-and three-word sequences" (Quirk et al., 1985: 669 and 671). The focus throughout will be on sets of words of this length, though, as the findings reveal, it is not only prepositions that are being discussed. This, too, fits what Quirk et al. (cf. 1985: 672) say, namely that a complex preposition may follow strictly the definition (above) or can be found on a cline of restricted syntactic constructions. Biber et al. (cf. 1999: 75 and 637) retain this approach and describe the material on the basis of their corpus findings.

In this section, the aim is to look for overall usage patterns that seem to appear universally across genres – both expressed in the use of collocations and colligations.

To do so, I shall first look at those items which seem to be, to a very large degree, tied to *of* or *to*. Such items are both high frequency and appear in the most frequent bigrams with *of* and *to*. Above, I have referred to such words, which, in over three-quarters of their usage, appear with *of* or *to* as **mono-collocates**. These will be looked at in more detail in 6.3.2. Sections 6.3.3 and 6.3.4 are an investigation of *of* and *to* usage, respectively, across genre boundaries.

6.3.2 Mono-collocational items with OF and TO

The clear majority of collocates found with highly frequent items like *of* or *to* are also collocating, to either side of the node, with a large, varied amount of other items. That a word is occurring with high frequency within a bigram does not serve as an indicator. For example, one of the most frequent collocates is the pronoun *her* for fiction texts (*of her, to her*) which, roughly occurs in 3–4 per cent of all cases of *of* and *to*. These bigrams, rank are amongst the most frequent bigrams. While not quite as frequent as *of* or *to*, *her* is also one of the most frequent items in the corpus, appearing around once every hundred words. And every 7th to 10th occurrence of *her* is either *of her* or *to her* (see endnote 3.3). This is highly frequent, but not mono-collocational. Furthermore, these bigrams are extremely rare in the other two genres.

There are, however, other items that collocate with either *of* or *to* to a very high degree or even appear (almost) exclusively in a bigram with one of these items. This kind of structure can be found in one or two of the sub-corpora; however, a number of items have been found that appear in combination with *of* or *to* to a very high degree regardless of sub-corpus (i.e. regardless of genre). As defined earlier, a mono-collocational item would appear either in 80 per cent or more of all uses, or, alternatively, where all other collocates are occurring with a frequency that is lower at a highly significant level. An example of an item that appears close to mono-collocational in one genre and where other collocates are significantly lower in occurrence is the bigram *to get*. *To get* appears in less than a quarter of all uses of *get* in spoken sub-corpora, and in around two-fifths of all uses in the podcast and fiction data.

The highest occurring ratio is found in BNC-F, where 42.61 per cent of *get* occurrences are *to get*; the nearest frequent bigram (left-collocate) is *you get* – which appears seven times less frequently than *to get*. This kind of ratio (again, with *you get* coming second) is found in the other sub-corpora, too. As such, *to get* can be classed as a bigram with a high degree of fixed collocational pattern for the item *get*.

A far clearer example of mono-collocationalism is found when we look at the usage of *seems*. While *seems to* in BNC-F, for example, occurs in over 40 per cent of all uses of *seems*, its collocational and colligational structure is not as fixed as observed in the podcast data. Here, *seems* occurs in over half of all uses as *seems to* (in the multiple-speaker data) and, amongst single speaker material, in over 68 per cent of all uses. Uniquely in the podcast data, however, the overwhelming pattern of usage is *it seems to* – a phrase clearly borrowed from academic use. The form found predominantly in fiction texts, *it seems a ...* is, proportionally, far rarer here.

A very specific case is *used to*. This is a less-frequent bigram in both fiction and podcast texts and it occurs in around half the uses of *used* amongst the podcasts.[2] The situation is different, however, amongst the casual spoken material. *Used to* occurs in 86 per cent (BNC-C) or even 94 per cent (4CC, which also has a one-fifth higher count for the item *used*) of all uses of *used*. The differences how these bigrams are used between the two sub corpora are marginal. The majority of bigrams appear in the form of the trigram **pronoun** (I, we, they, he she, you, it) – **used to**; next, looking at the right-extension of the bigram or trigram, the structure becomes **pronoun-used to-be/go/have**: the prime verbs. The differences of the proportional frequencies of the actual co-collocates between the two sub-corpora is only marginal. The far stronger use of this particular *to* cluster can be explained as basic pragmatics: often, interlocutors would ask about life-events (not very different from a typical conversation: "So, how was your weekend?"). Consequently, observations from the speaker's past are recounted: "Our Annie used to carry her own"; "We used to go to the Isle of Wight"; "We used to be frightened of the woods", and so forth.

A similar use of a *to* bigram can be found in the use of *want to*. Apart from the 19C and 4CC sub-corpora, this appears within the ten most frequent *to* bigrams in all text collections. The way this grammatical form monopolises the item *want*, however, is clearly different according to the genre. *Want to* occurs in less than 40 per cent of all uses of *want* amongst the spoken data. It is found in just under 60 per cent of all fiction corpora. Amongst the public speeches, however, it is found in almost three-quarters of all uses.[3] This makes it a mono-collocational use. Amongst the single speakers, there are 761 concordance lines for *want*; 575 of these are *want to*. The nearest collocational uses are marginal by comparison: 71 occurrences of *I want* and 21 occurrences of *want the*.

The colligation is fairly stable: **Pronoun+want to-V-Inf**. The pronouns here are placed with a "+" as they might not be in L1 position – when the negations *don't* or *didn't* are applied, for example. The pronouns are the same in both sub-corpora, too. In order of precedence, we find *I*, then *you* or *we*, finally *they* and *people*. Similar to the occurrences of *used to* in the spoken corpora, the employment of *want to* clusters is explained through the pragmatic aim of the speakers. *I* and *We want to* stand for the plans the speaker presents to the audience: "We want companies to get together"; "I want to focus on the Doha round." When the speaker employs *you*, she or he addresses the audience: "Would *you* want a re-moralised politics?"; "If *you* want, I can demonstrate it." This is in sharp contrast to using *they* or *people*, words that are employed to demonstrate a contrast between the speaker (the speaker's view) and another group: "It doesn't matter if they want to see that and if that turns them on"; "Poor Bangladeshis are poor because they want to be" (sic!); "If people want to come and live in the UK"; or "and that's what people want to do."

To compare the most prominent mono-collocates with *of* and *to*, the comparison includes here data from the *British Academic Written English* (BAWE) corpus and the *British Academic Spoken English* (BASE) corpus as well. This serves to broaden the basis on which the claims are made and reveals further, pragmatic, functions of such collocates. As a further step, the individual usage patterns are divided into written corpora (19th- and 20th-century British fiction and academic written texts) and all forms of spoken including prepared speeches (single-speaker public speeches), semi-prepared (academic spoken presentation, panel and Q&A sessions of public speeches) as well as casual, informal conversation (BNC-C and 4CC material).

Looking at the most frequently occurring bigrams of *to*, there are two items with strong mono-collocational tendencies. These are the words *going* and *able*. As Table 6.1 shows, *going to* is a preferred form of using *going* throughout. This is particularly visible for 19C fiction; less so in academic written material. *Going to* is the most common form of employing *going*, with the next most-frequent cluster being *is going* which occurs in less than 20 per cent of all uses of *going*. However, this is clearly genre specific: *going* is five times more frequent in 19C, ten times

Table 6.1   TO dominant mono-collocates: written

Sub-corpus	N GOING / GOING TO	% of going is *GOING TO*	N ABLE / ABLE TO	% of able is *ABLE TO*
BNC-F	17,829 / **11,892**	66.7	4,133 / **4,013**	97.1
19C	6,970 / **5,436**	78.0	2,535 / **2,263**	89.3
BAWE	848 / **481**	56.7	3,129 / **3,070**	98.1

Table 6.2   TO dominant mono-collocates: spoken

Sub-corpus	N GOING / GOING TO	% of going is *GOING TO*	N ABLE / ABLE TO	% of able is *ABLE TO*
SSM	800 / **550**	68.8	460 / **434**	94.3
MSM	615 / **495**	80.5	118 / **118**	100.0
BASE	5,298 / **4,184**	79.0	650 / **626**	96.3
BNC-C	10,387 / **4,327**	41.9	952 / **914**	96.0
4CC	2,131 / **780**	36.6	148 / **146**	98.6

more frequent in BNC-F than it is in BAWE. This indicates that *going* and, consequently, *going to* are dispreferred choices of wording in academic texts, while such wordings are fairly commonly found in fiction texts. Table 6.2 appears to show that the opposite is true when it comes to *going to* in spoken presentations. In fact, *going to* is the fifth-ranked bigram overall in BASE, tenth-ranked in MSM. During spoken presentations, as we have described in detail in Chapter 4, the phrase seems to be used to guide the listener on to a new topic. The difference between SSM and MSM or BASE could thus also be explained: speaking more freely, presenters keep returning to this phrase to catch the audience's attention. Within the casual spoken material, this can also be seen as the dominant usage. The nearest collocate, *on* (*going on*) occurs only infrequently: 1 per cent in 4CC, 0.6 per cent in BNC-C. In all sub-corpora, the colligational form expressed mostly is *going to–v–Inf.*: "They're going to do it"; "All schools were going to be closed." As we have seen earlier, the most common trigram for this form is *going to be*. Far less frequent is the form *going to–NP*: "Going to church"; "I'm not going to the football, mum," All of these express an action to be undertaken in the near future. Thus, this *to* MWU expresses a near-certain capacity to do something, which links it to the other mono-collocate: *able (to)*.

A strong mono-collocate is found in *able to*, which is shown to be the only, or almost only, form a reader or listener would encounter of the item *able*. Between half and three-quarters of all such bigrams is the trigram *be able to*; colligationally, *able to* is almost always preceded by a form of *be*: *be able to, been able to, being able to, was able to, were able to,* also *was not able to*. Furthermore, they are followed mostly by a V-Inf form. This means that *able* is couched, in most cases, by V-Inf constructions: "I shall *be able to* weep for her at night"; "I just hate not *being able to* put my finger on the map."

Overall, mono-collocates, whether genre-specific or found across corpora, centre on a *to*-Infinitive – getting or wanting things, or being able to do things. It is also important to highlight the temporal aspect that goes with the use of *to* mono-collocates. While *used to* is solely employed as a narrative device, re-telling of what has happened in the past (and is mainly employed in casual speech), *be able to* also fits into a time-reference framework: it usually appears with a reference to the future, as in "You'll be able to" or "John wanted to be able to push the furniture." Alternatively, there are modal conditionals that imply actions in the future: "You wouldn't be able to see, or avoid to be able to see." At the same time, it indicates a past action, like in "It was the best he had been able to come up with." The other two *to* mono-collocates indicate future events – *want to* (sometimes fitting in with other frequent bigrams as in "I *want to be able to* look out of the window") and *going to*.

Looking at *of* mono-collocates, there is a qualitative difference from how they occur with the item *to*. There are a number of bigrams that indicate strong predominance of the item-with-*of* usage, for example, *one of,* occurring in around a quarter of all uses of *one*.[4] Another case is *out of,* occurring in just under a third of all uses of *out*. Diverging from *to* mono-collocates, however, we do not find a single example where usage of *of* is significantly genre-specific. We can see one or two sub-corpora that employ this strength of collocation to a lesser extent; yet no genre or sub-corpus presents a pattern of mono-collocation that is noticeably divergent.

Overall, we can see that amongst the usage of *of* bigrams there are mono-collocates which are not very visible in one or two of the six sub-corpora. As with *to*, there are two items which appear fairly clear as mono-collocates with *of*. These two groups are shown in Tables 6.3–6.6. What these bigrams highlight is the strong use of MWUs for vagueness markers and discourse markers. The data presented here needs further explanation. Overall, *lot of* and *kind of* are more frequent in spoken usage than in written usage and the fixed bigrams are also more prominent in spoken English. While *lot of* and *kind of* may not seem mono-collocational at all times, they are by far the dominant bigram of *lot* and *kind* in all the sub-corpora. *Kind of* is almost always used amongst the multiple-speakers and BASE speakers could be interpreted as a recent dominant form: the data is from 2003–2012 rather than dating back to 1948. This view would be supported by the fact that, amongst the

Table 6.3 OF mono-collocates as vagueness-markers: written

Sub-corpus	Freq. LOT / LOT OF	% of lot is *LOT OF*	Freq. KIND / KIND OF	% of kind is KIND OF
BNC-F	4,863 / **2,475**	50.9	5,385 / **3,544**	65.8
19C	845 / **321**	38.0	4,701 / **1,387**	29.5
BAWE	768 / **465**	60.6	836 / **668**	79.9

Table 6.4 OF mono-collocates as vagueness-markers: spoken

Sub-corpus	Freq. LOT / LOT OF	% of lot is *LOT OF*	Freq. KIND / KIND OF	% of kind is KIND OF
SSM	464 / **316**	68.1	721 / **605**	83.9
MSM	346 / **269**	77.8	269 / **259**	96.3
BASE	1,309 / **945**	72.2	1,940 / **1,862**	96.0
BNC-C	3,996 / **2,065**	51.7	590 / **467**	79.2
4CC	1,878 / **1,184**	63.1	591 / **557**	94.2

Table 6.5 OF dominant mono-collocates as discourse markers: written

Sub-corpus	Freq. COURSE / OF COURSE	% of course is *OF COURSE*	Freq. SORT / SORT OF	% of sort is SORT OF
BNC-F	10,371 / **9,872**	95.2	5,020 / **4,081**	81.3
19C	6,038 / **3,902**	64.6	3,719 / **2,843**	76.4
BAWE	991 / **384**	38.6	390 / **277**	71.0

Table 6.6 OF dominant mono-collocates as discourse markers: spoken

Sub-corpus	Freq. COURSE / OF COURSE	% of course is *OF COURSE*	Freq. SORT/ SORT OF	% of sort is SORT OF
SSM	731 / **592**	81.0	386 / **343**	88.9
MSM	157 / **146**	93.0	247 / **242**	98.0
BASE	1,968 / **1,297**	65.9	3,738 / **3,601**	96.3
BNC-C	1,951 / **1,361**	69.8	4,640 / **4,120**	88.8
4CC	965 / **695**	72.0	1,807 / **1,740**	96.3

casual speech data, the more recent 4CC material appears in a similar relation to the slightly older BNC-C material. Another reason to be considered is that *kind* and *sort* appear with the same frequency in the multiple-speaker corpus, but *kind* is nearly twice as frequent than *sort* (721 to 386 occurrences) in the single-speaker data. Given what we have seen by way of preference in the 19C corpus, *(a) kind of* could be deemed as more formal and appears therefore in edited written-to-be spoken material.

In both written and spoken data, the vagueness marker *lot of* is preceded by an article and followed by a noun: "a lot of work", "between the lot of them". All of these forms appear around ten times more often than utterances of scripts that say *a lot more* .... . This is in contrast to *kind*, which is more complex, as it allows modifiers as well. This means we see both "the kind of man" and "for I am a plodding kind of fellow".

The most striking feature is, however, that the 19th-century literature material makes use of both *lot* and *kind* in a different mould to all other sub-corpora. A closer look at the concordance lines reveals why. Apart from three cases[5] where it refers to "my lot", *lot* is always used as referring to a countable unit in the podcast data: "a lot of things"; "get a lot of money". This is not at all the case in 19C, where 175 concordance lines say *his/my/her X's* lot – referring not to a countable unit but as a substitute term for family or gender or social group and fate or fortune "he never worried about the fortunes of his lot"; "that it make my lot less hard". *Kind of* is used in a similar way. In 4CC, there are only six occurrences where "kind" is used in the sense of "nice" or "helpful". By contrast, in 19CC, the bigram *kind to* alone occurs 356 times. A cursory investigation, looking at one-fifth of the concordance lines, appears to confirm that half of the time "kind" means "nice" and the other half it substitutes for "type". Looking at the 20th-century BNC Fiction material, this balance does not exist anymore. *Kind of* is used proportionally more than twice as often; yet the bigram *kind to*, occurs significantly less often. This leads to the discovery of an overall trend: the younger, more contemporary the material, the higher the frequency of use for the less formal *lot of* and *kind of*. This is not only true for 19th- versus 20th-century literature. The single-speaker podcasts cover the period between 1948 and 2013; the multiple speaker podcast material comes from 2006–2013. The BNC-C material has a cut-off point in the early 1990s; BASE material was collected in the early 2000s; and 4CC has recordings which were taken as recently as 2013. When we look at *of course* and *sort of* (both also deemed rather less formal) we can see, in Tables 6.5 and 6.6, that this trend is shown here as well, albeit less starkly. This move towards greater informality has been documented before by, amongst others, Mair (1997) and Biber et al. (1998).

Of course presents an example where we can see a strong tendency towards mono-collocationalism. The lowest such use is found both in the oldest material, 19C, and, in particular, in academic writing (BAWE). This lower usage indicated a higher degree of formality and also points to the fact that *course* is used here in a non-discourse-marker form. Therefore, 23 per cent in BASE (12 per cent in 19C) of all uses of *course* refer to *the course*: "*the course* of events", "in *the course* of a few hours", something that is close to "during" and time-event related. In fact, when looking at trigrams, *the course of* occurs notably more frequently as the use of the discourse marker with *of course I*. By contrast, only 3 per cent of concordance lines of *course* are the bigram *the course* in BNC-F.

In the fiction texts as well as in the casually spoken material, *of course* tends to be followed by a pronoun: *I, you, we* or *they*. The BAWE material, by contrast, is not followed by any pronouns; instead, it is mostly an insertion. The total figure[6] for *course* is, as Table 6.5 shows, very low: *course* and *of course* are deemed to be a not very academic turn of phrase. The prepared speeches are different again, as *of course* is almost exclusively a discourse marker employed to strengthen the impact of the utterance by referring to a shared opinion or knowledge between the speaker and the audience: "But the consequences *of course* were much more visible", "and we have *of course* a wonderful example on our doorstep", "She's Geri Halliwell, former Spice Girl *of course*." This highlights the pragmatic value of the phrase, which is used, if nothing else, for rhetorical effect. Nevertheless, Table 6.6 highlights differences in degree that seem to escape easy interpretations. The degree of mono-collocationalism is lowest for BASE for similar reasons as in BAWE – the reference here is to *the/this course* (of action, etc.) and therefore *course* is not used as a discourse marker. Yet this does not explain why *of course* is relatively infrequent in the casual spoken data (BNC-C and 4CC). The reason for this is that the transcriptions do not fully represent the spoken units. Fast, casual speech has, characteristically, forms of contraction and elision (cf. Collins and Mees, 2009). Thus, the grammatical item *of* appears to be not pronounced or have, as a spoken feature, no longer a place in the produced utterances. Consequently, transcripts provide concordance lines like this: "Yeah, course you can. Course you can"; "Course I will"; "Well, course we never sent one."

The evidence is stronger still for the claim that there is mono-colloquialism is the item *sort*, which is very frequently used in the MWU *sort of*. Table 6.5 shows that, again, the lowest collocational strength is found amongst academic written texts and the 19th-century writings, where "sort" similar to " lot" can mean something like "type": "a sort of speedy process"; "some sort of shaman" (BAWE). Likewise, "we found him a commendable sort"; "it was clear she required nothing of that sort" (19C). As with *of course*, both *sort* and *sort of* are extremely rare items in academic writing – similar reasons apply for these two words. Yet, eight out of ten uses in the fiction genre, rising to nearly nine or more out of ten in the prepared and casual spoken data, employ the vagueness marker *sort of* when using the item "sort". So a verbose, indirect statement like this appears: "'Yes, certainly', said the girl with a sort of demure alertness which was somewhat amusing." Like *kind of*, *sort of* is mostly preceded by the determiners like *a, the,* or *that*. While mono-collocation is strong in the written data, it is almost total (between 90 and close to 100 per cent) in the spoken material, as Table 6.6 demonstrates. There is also a further form of vagueness employed, as all corpora have a fairly high amount of concordance lines (around one in ten) where *sort of* is used as part of either *sort of thing* or *some sort of*. Even beyond the confines of a spoken interview setting, there is use of the interrogative *what sort of* (appearing in 6 per cent of all uses of *sort* in 19C). Furthermore, *sort of* modifies the noun phrase which follows, so we have sentences like "What *sort of* thing?"; "He had given her a *sort of* intimacy with his ways"; "It was almost *sort of* a protest regatta."

Summing up, we have seen that *of* mono-collocates appear across all corpora. The difference in collocational strength appears to be due to changes in use over time. The data provided here support the claim that there has been a noticeable shift towards a more informal use of language over the past century and a half; indeed there has even been a noticeable shift over the recent decades. In the phrases investigated here, a move towards greater conformity over time has been detected: words which used to be found with a wider combination of other items, like "lot" or "course" are being found increasingly to collocate with *of* most of the time. As such, we have the discourse marker *of course*, which fulfils its pragmatic functions most clearly within the podcast data. Otherwise, the most frequent mono-collocates with *of* are all vagueness markers. It has to be seen that these markers display stronger collocational bonds, and become more mono-collocational, the higher the degree of vagueness appears to be. While *a lot of still* seems to be employed for countable units, *a kind of* moves more into the domain of abstract impressions. More vague still, judging by the occurrence patterns in the concordance lines, is the phrase *a sort of*. This latter one is also often found with other items which indicate vagueness, like *some, any* or *different*.

To conclude this section, it can be said that *to* and *of* mono-collocation does exist. It can either be genre-specific (it appears to be less corpus-specific) or can be found throughout the whole collection of texts investigated. The words are found in a strong bond with either *to* or *of* to an extent that they appear in bigrams in well above 80 per cent of all uses of the word in question; alternatively, all other collocates are far rarer in direct combination with such words. Mono-collocates appear to create MWUs that are essential building blocks of communication. They can, in particular, express pragmatic needs (*seems to* and *of course* in the podcast speech data) or, in general function to express narrative time-frames (*used to, want to, going to*) or are employed in texts to let the author or speaker be vague when a more detailed description is either not needed or wanted (*lot of, kind of, sort of*). We have seen that such bigrams can, on occasion, claim 100 per cent (or close to 100 per cent) of all uses of a specific item.

This supports the view that neither *of* nor *to* can, justifiably, be seen as stand-alone items: these two words have a specific role and a specific function in combination with at least one other word. Even where there is no 100 per cent agreement of collocation, the colligational structure appears to cement *of* or *to* into a fairly fixed MWUs.

6.3.3   The usage patterns of OF

6.3.3.1   *OF patterns in general*

The aim of this section is to demonstrate in how far *of* is found in collocational and colligational structures to a degree that a it presents a salient feature of *of* usage. At the same time, this should reveal particular patterns of use that are markers of particular genres, as represented by the material investigated here.

Looking at all six sub-corpora, the *of*-with-*the* structure is clearly dominant. *Of the* appear in over a quarter of all uses of *of* – though not in casual spoken, an issue I shall discuss below. *The*-N-*of* is the predominant colligational pattern for *of* trigrams: *the end of, the sort of, the rest of*, etc. This form occurs in just over a third of all *of* trigrams for the fiction and single-speaker podcast data. It is, however, only found in 23 per cent of the multiple-speaker podcast and in just over 10 per cent of the casual spoken data.

There is, therefore, a distinctive divergence of usage between more prepared texts (in a way: more formal usage) of *of* and the more casual, less prepared and spontaneous use. This is clearly reflected in the frequency of the item *the* in the sub corpora, as Figure 6.1 shows. While the more formal texts have *the* as the most frequently occurring item, and this appears to run in tandem with employing *of the* and *the x*

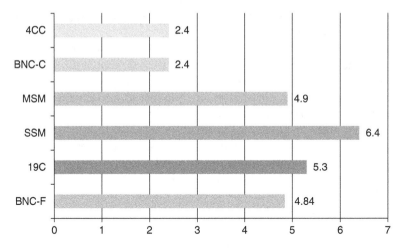

Figure 6.1 Frequency (in per cent) of THE in all sub-corpora

of constructions, *the* is not the most frequent term in casual spoken English.[7] Given that *the* appears proportionally less than half as frequent in the spontaneous spoken data, it should come as little surprise that *of*-with-*the* constructions are, accordingly, less common. This, however, is not the full picture. In fact, the most salient *of* bigram construct is *of*-**det**: *of the, of a, of that, of this*. While *a* is less than half as frequent in the prepared (written and spoken) text, it is only slightly less frequent in BNC-C and 4C. Subsequently, *the*-**N**-*of* constructions are twice as frequent as *a*-**N**-*of* ones in BNC-F and SSM and four times as frequent in 19C and MSM. Amongst the freely spoken data, however, the relation is different: for every ten uses of *the*-**N**-*of* there are 13 uses of *a*-**N**-*of* in BNC-C and 4CC. This indicates that there is a greater degree of indefiniteness amongst the casual spoken data. At the same time, we can see that the frequency of determiners like *a, the, this, that* are closely tied to their use with *of* in all sub-corpora: the ***determiner*-with-*of*** bond.

Looking at the trigrams of all sub-corpora, *of the* is part of a noun-phrase, in particular *one of the* (most frequent *of* trigram in 19C, single-speaker podcasts; second most frequent in BNC-F, multiple-speaker podcast and 4CC and fourth-most frequent in BNC-C) – *one of the most, is one of the, and one of the*. We find that, indeed, *one of the* is prototypical for the most frequent type of use *of* is employed in: to describe a **part of** relationship. In the same category, we find: *couple of, lot of, rest of, some of, part of, sort of, kind of*. All of these appear amongst the most frequent bigrams regardless of genre; it is the longer clusters that show divergent use and reveal genre-specific employment of *of*. This fits with the semantic association that *of* is used, to a very large extent, to describe a "part of" relationship.

Another trigram which employs *of the* appears less frequently yet is still found amongst the top 12 3w clusters with *of* is *out of the*. This particular usage is interesting because here *of* is the link element between a prepositional phrase – out of – (*get out of, was out of*), and a noun phrase – of the – (*of the house, of the room*) which creates the complex construction of **V-Prep-of-det-N** (*get out of the house*).

One other important use of *of* is in *of course. Of* course is usually followed by *it* or a personal pronoun but can be employed in a way that is flexible enough not to appear with high frequency in longer clusters. The bigram is amongst the top seven to ten most frequent *of* bigrams in all sub-corpora bar the 19C. Here, and in the single-speaker podcast data, it appears in just over 1 per cent of all *of* uses, while it is 2 per cent for the multiple speaker podcasts, 3 per cent in BNC-F and BNC-C and over 4 per cent in 4CC. This indicates that it is an established, formulaic form using *of* that appears to reflect the degree of formality and, in a way, age of text. The more formal the text is, the less use is made of *of course*; more recent material shows a proportional increase of this phrase. This reflects the pervasive employment of *of* as a part of a **discourse marker.**

Focussing on bigrams only, we can detect one clear written versus spoken division: while the points made above are true for *of* usage in general, the written fiction texts make far greater use of **of**-pronoun (*of his, of her, of my, of them, of their*) amongst the most frequent bigrams than is found in all spoken data. Spoken data only record *of them* or *of their* in this particular category and prefer a form that is rare in fiction texts: *of people*. In other words, spoken English has a clear preference of using a (more vague, more anonymous) third-person plural referent. This also fits with a stronger use of vague countables – *some of, lot of, kind of* which are more a feature of the public speeches than the casual spoken data. Across all trigrams, they are, however, generally found: *a couple of, part of the, a bit of, a lot of, the kind of, the sort of, sort of thing.*

The other phrase that is consistently found in all sub-corpora is *(at) the end of (the) (day)*. In all corpora, this form is more frequent than (in) the middle of (the) – the other phrase-like cluster being found in every sub-corpus.

6.3.3.2   *OF patterns with R3 items*

One colligational pattern that stands out when observing *of* usage is its combination with those words found in the third position to the right

Table 6.7   Frequent OF occurrence with R3 items

Corpus/Word	N *AND*	%	N *THE*	%	N *IN*	%	N *THAT*	%	N *WHICH*	%
19 C	20,966	5.68	13,202	3.58	6,250	1.69	4,520	1.22	4,935	1.34
BNC-F	16,154	4.80	14,866	4.42	5,714	1.70	3,755	1.11	1,594	0.47
SSM	2,098	4.48	1,966	4.20	1,161	2.48	756	1.61	450	0.96
MSM	286	4.05	274	3.88	249	2.17	249	3.52	47	0.67
4C	563	3.42	418	2.54	233	1.42	330	2.00	37	0.23
BNC-C	1,363	3.22	1,155	2.73	484	1.14	902	2.13	74*	0.17

(R3) "I'm quite aware *of* the fact *that*". Such structures, in particular relative clauses with the relative pronouns *that* or *which* can occur frequently. The resulting finding is that *of* tends to be followed by relative clauses. *The, and* and *in* are amongst the most frequently occurring R3 words following *of, as* Table 6.7 shows. *Of* W$_1$ W$_2$ *which* is the most common occurrence pattern for *which* (the exception here is BNC-C, where *which* in R4 has 77 occurrences).

Overall, it can be seen that R3 words with *which* are proportionally significantly less frequent in the spoken corpora. Instead, there are *that* clauses, which occur twice as often in the casual spoken (4C and BNC-C) and semi-prepared-spoken (MSM) than in all the other, prepared, texts. This fits with the description given by Carter and McCarthy (2006: 387), that *"that* is more informal than *who* or *which"* and Biber et al. (1999: 615), who say that *that* is more common in casual conversation. Two further genre-specific trends can be seen: First, there is a notable stronger use of *of* W$_1$ W$_2$ *in* in the public speech material than in all other corpora. Most of these are straightforward prepositions; there are also some discourse markers, like *in fact, in some ways, in general*. This is in contrast to the casual speech corpora, where *of* W$_1$ W$_2$ *in* is mostly used with *in* as a preposition. Second, the very strong usage of *of* W$_1$ W$_2$ *which* and also *of* W$_1$ W$_2$ *and* in 19th-century British literature. This indicates a preference of complex sentences, where relative clauses are added, as in this example: "This gentlemen lived on an annuity *of* seventy pounds, *which* would terminate when he died." On usage patterns, Biber et al. (1999: 615) say that *"which* commonly occurs with non-restrictive relative clauses – 25 per cent to 35 per cent of the time, depending on the register. In contrast, *that* rarely occurs with non-restrictive clauses." It must be noted, too, that the SSM also shows a strong tendency to employ *which* relative clauses – and these are part of extremely long, descriptive sentences. This, again, reflects that such speeches have been carefully prepared beforehand and do not reflect spontaneous speech. The strong preference for *of* W$_1$ W$_2$ *and* reflects the strongly descriptive nature of novels, in particular the British fiction of the 19th century, where additional information is added to what is, quite often, a list of attributes – like in this example: "He rises and fetches it, slips it quickly out *of* its coverings, *and* puts it into her hand." While *and* is employed to ensure there is an unbroken flow in the description (here: of an action), *and* stands in no further semantic connection to *of*.

6.3.3.3   *OF patterns in long clusters*

Previous chapters have seen a salient distribution pattern that present *end of* as more frequent as *middle (midst) of* and this, in turn, is more frequent than *beginning (start) of*.

As section 6.3.3.2 has already highlighted, longer *of* clusters serve as clear demarcation of specific genres. In the fiction material, a lot of descriptive usage – in particular, of spaces rather than people – can be found. So there are references to outdoors: *the end of the road, the edge of the cliff*. More pervasive are descriptions of houses and rooms however: *the other end of the room, in front of*[8] *the door, at the back of the house, the other side of the room, the far end of the corridor* ... This is accompanied by references to time: *in the course of the evening, in the course of the day, a quarter of an hour*. Such *of*-phrases are described, according to Biber et al. (1999: 635), as having "a range of uses in expressing a close semantic relationship between the head noun and the following noun phrase where there are parallels with noun and adjective pre-modification rather than with the genitive". It is, in light of this, important to note that "the rest of the house" is used as well as the "the other side of the room", whereas a genitive construction (*the house's rest; *the room's other side) would be deemed as irregular – cf. Sinclair (1990) and Hoey (2005).

In the prepared speeches, however, *of* for *part-of* usage dominates: *in the terms of the agreement, one of the most urgent, some of the things that, in the case of the*. These are all fairly abstract forms, referring not to spaces and time-frames that people deal with on a daily basis; these *of* forms refer to (abstract) ideas, concepts and models. Here, too, the phrase *the other side of* occurs relatively frequently yet is employed for a wider (and larger) set of spaces: *the other side of the fence, the other side of Liverpool, the other side of the world*. It must be noted, however curious this appears to be, that *of the world* is a documented fixed phrase in English. Albeit with different frequencies, it can nonetheless be found in each of the seven sub-corpora. Amongst all uses of *of*, it occurs from a very meagre 0.02 per cent in BNC-C and a significantly higher 0.12 per cent in 4CC (casual spoken); 0.20 per cent in BNC-F, 0.30 in 19C and 0.39 per cent in ANC (fiction); to a highly relevant phrase in public speeches (it is one of the most frequent trigrams here as well): 0.55 per cent in the multiple-speaker podcasts and 0.66 per cent in single-speaker speeches.

Lastly, casual spoken English seems to make very strong use of forms of *a lot of* and *think of*. Consequently, we find *got a lot of, quite a lot of, a hell of a lot of, a lot of money, a lot of people*. As has been mentioned before, this highlights a clear concern with third parties. Furthermore, *do you think of, I can't think of* or *what do you think of* appears to a reference to something non-definitive, as does *that sort of thing*. It is interesting to note that this is the only bigram found that matches the list of *prepositional particles – phrasal* verbs given in the Collins COBUILD Dictionary (Sinclair et al., 1989). By contrast, however, there is the very twee and very British formula that is amongst the most frequent long *of* clusters in both BNC-C and 4CC: *(want) a cup of tea*. This is in sharp contrast to the fictional texts: BNC-F records it 517 times (*of the car* is slightly more frequent with 551 instances). In 19C, *cup of tea* occurs a mere 150 times – while *of the house* occurs 1,310 times. Yet this is fairly good when compared to the ANC, where *cup of tea* is recorded just once – compared to six concordance lines referring to *cup of coffee*.

6.3.4   The usage patterns of TO

As has been outlined previously, the occurrence patterns for *to* differ markedly from *of*-patterns. Nevertheless, this section will show that there are salient uses found regardless of genre as well as text-type specific ways of employing the item *to*. We have seen that *to* followed by *the* is not a dominant feature as *of the* is. *To the* occurs in 11.5 per cent of all fiction *to* bigrams, slightly less (10.5) in prepared speeches. The MMS data appears closer to spoken corpora: around 7 per cent. Nor is the difference in frequency or statistically significance very large when we look at the next-most frequent bigram, *to be*. In fact, when looking at the 12 most frequent clusters, *to the* tends to be the only non *to*-Infinitive construction. Amongst the bigrams, all prime verbs as well as *to see, to go,* and *to get* are found across the data. These are accompanied by constructions that post-position *to*: *going to, want to* and *have to*. Amongst the podcast data, there is also the bigram *need to*. All of these occur amongst the ten most frequent bigrams in all sub-corpora, with the exception of 19C (there is a specific reason for that, which will be discussed separately).

Overall, when looking at *to* bigrams, the following claims can be made: firstly, the majority of the most frequent uses of *to* are *to*-Infinitive **constructions**, and the most frequent amongst these use the prime verbs *be, do* and *have.* This appears to contradict research by Rudanko (1998) into the historical shift from *to*-Infinitive to ***to*-ing** constructions: "It is argued that as far as they are concerned, the element *to* has ceased to be an infinitive marker during the last three centuries and is instead exclusively a preposition in present-day English." However, Rudanko has chosen a very small selection of target items ("take", "submit", "confine", etc.) rather than starting, as I did, from the usage of *to* itself. It is, however, in line what Biber et al. (1999: 89) state:

> The **infinitive marker** *to* is a unique word which does not easily fit into any of the other classes. Its chief use is as a complementizer preceding the infinitive form of verbs. (...) The infinitive marker *to* also occurs as part of other multi-word lexical units, including *ought to, used to* and *have to.*

This description reiterates what we have found so far, stressing the point that *to* appears as part of MWUs and furthermore makes reference to *used to and have to* – lexical units we have seen to be predominant in spoken English.

Secondly, a sizable chunk of the most frequent *to* constructions are employed to refer to **future plans, events or moves**; these are expressed by using the forms of *going to, want to* and *have to.*

Thirdly, the pattern of *to* occurrence varies far more – looking at collocations and its pragmatics – than what we have seen with *of.* Consequently, *to* is not merely a genre-specific indicator of use: ***to* is a corpus-specific indicator of usage patterns**. This third point is best explained when looking at the most frequent *to* bigrams in 19C. Indicators for future actions may use *going to, want to, have to* as in the other five sub-corpora. However, all these constructions are, proportionally, far rarer in older works: *going to* is found in 0.9 per cent of *to* concordance lines in 19C; in 2.9 per cent in BNC-F. However, Victorian literature still employed *to* phrases to describe similar events. However, instead of *going to,* we find *will* with *to* as in: "Perhaps she *will* refuse *to* admit me"; "I *will* never yield her *to* Horace." Consequently, *will* in position L2 (the most frequent) to L5 (the least frequent) to *to* can be found to add up to 5,135 concordance lines – 1.44 per cent of all *to* uses.[9] ***Will+to*** are, however, far rarer in BNC-F (0.7 per cent), while it is almost unused in the spoken 4CC (N=52 while *going to* occurs 780 times). This means, on the one hand, that constructions with ***will+to*** are corpus specific – are only found to be a frequent feature in 19th-century British fiction, but not in the comparators. It also means that our third point is valid for 19C, though it is realised through a different grammatical form. 19C is unique in another way: even compared to BNC-F, 19C employs *to* in a far greater degree as a preposition: *to*-personal pronoun *(to me, to her, to him, to his)* can only be found here.

Four of the six most frequent clusters follow this pattern, whereas in BNC-F, there is only one: the third-ranked *to her*. This leads to the fourth point: overall, **to is not employed as a preposition amongst the most frequent bigrams**.

Amongst the trigrams, *to*, more clearly than *of* bigrams, show differences between British written texts and British spoken material. For this, the six corpora fall into two distinct groups: the prepared and edited texts (19C, BNC-F, but also SSM) and the material which is, to a smaller or larger extent, spontaneous and online in production: (4CC, BNC-C and MSM). The latter are far more formulaic and fall back on prepared trigrams, whereas the former show greater creativity and variety of application. This is reflected by the higher proportional frequencies found amongst the second group (see Table 6.8 and Figure 6.2). Table 6.8 is remarkable in that it shows how low the most frequent trigrams are in their respective use for the first group.

That this is particularly low for 19C could be explained by the fact that these are full texts and a yet more elaborate use of language. The multiple-speaker podcast data is prepared speech as well as (formal and informal) free speech, and uses the same clusters of words to a greater degree still; free casual speech is the only set of data that provides reliable frequencies, as around three of every 100 uses of I *to* would be *I've got to* or *We used to*.

Amongst the collocationally fixed sets found throughout the corpora, there are only very few: *(to) be able to* are found in the top three trigrams/4w clusters in all but the casual spoken corpora; it is ranked sixth in BNC-C. The reason for it not being that frequent in 4CC can be found in the underuse of Lancaster, Liverpool and young London speakers (cf. Pace-Sigge: 2013). Throughout, proportional frequencies are high as Figure 6.2 shows. *To go to* is ranked third in 4CC and BNC-C, fourth in

Table 6.8 Most frequent TO trigrams

Corpus	BNC-F	19C	SSM	MSM	BNC-C	4CC
most frequent 3w	BACK TO THE	TO GO TO	BE ABLE TO	GOING TO BE	I'VE GOT TO	WE USED TO
N	2,864	1,545	256	107	1,890	692
% of all TO	0.69	0.43	0.77	1.5	2.7	2.8

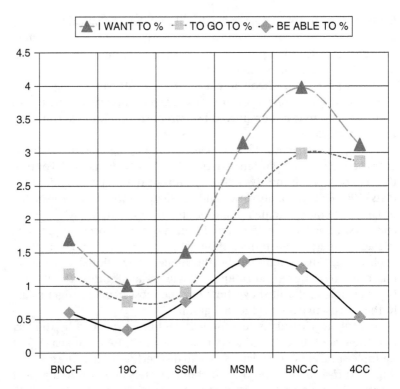

Figure 6.2   Most common TO trigrams – percentage of all TO usage

BNC-F and seventh in MSM, but is far less frequent in SSM. In five sub-corpora, *to go to the* is amongst the top five *to* 4w-clusters. Both *to talk to (you)* and *I want to* are evident in the majority of the sub-corpora. As has been highlighted in Chapter 3, 19C uses *to talk to* yet has a preference for the alternative form *to speak to*. *I want to* is ranked between fourth (prepared speeches) and tenth (BNC-C) amongst *to* trigram use. It is less prominent in 19C, where it ranks 15th. In 4CC, however, it is rarer.

Shifting the focus onto genre-specific use, *I want to talk (speak) to you* is a predominant form in British fiction, together with *I want you to* and its negation, *I don't want to*. We also find, slightly less frequently, *you don't want to*. Across these corpora, there are a large number of phrase incorporating *to*: *going to do, something to do with* and, in particular, negated forms: *I don't know what to do, nothing to do with*.... Furthermore, there are forms of *seem* to* ("it seems to me"; "it seemed to be"). None of these particular uses are very frequent in the other four corpora. Amongst the casually spoken data, *to* is mostly used for the *to*-Infinitive; BNC-C often refers to forms of obligation (*I have got to go, You have to imagine, I need to do it*), whereas reporting with the form *used to* dominates 4CC. As has been pointed out in Chapter 4, the podcast data employs *to* to a large degree as pragmatic discourse markers that highlight important parts for the audience to listen out to. In a way, these are pointers to alert the audience to important parts of the speech: *I would like to* (second and third most frequent 4w clusters); *it seems to me that, this is going to be, we have to, when it comes to* or *I just want to*.

Looking at the colligational use of *to*, the predominant form in all n-grams includes *going to: he was going to, I am going to, are you going to, we're going to, I was going to*. Thus, **personal pronoun–AUX–going to**, indicating an action in the near future, is the dominant use of *to*. There is, however, one striking exception amongst the corpora: 4CC. Looking at the usage pattern in detail, *going to be* is never uttered by any Liverpool or younger London (both Hackney and Havering) informant. Given that we find, instead, a very much stronger use of *used to* formulae in 4CC, this lack of near-future descriptions must be pragmatic. Reasons can only be speculated upon. However, given that there is also a distinct lack of *to be able to* phrases, it is either the setting where these recordings come from or a lack of confidence in the respective groups of speakers that is thus reflected.

One key *to*-Infinitive form is *to do*. While all corpora have the 4w chunk *to do with the* (a combination of **something vague followed by something specific**), this particular usage is less used in casual spoken English, while it is the most frequently, by a wide margin, occurring form with *to do* in the podcast data. It is also fairly frequent in the BNC-F and 19C corpora, yet not quite as frequent as *nothing to do with* (as has been mentioned above). It must be noted, by way of contrast, that *everything to do with* is almost a hapax legomenon: it occurs not once in the multiple-speaker-podcasts or 4CC (nor in the ANC), only once in 19C, twice in BNC-S and single-speaker public speeches. The only exception is the largest corpus, BNC-F, where it occurs 18 times. We are able to generalise, that it is a salient feature that *thing-to do with* is a common form of *to* usage: *nothing/things/anything/something to do with*.

Another marked form of *to* comes in the shape of infinitive clause with a subject predicative: **to–W$_1$–to** or **V-Inf–TO–Preposition**, as in *to go to Manchester, to talk to his mother, to come to her, whoever has to listen to that*, etc. This particular colligation appears in around 3 per cent of all uses of *to* investigated.[10] As we have said above, *to go to* is rather infrequent in prepared speeches. However, of all the trigrams that use this format, *to go to* is clearly the single most frequent form. It appears in around ten per cent of all such uses in the fictional texts and in nearly 15 per cent amongst the Q&A/plenum data. It is by a long stretch the most relevant such form amongst the spoken data, where around a third of all of these colligations are in the expression *to go to*. In both 4CC and BNC-C, the next common such cluster, *to talk to* appears around five times less frequently. *To go to*, as has been pointed out, is also employed in a different function: **V-Inf – TO – near future event**; this is often indicated by the 4w form *to go to the*. Overlap between the category (preposition) and the function (near-future event) is a regular occurrence: "Here's two pounds fifty to go to the pub with Neil"; "I got to go down to Horley and I've got to go to the bank"; " 'Cos you have to go to the other colleges to go get your certificates."

6.4   Summing up

We have seen that the items *of* and *to* can be compared in both a vertical and a horizontal way. There are clear collocational and colligational patterns that appear to be universally found. At the same time, genre-specific markers are also evident. These may be dependent on the time of production (for example: 19th-century compared to 20th-century fiction) or reflective of the pragmatic usage of a speaker (as seen in public speeches). Beyond that, there are specific differences that are characteristic to spoken forms of use.

The clearest colligational pattern seems to come apparent in the mono-collates found with *of* or *to*: single items which are very close in their frequency to the bigrams or where the bigram with *of* or *to* is by a large margin the most frequent bigram. Sometimes, the spoken form takes the item so much for granted that the speaker seems to swallow the whole word – *of course* being an example described here.

OF-MWUs have been found to appear as follows: The predominant trigram colligation is ***the*-N-*of*** in the fiction and single-speaker podcast data. This form occurs in just over one-third of all trigrams. This patterns is, however, at variance in spoken data, being only found in 23 per cent of the multiple-speaker podcast and in just over 10 per cent of the casual spoken data. Casual spoken reflects a greater degree of vagueness: while *the* is more frequent than *a*, *a*-N-*of* is the pattern found to be more frequent.

In its use, *of* reflects part-of (*part of, kind of*), preposition (*edge of the cliff*), and discourse-marker (*of* course) use as the three most frequent forms occurring. It also occurs frequently in the structures of relative clauses with *that* or *which* – as, for example, in "I'm quite aware *of* the fact *that* ..."

TO-MWUs can be described as follows: It can be seen that *to* usage is an indicator of pragmatic usage pattern that is often genre- and, to an extent, corpus-dependent. It has to be seen, however, that the *to*-Infinitive is by a long stretch the most used form of *to* while *to* as a preposition is less frequent. In fact, to-as-preposition tends to be preceded by a *to*-Infinitive. Overall, in all corpora *to* is used with a high degree of regularity and frequency in order to express vagueness; and *to* is also very often employed to refer to a near-future event. This can be expressed in a form that appears to go out of use: *will* + *to* as found in 19C. It can be, mostly, in the form of *going to*. It can also be, and this is most strongly occurring in casual speech, with *want to* or *have to*.

7
Implications for the Teaching of English

7.1 The background

Amongst learners of English, prepositions are an important element of the language as, more often than not, the constructions found in the target language are different to what is known in the learner's L1 (cf. Swan and Smith, 1987). Sinclair (1991: 81–82) has highlighted that pre-corpus dictionaries were fairly useless, were a learner to consult them to find out how to use *of*. Similarly, grammar books have "*of* pop up all over the place, attracting dozens of special statements ... in one recent grammar, there are over 50 entries of *of* spanning the entire book with substantial entries in over half the chapters". I can only fully concur with Sinclair that such an approach might be deemed fully comprehensive – yet it does little to assist a learner. I hope it has become clear from the research presented here that *of* is not only, nor mostly, used as a preposition. When we look at the nesting of *of* and *to*, and focus on the most frequent occurrences, clear patterns of usage have emerged. These are relevant for the understanding and teaching of a language:

> Focusing on patterns can, we believe, provide a more comprehensive and useful description of English than has been available to teachers up to now. What is so new about this work is that it does not rely on a distinction between grammar and vocabulary, but provides connections between the two. (Hunston, Francis and Manning, 1997: 208)

Tim Johns (cf. Johns, 1991; McEnery et al., 2006; O'Keeffe, McCarthy and Carter, 2007; Flowerdew, 2012) was an early advocate of employing corpora and corpus-based data in the classroom. Students were presented with concordance lines, and given the chance to "play Sherlock Holmes" and find salient patterns of use and meaning for the words presented. Thus, Johns (1991) describes the differences found for *persuade* and *should*. His students were able to distinguish different semantic categories that occur overall (while singular events are felt to be less relevant). While Johns focussed on lexical words, this book has focussed on two grammatical words. Two lecturers at the university of València have, indeed, applied a similar approach to teach prepositions: "A cross-curricular approach in the use of prepositions [in subject modules] such as *Lexicology* and *Critical Discourse Analysis* ... where students are shown how to conduct research that will yield revealing insights into the highly context-dependent meanings of common prepositions" (Dolón Herrero and Fuster Márquez, 2012). As such, the work presented here functions as an extension of the work presented by Renouf and Sinclair (1991). With reference to Johns, the approach taken in this book has been the same: lines of concordances and occurrence-patterns of collocates, clusters and colligations have been compared in order to describe the most commonly found patterns for the items *of* and *to*; providing the further step of highlighting differences and commonalities apparent between different genres. All this is hoped to be conductive to the task of both teaching and learning English as a language. In a way that can be seen as similar to the view expressed by Hunston et al. (1997) above, Michael Hoey is concerned with how learners first encounter language:

> What distinguishes learners (or, more accurately, types of learning) is not therefore whether they are native or non-native but how primings come into existence. When a speaker is surrounded by evidence – all of it good, in marked contradiction made by Chomsky (e.g. 1965) – the primings get up inductively at variable speeds. (Hoey, 2005: 184)

This approach can be adopted with the help of this book. Were a learner of English given all the possible functions that either *of* or *to* seem to fulfil; were a learner to decide how and which preposition works best in context, the resulting thought-processes would take far too long to provide a basis for fluent communication. If, on the other hand, there is an awareness of relative frequencies, a knowledge of common pre-fabricated chunks, a learner can make a fairly quick decision and move towards fluency faster. As Cheng points out (2012: 102), "Language comes quite often in the form of repeated phrases made up of two or more adjacent words." Similarly, Stubbs (2001: 59) speaks of "the pervasive occurrence of phrase-like units of idiomatic language[s]".

Furthermore, Hoey's view of "learning through being primed" fits fully with Rice's findings on learning patterns of native speakers. The description given by Cheng, Sinclair, Stubbs and others of language being idiomatic, lexical-based rather than structured in the way of traditional grammars is supported by Rice's research findings, looking at young children's native language acquisition. She highlights that her

> ... findings suggest that much of language acquisition is driven by external/environmental factors more than internal/cognitive factors. Equally, it appears to be lexically driven rather than syntactic, which in turn reinforces the notion that the mental lexicon (rather than an internalized grammar) is the right target of our theoretical attention and research. (Rice, 1999: 275)

Consequently, it makes sense to teach language in a spirit that takes into account its phraseological tendencies. Flowerdew proposed (cf. 2009: 335) a teaching syllabus that is not grammatical forms but "designed around the most important recurrent patterns ... designed around lexical patterns and not simply single words". Flowerdew describes that such an approach to teaching language has already, in a similar form, been developed by Nattinger in 1980.[1] The evidence provided in this book can thus form one solid basis founded on natural language usage.

One further issue has been highlighted by Hoey (2005), McEnery et al. (2006), Cheng (2012) and Flowerdew (2012), amongst others: that learners must be aware of the fact that different genres produce different word uses – "different corpora show different results" (see also Pace-Sigge: 2013). Therefore:

> Learners seek to acquire the primings associated with those areas of life in which they wish to seem competent and in which the effects of seeming incompetent may be practical as well as social. For each learner, this may vary. (...) Crucially, as any language learner will confirm, the primings we have may serve us in one situation and fail us in another. (Hoey, 2005: 185)

The Function and Use of TO and OF in Multi-Word Units cannot possibly claim to be able to provide every learner with word uses for all areas of life. Nevertheless, it can provide one extremely useful tool for those areas that learners of the English language will see as an important part of their studies, namely, the way *of* and *to* wording patterns appear in highly relevant forms of text. First of all, when discussing English Literature – which is a subject in *English Language and Culture* courses. Next, such usage patterns are useful for a learner because they give her or him a notion of and a feeling for the pragmatic markers and common features in public speeches which are commonly employed. Also, albeit to a smaller extent, this book provides some indications of common phrases in academic writing and speaking. Not only university students but everyone who is fulfilling a public role is, in the 21st century, expected to deliver speeches to non-specialist audiences in English. Last but not least is the core[2] communicative form: casual speech. The data described here does not only serve to show what is specific to spoken conversation: it also gives a notion that particular turns of phrase are geographically more prominent in some areas than others (see also Pace-Sigge, 2013). Furthermore, it can be employed, by learners and teachers alike, as a negative template: usage forms found for *of* and *to* that are fairly common in casual talk may not be fully acceptable in more formal uses – particularly not in formal texts.

7.2   The core clusters

Below, some core clusters in the different genres will be shown to highlight prominent usage patterns of *of* and *to* (for full tables, please consult Appendix 6.i–6.iv). This is not meant as a repetition of what has been described in detail in the previous chapters. Instead, a number of the most frequent MWUs will be directly compared here to highlight the crucial degrees of overlap in their usage, while also raising awareness as and where divergence is present. This divergence needs to be explained to make such sets of words with the item *of* or the item *to* relevant for teaching purposes.

7.2.1   The core clusters: OF

Looking at *of* usage in fiction (Tables 7.1 and 7.2), it can be seen that there is a great deal of consistency in the usage of the item in fictional texts. That the percentages are different can be explained by the fact that BNC-F has excerpts and 19CC uses full texts (see Chapter 3). However, in their rankings – how frequent these MWUs appear in relation to each other – differences are marginal. The one exception is *part of the* which is more prominent in 19CC (*a couple of* is far more prominent

Table 7.1 Key trigrams (OF) in fiction

trigram	R	OF BNC-F %	R	OF 19C %
OUT OF THE	1	1.91	2	0.98
ONE OF THE	2	1.76	1	1.25
PART OF THE	12	0.41	3	0.46
THE END OF	4	0.73	4	0.41
SIDE OF THE	7	0.66	7	0.34
END OF THE	9	0.62	12	0.30
SOME OF THE	11	0.46	8	0.34
THE BACK OF	10	0.62	10	0.31

Table 7.2 Key long clusters (OF) in fiction

4w/5w	R	OF BNC-F %	R	OF 19C %
THE END OF THE	1	0.39	2	0.16
AT THE END OF	3	0.32	1	0.17
THE REST OF THE	2	0.35	3	0.15
IN THE MIDDLE/MIDST OF	4	0.31	4	0.14
AT THE END OF THE	1	0.18	1	0.07
IN THE MIDDLE OF THE	2	0.16	2	0.07
THE OTHER SIDE OF THE	3	0.16	3	0.06
ON THE OTHER SIDE OF	4	0.12	5	0.05

in BNC-F though) – which highlights how more contemporary texts are less formal.

Overall, the impression given is that there is a great deal of agreement between the two corpora of British literature. Semantically, *of* is employed to describe *part of* (*one of, some of,* in a way, also, *side of, back of*) relations. These, together with the trigrams *out of the, end of the* hint at a strong predominance of *of* in prepositional usage in fiction texts. The longer clusters reflect an even greater degree of consistency in use. The *part of* descriptors remain the most frequent ones. As we have seen throughout, *at the end of (the day/the street)* is a highly idiomatic turn of phrase which is used more frequently than *in the middle of*. In Chapter 3, we have highlighted that *in the midst of* was the preferred phrase in the older texts, though, even then, *in the middle of* was in fairly frequent use. *In the beginning of* is, by contrast, far less commonly used. Two key characteristics are also worth knowing: first, *the other side of* is far more of a fixed phrase than *the side of*. Second, one can see the extremely prominent use of personal pronouns in singular and plural forms (see Appendix 6.i). Therefore, a lot of examples like *of his, of her* and *of them* relate to the very strongly interpersonal nature of the texts at hand.

The colligation pattern for the item *of*, which has been found in use throughout, is strongly linked with noun phrases. *OF THE* appears (with the exception of the casual spoken data) in one quarter of all trigrams of *of*. Therefore, there are ***of the x*** or ***the x of*** or a combination of both: ***the x of the y***. Given this particular link, learners have to be aware of the fixed word-order here. ***The of*** is not an available option.

As the 5-word long clusters indicate, the positioning function displayed by the preposition *of* does also frequently occur in concert with other prepositional markers. Hence, we find ***at y^1 z^1 of; in x^1 z^2 of; on x^1 y^3 z^3 of;*** *at the end of, in the middle of, on the other side of*. A learner will have to be aware that *at the, in the* and *on the* stay fixed, yet the second preposition clearly relates to the noun.

Tables 7.3 and 7.4 look at spoken *of* usage. In this case, the most formal cases – prepared speeches by single speakers (SSM) are compared with a corpus of casual spoken British English, which includes the most recent material. When we look at the data with the aim to teach non-native speakers about the most natural-sounding, fluent usage of spoken *of*, we can see that the case is no longer as clear-cut as above. There, the same genre showed relatively minor differences of usage over a century of usage. Comparing a rehearsed, edited and prepared spoken set of utterances with un-rehearsed, spontaneous online casual speech shows clear differences. Two core phrases that have also occurred frequently

Table 7.3 Key trigrams (OF) in spoken usage

trigram	R	OF SSM %	R	OF 4CC %
ONE OF THE	1	1.34	2	1.96
A LOT OF	4	0.64	1	6.60
OUT OF THE	9	0.31	12	0.79
THE END OF	6	0.48	10	0.89
SORT OF THING		0.05	6	1.20
SOME OF THE	3	0.71	14	0.74
A COUPLE OF		0.12	4	1.47
IN TERMS OF	5	0.61		0.19

Table 7.4 Key long clusters (OF) in spoken usage

4w/5w	R	OF SSM %	R	OF 4CC %
AT THE END OF	2	0.21	5	0.51
ONE OF THE MOST	3	0.17		0
IN THE CASE OF	4	0.16		0
ON THE BASIS OF	6	0.13		0
A BIT OF A		0.04	2	0.57
QUITE A LOT OF		0.01	4	0.51
THAT SORT OF THING		0[3]	8	0.46
AT THE END OF THE	*1*	*0.10*	*1*	*0.30*

in the written data are stable in use in the spoken material as well: *one of the* and *at the end of the* – these are also amongst the most frequent trigrams and 5w clusters in MSM and BNC-C. To a lesser degree, this is also true for *out of the*. Otherwise, however, the casual conversation data has very specific phrases, which are less – if at all – used in formal presentations. Thus we have a greater degree of phrases with vagueness markers in the casual 4CC material: *a lot of, a couple of, sort of thing*. Note how *a lot of* appears in nearly seven of all 100 uses of *of* here. *Some of the* appears with the same relative frequency in both the single-speaker public speeches and the 4CC casual conversations. Yet it must be noted that, amongst trigrams, this phrase is far less likely to be heard in casual speech. *In terms of*, however is a clear marker of formal spoken usage.[4] The same is true when longer clusters are considered: *a bit of a, quite a lot of* and *that sort of thing* are fixed chunks usually heard in casual spoken English. They are almost fully absent in prepared speeches. The public presentations, on the other hand, show usage of the phrases *one of the most, in the case of* and *on the basis of*. All of these can be identified as pragmatic speech markers, where the speaker will demonstrate a point by exemplifying it. Further details are in Chapter 4.

   One colligation feature must be mentioned: While *a lot of* is found in all sub-corpora, trigrams and longer clusters that use the indefinite rather than the definite article (a/an rather than the) occur more frequently in casual spoken concordance lines. Unsurprisingly, these indefinite articles tend to go with vagueness markers: *a bit of, a couple of*. It must be noted that those two phrases are fairly specific in what follows. *A lot of* is different, as the longer BNC-C and 4CC clusters reveal: a lot of *people*, a lot of *money*, a lot of *them* are all possible and frequently heard. Yet only *them* could be preceded by *a bit of* or *a couple of*. SSM data is, by contrast, very specific and longer clusters retain the feature of exemplification: *one of the most important, the rest of the world, the other side of the*, etc. (see Appendix 6.ii for details).

7.2.2   The core clusters: TO

A review of Chapters 3 to 6 reveals that, on the whole, *of* structures are more stable across sub-corpora and genres than *to* structures. One possible explanation can be found in the fact that a sizeable amount of *to* usage is found to be within *to*-Infinitives. Given that verbs differ considerably according to context, one might expect that there are, in fact, only very few clusters, indeed, longer clusters, that are found repeatedly in texts that differ in their intended audience, time of writing, as well as in their pragmatic and discourse aims. Yet in all the clear divergence displayed, one cannot overlook the great deal of convergence within the phrases that occur most frequently in all corpora.

Greater divergence means there are fewer trigrams and longer clusters of *to* in common between 19C and BNC-F: this is shown when Tables 7.5 and 7.6 are compared with Tables 7.1 and 7.2.

Yet the trigrams listed in 7.5 show that a relevant number of *to* phrases occurs both in their relative frequency and, possibly even more so, their relative rankings are very much on a par with each other. The one clear marker of diachronic change is *to talk to*. A learner of English would need to be aware that the phrase *to speak to* – as in *I like to speak to you* – would sound stilted, slightly archaic today. In fact, looking at the prosody of the two phrases, the semantic associations with *to speak to you* rather than *to talk to you* reveals a greater degree of seriousness: *The police wishes to speak to a man last seen with the victim at...*, rather than *I would like to talk to you tonight.*

Another such key difference is the far stronger usage of the form *going to* in contemporary fiction. This is discussed, in detail, in Chapter 3.

Amongst the key phrases, *(to) be able to* stands out. It has been shown earlier that this phrase has strong mono-collocational properties. Section 6.3.2 discusses the phenomenon of mono-collocates in detail, and learners have to be aware of idiomatic phrases that are fixed and almost exclusively employed in set multi-word sequences.

The widest divergence in *to* usage is found amongst all forms of spoken English. Consequently, only the least prepared of the formal speech data – panel speakers and Q&As – can be compared with the more conservative, older casual spoken material in the BNC-C. The results can be seen in Tables 7.7 and 7.8.

Yet before I come to these, I wish to highlight the rather surprising fact that, in the face of a wide range of possible verbs, the *to*-Infinitive appears, across spoken corpus data, very strongly fixed on the prime verbs and some other verbs that are essential building blocks of the English language as they fulfill a variety of semantic functions. For this, the bigrams in Table 7.9 show occurrences in all spoken corpora. Here, it can be seen that *to the* – indication of prepositional use – is more a marker of prepared than non-prepared speech. Consequently, it is significantly more prominent in SSM: a noteworthy issue for students of English. Amongst the verbs, the prime verbs are all key: *to be, have to*. It must be pointed out that *to have* is in all cases more frequent than the latter. Students must be aware of the specific colligational patterns that are thus used. Furthermore, there are typical references to activity: *to do* (whereas *do to* is far more rare) and *to go* (*go to* is less used). The

Table 7.5 Key trigrams (TO) in fiction

trigram	R	OF BNC-F %	R	OF 19C %
BE ABLE TO	3	0.60	3	0.34
TO GO TO	4	0.58	1	0.43
TO BE A	6	0.52	2	0.43
SEEMED TO BE	11	0.42	8	0.28
TO TALK TO	8	0.45		0.13
TO SPEAK TO		0.21	5	0.34

Table 7.6 Key long clusters (TO) in fiction

4w/5w	R	OF BNC-F %	R	OF 19C %
TO BE ABLE TO	2	0.19	2	0.13
TO GO TO THE	4	0.15	6	0.08
I WANT YOU TO	11	0.11	10	0.06
TO TALK TO YOU	10	0.11		0.02
TO SPEAK TO YOU			7	0.07
WHAT ARE YOU GOING TO	2	0.04		0

Table 7.7 Key trigrams (TO) in spoken usage

trigram	R	OF MSM %	R	OF BNC-C %
BE ABLE TO	2	1.37	6	1.26
YOU HAVE TO	4	0.96	4	1.48
I WANT TO	6	0.89	10	0.99
TO GO TO	7	0.88	3	1.73

Table 7.8 Key long clusters (TO) in spoken usage

4w	R	OF MSM %	R	OF BNC-C %
TO BE ABLE TO	1	0.93	9	0.31
I DON'T WANT TO	2	0.33	3	0.40
TO GO TO THE	6	0.28	2	0.45
IT SEEMS TO ME	8	0.24	8	0.04

relevance and usage patterns of *going to* have been discussed in detail in Chapter 3. Suffice to say here that *going to* amongst trigrams is the most frequent constituent part in MSM and, in longer clusters, appears to be a key pragmatic marker in all forms of public speeches. *Going to*, in one sense of its use, has a nesting that is similar to the use of *want to* – this is discussed in detail in Chapter 5. Table 7.9 presents also a clear outlier in *used to*. This verb appears in 4CC very strongly as it is employed to re-tell stories – a lot of the 4CC material is based on interviews where the participants are asked to recall earlier experiences and memories. The relevance for teaching is the point that *used to*, as in *I used to go to...*, is probably the most common past tense *to*-Infinitive in spoken English.

Looking at Tables 7.7 and 7.8, it is noteworthy that *(to) be able to* is the one fixed phrase that is also most frequently found in the fiction data. In clear contrast to the fiction data, spoken usage makes far greater use of personal pronouns in conjunction with the *to*-Infinitive. At the same time, there are the phrases *I want to/I don't want to* – usually referring to future action – which indicate the first-person singular preference found in speech. A student may want to take note that the imperative *you have to* is often employed, yet only implies a weak directive form: unlike, for example, *you must shut the door after you*, it is much more likely to be found in phrases like *you have to imagine*.

Finally, comparing casual and more formal speech, a student might need to know that *to go to* (infinitive followed by a preposition) is clearly a marker of an actual action: something somebody did and tells the listener about. As such, it is far less prominent in public speeches. The use of hedging, however, as seen in the phrase *it seems to me*, would be unexpected in casual spoken English while it is expected to be found in public speeches.[5] The same is true for the polite formula *I would like to*.

Table 7.9 Key bigrams (TO) in spoken usage

BIGRAM	R	SSM %	R	MSM %	R	BNC-F %	R	4CC %
TO BE	2	7.93	1	8.13	5	6.09	4	6.65
TO THE	1	10.71	2	7.41	3	6.61	2	6.89
GOING TO	11	1.62	3	6.97	6	5.89	11	3.21
TO DO	4	2.11	4	4.39	4	6.48	5	5.12
HAVE TO	5	1.99	5	4.17	1	8.19	7	4.16
WANT TO	9	1.71	6	4.08	9	4.76		1.71
TO HAVE	7	1.59	9	2.85	12	3.38	12	3.12
TO GO		0.64	11	2.42	2	6.69	3	6.88
USED TO		0.63		0.96	10	3.90	1	15.65

7.3   Summing up

To conclude: in line with Johns, Nattinger and Flowerdew (see above), and Hunston and Francis (1999: 10ff.), a case can be made to include *lexical phrases* in the teaching and learning of languages. Furthermore, a clear link to psycholinguistics can be established where the process of learning a language is concerned. McDonough and Trofimovich (2009) make the case to employ formulaic patterns in L2 classroom teaching, and Hoey (2014) highlights the importance of fixed sets that a listener/speaker gets primed through repeat usage. All these sources concur that there is a fixed link between lexis and grammar and that any system that would teach dictionary-entry-like single words would be counterproductive:

> In short, then, we argue that patterns are the building blocks of language, and that they eradicate the artificial divide between vocabulary and grammar that impoverishes the teaching of both. Each word has its associated patterns, and it is these patterns that go together to make idiomatic English. Patterns are not simply idiosyncrasies of form: they also have meaning. (Hunston et al., 1997: 215)

This book has been written in the spirit expressed above. The aim is to provide an L2 learner with relative guidance as to which forms are most frequent overall and most frequently found in a specific genre. Consequently, a learner should be able to have found fitting guidance as to when to employ either *of* or *to* within a suitable pragmatic framework. In fact, this work provides a foundation that indicates what grammatical forms these items appear in and provides an insight into which structures and which formulae are most appropriate in different types of text.

8
Conclusion

Sinclair (1991: 81) voices the concern that items like *of* have no place in a dictionary but should only be dealt with in grammar books. It can be said, looking at the most frequent expressions with these items, that they have a strong semantic role and that this kind of role is expressed in their central position within fairly fixed MWUs. This fits with the observations by Pawley and Syder (1983), de Monray Davies (1998) and those made by Wray and Perkins, who strongly relate their work to Sinclair (1991):

> There is undoubtedly some sort of relationship between frequency and formulaicity, both in the sense that some formulaic sequences are very frequent, and that formulaic output is frequently called upon. (Wray and Perkins, 2000: 7)

This book does not claim that the functions *to* or *of* have subscribed to them by O'Dowd and many others are wrong (see also Wray and Perkins, 2000: 11–12). Yet, the approach used here is different: in general, this is a corpus-led investigation to see in which functions *of* and *to* are most frequently found used in across three genres of text. The results highlight, when we look at collocations only, some specific differences between usage patterns depending on the source; they also show that some semantic associations (like the "wake-up calls" in speeches and the frequent references to space, in particular, houses, in fiction) are clearly linked to the pragmatic aims of the texts – this, again, confirms the claims made by Wray and Perkins (2000). Yet when the question is what the main colligational functions for either *of* or *to* are, a fairly uniform picture emerges, which is beyond the confines of genre but highlights the overall use of the items in contemporary modern English.

Real, natural-occurring corpus data has been shown previously to work as a tool to create prototypical constructions (Gries, 2003; E & Tyler, 2003 amongst others).

Looking at the data presented, the first question is, of course, in how far this confirms, contradicts or expands upon the work by Sinclair, Biber and Hoffmann?

The OSTI report (Sinclair et al., [1970] 2004: 158–159) gives L2 to R2 patterns for *of* and *to* in spoken and written texts. *Of the* and *of* followed by pronoun *them* is clearly marked in both works. This book shows that *sort of, lot of, some of, kind of* and *part of* are more predominant in prepared-spoken than in casually spoken material; *one of* and *out of*, however, are even more prevalent in spontaneous than in careful speech. *Of course* has even today highly frequent usage in fiction (BNC-F) while *of people* and, to a lesser extent, *of work* is found in the material investigated here. By contrast, *front of* is only prevalent in the fiction texts. The OSTI report also misses some phrases that are found in the casual spoken data presented here: *of a, of it, a couple of, a cup of tea*. Sinclair (1991), revisiting the issue, has taken several selections of *of* usage from his corpus and analysed these in detail. The approach in this book has been different, as the most frequent uses within several corpora have been investigated. Consequently, there is little overlap in the examples given in detail. There is, however, a lot of agreement when it comes to the structures found. The 1991 book highlights that *of* is found outside nominal groups and, indeed, our data confirms that discourse phrases like *of course, sort of*, etc. are a particularly frequent form of use. Similarly, the notion of *part of* is being expressed in a variety of ways. The nominal groups and "support nouns" (*example of, kinds of*) described by Sinclair have been found here, too.

Amongst *to* usage, the OSTI report is supported by this book's findings with regards to *want/got/go* lemmas with *to* and also lists *used to* and *able to* – the latter one a phrase found in all corpora investigated here. However, the modals in L2 (*would, could*) are rare in spontaneous speech, while being a clear marker of the podcast material. Sinclair et al. listed both *have to* and *to have*. These are like *to be, to go* and *to get*, also prominent in my data. *Need to* occurs in the public speech data, but not very much in the casual spoken texts. Still, bigrams like *to run, to make, to start, to do*, etc. are clearly less frequent in my material. It is also interesting that *of her/to her* are highlighted by Sinclair et al. when it seems to be highly frequent only in the fiction corpora viewed for this book. Interestingly, Biber (2000: 298) says that *seem to* appears 100 times in 1 million words in both academic prose and spoken conversation.

Sinclair records it in neither sub-set and the material investigated here only has *seems to (it seems to me)* in the prepared speeches and *seemed to (be)* in 19th-century literature. With regards to Sebastian Hoffmann's (2005) work on complex prepositions, *in terms of,* listed as the most frequently occurring form in the BNC, is only prominent in the podcast data, but less used in the fictional texts and even less in casual conversation. Similarly, *in front of* is fairly frequent in the BNC-F data, but not as prominent in any of the other corpora. The only other complex preposition found to be fairly frequent is *in spite of* (found in 19C); none of the *to* complex prepositions are highly frequent in the data focussed on here. It can be confirmed, however that the "phrase-left intact" Sebastian Hoffmann (2005) talks about with reference to complex prepositions is also true for the stable kind of nesting of phrases other than complex prepositions. On the other hand, Thomas Hoffmann's (2011: 278) claim that "individual speakers will obviously have entrenched different constructions to different degrees" is neither backed up by Sebastian Hoffmann's work, nor the work here presented. It could be therefore modified to express the following: "a lot of speakers, despite being individuals, have entrenched a lot of constructions; individual use will differ to various degrees on the speaker's conscious effort." Indeed, Hoffmann (2011: 276–277) provides a number of examples that show that there is a break in such fixed phrases that has been deliberately undertaken. The majority of the ICE_GB data presented by him is supporting the view that a lot of such phrases are fixed to a large degree. Moreover, Sebastian Hoffmann's research into the grammaticalisation of the phrase *in view of* shows that there is a clear tendency of such constructions over time to move from the literal meaning (recorded between 1650 and 1800) to the usage form of a complex preposition (first recorded in 1800–1850) and far more prevalent in the modern use of the phrase (cf. Hoffmann, 2005: 54ff.). One other finding by Hoffmann can be confirmed and expanded beyond the occurrence in prepositions by the findings presented here: "A closer look at ... complex prepositions showed that considerable differences with respect to their genre specific use can in fact be observed." As shown, there are other MWUs that occur frequently independent of genre. A case can be made that writers and speakers are primed to employ the same *of* or *to* constructions that occur regardless of speaker, topic or context, at times even when speaking or writing within a considerable distance of time. These are Multi Word Units that the speakers or writers must have encountered themselves previously. Subsequently, the speakers or writers will have found that their audience recognised and understood these entities. As a result, the users keep employing them. Therefore, notably strong uses of, for example, *at the end of the day* (fiction), *I want to talk about* (public speeches) and *have a cup of tea* (casual speech) can be found. The same is true for the strong use of *part-of* constructions, rather than place- or time-directed prepositions. This fits with the assessment of primings as given by Hoey (1995: 90):

> What we are now contemplating ... is the possibility of finding bonding across texts written between three and fourteen years apart, solely because of the mental concordances of the authors retained records of the texts they had read, which in turn were written in the light of *their* author's mental concordances, which (perhaps) included sentences drawn from a common primary source (author's highlights).

Over the following years, Hoey had looked into this phenomenon, and the result was his theory of Lexical Priming. Consequently, he expanded and refined his earlier idea:

> It is more than likely that many users of a language never construct a complete and coherent grammar out of their primings. Instead they may have bits of grammars, small, self-contained mini-systems that do not connect up but represent partial generalisations from individual primings. (Hoey, 2005: 181)

Thus, public speakers appear to have taken up a set of formulations that draw their listeners' attention at crucial points within their spoken presentation. These could have been either acquired through listening to other speakers or by gauging audience reception – this certainly demands further investigation. Yet the fact that these signposts do appear in a large variety of public talks by different speakers indicates that they are primed to employ them as much as the audience appears to be primed to react to such signposts. All this would fit in with what Hoey refers to as *harmonising primings* (ibid.), which are also extremely apparent when viewing the literature data.

It has long been debated amongst corpus linguists (see Scott and Tribble, 2006: 58 or Gries, 2009: 25, amongst others) what counts as a *word* or, indeed, an *item* when data is analysed. This is important, as frequency often is the starting point for all analysis in the field. While hyphenation and compounding can alter results and while a strong case can be made to include both punctuation marks and non-dictionary items, the simplified answer is: a word is defined as the piece between two spaces. This is the kind of "meaningful unit" that is often referred to – and this is, of course, the unit appearing in dictionary entries. It must be recognised, however, that this is a cultural artefact. Greek texts (even as late as in Roman Greece), hammered in stone were a consecutive line of letters – there were no spaces, but the readers nevertheless made sense of the long line of letters. All Arabic letters are consonants – the vowels are still produced, but not scripted. Chinese characters are logograms, where a single character is a syllable. This demonstrates that alternatives to the accepted western way of spelling out meaningful units are found in use elsewhere. Crucially, though, words are very dependent on the level of inflection present. Were we, for example, to compare a language with little inflection (English) with one that is highly inflected (Latin), a clear difference is observable:

vadimus ad domum dei – going **to** the house **of** God

This, if anything, serves as a clear demonstration that English employs multi-word units where an inflected language retains the single-word character, relying on morphology for such grammatical functions. In this book, a case is being made that *of* and *to* are *not* freestanding agents that can provide a meaningful unit. As Sinclair demonstrated with the original Collins COBUILD Dictionary (a tradition proudly upheld in the Longman and Macmillan Dictionaries), *of* and *to* most regularly appear in a narrowly defined colligational way most of the time. These colligations are, to a certain degree, fairly fixed to set collocations; at times in a way that these collocations are almost mono-collocations made up out of a defined set of words and the items *of* or *to*. Indeed, an argument can be made that the existing form of representing items is doubly misleading. For one, in order to be meaningful, items like *of* and *to* have to be integral parts of lexical items which are MWUs. Furthermore, all orthographical representations of items are a simplified and codified (and therefore: fossilised) approximation. Such a difference in the production of an item can sometimes be seen in (present-day) homonyms: *Too* entered ModE as an emphatic form of *to*, meaning "in addition to" (Hook, 1975: 89). This is a poignant demonstration how a sounding of one particular word was mirrored in its (still retained) spelling. All in all, this shows that words change their collocations and meanings through usage.

Mindt (2013) provides a possible explanation for what Gimson describes as *strong* or *weak* forms when describing "connected speech" (or: spontaneous online production). Gimson lists both *to* and *of* as items which appear in both strong and weak forms. In the case of *of*, the production would be sounded either as /əv, v, ə/ (weak form) or as /ɒv/ (strong form). He points out that "the use of strong or weak forms does not appear to be a matter of style... The alternation of strong and weak forms is entirely regular" (*Gimson's Pronunciation of English*. See Cruttenden 2001: 294). Bybee's thoughts (2003; 2006) on grammaticalisation expand this. Mindt, in her investigations of qualitative differences in the phonological production of the item *to*, describes that there are detectable differences depending on the category the item is employed in, as shown in Table 8.1. Linzen et al., looking at lexical and phonological variation in Russian prepositions, find a parallel process:

> Most striking is the example of the root [dnj-] "day", which contains a yer, but behaves differently after the preposition[s] depending on whether that preposition means "with" or "from", ruling out any purely phonological explanation. (Linzen et al., 2013: 506)

This leads to two approaches. When considering the teaching of English, students could be made aware that the same spelling does not represent the same lexical items: an insight that goes back to John Firth. Yet in relation to the item *to*, the actual production with the sound can be highlighted as a point of differentiation; with reference to Linzen et al., a point can be made that this particular phenomenon is not unique to English. In fact, similar characteristics in the student's first language (L1) should be brought to the fore to provide the learner with an easy way to bridge the gap with the known priming (the learner's L1) and the to be acquired priming (the target language).

Looking at the theoretical explanation of such variations, we can define differentiation. Depending on the function, it can be tentatively said that the sounding of the word differs, albeit in a barely perceptible way. This can lead to the conclusion that, while *to (preposition)* and *to (Infinitive)* are represented in the same way orthographically, they

Table 8.1   Different phonological realisations of TO (based on Mindt, 2013: 119)

	PURPOSE/ADDING TO	CATENATIVE VERB
length of COME	0.30 s	0.26 s
length of vowel sound in COME	0.14 s	0.11 s
vowel in TO	0.24 s	0.13 s
vowel quality in TO	similar to /ə/	similar to /u /
pitch accent	*to V* higher	*to V* lower

should be treated as two separate items. This chimes particularly true in the light of the view given by Biber et al. (1999: 76) that "many of the *same orthographic words* can function as preposition, subordinator, adverbs ..." (author's emphasis). Combining these findings with the corpus-based investigation of the item *to* in different types of corpora seems to strengthen this view. There are different kinds of multi-word units with *to* as a key element for different kind of functions. Hence *been able to* has *to* functioning as a different type of item to that in *turn to her* and *used to be* – despite the fact that the item is always preceded by a verb-phrase. The author agrees with Mindt that these different functions would be expected to show slight differences in the production of the item *to* within any MWU. Orthographically, such differences would not be noted. We should therefore, I propose, see such grammatical words in a way similar to polysemous lexical words: different meaning, same spelling. Within an MWU, however, a delineation between different functions would be created by the collocational and colligational environment the item is in, according to Hoey (2005: 13): "When a word is polysemous, the collocations, semantic associations and colligations of one sense of the word differ from those of its other senses." This quote has to be read with the three claims that Hoey makes: that every word is primed to occur with particular other words, particular semantic sets; that these words are primed to occur in *or* to avoid grammatical positions or functions; and that these are the word's collocations, semantic associations and colligations (cf. Hoey, 2005: 13). Later on, Hoey refers to Sinclair who, in 1987 (as a comment on the Collins COBUILD Dictionary), "notes that each meaning of a word can be associated with a specific collocation or pattern". Discussing polysemy, Hoey gives a more detailed description:

> Experience suggests [and this is supported by Sinclair's work, too] that ambiguity in language in use ... is a rarity. This suggests that Sinclair's claim can be couched contrastively, such that the patterns of one use of a polysemous word always distinguish it from those of other uses of the word.
>
> We are, I want to suggest, primed to recognise contrasting patterns and to reproduce them. More precisely, colligations a word is primed for will systematically differentiate its polysemous senses. (Hoey, 2005: 81)

This fits neatly with the findings of Rice on child-language acquisition of items like *to* or *of*. Hoey (2005) and Pace-Sigge (2013) have laid out in detail how the employment of sets of words reflects the primings that speakers and writers have acquired through their exposure of often-repeated forms and phrases. What I have hoped to achieve here is to indicate that both *of* and *to* are respectively expressed by a single token – yet these tokens do not represent that they are not the same type. They are, depending on their associated words, differing lexical items, fulfilling different functions.

Further research is, however, still needed. The corpora employed here are fairly small – it is always difficult to create a suitably balanced large spoken corpus – and genres like academic English or newspaper prose have not been included. Likewise, it will be necessary in future to look also at medium–high use of MWUs with *of* and *to*. None of these approaches were available within the confines of this publication, yet I hope that the present study will serve as a workable platform from which further research can be undertaken.

Appendix

1.1 Frequency of OF *and* TO usage by genre

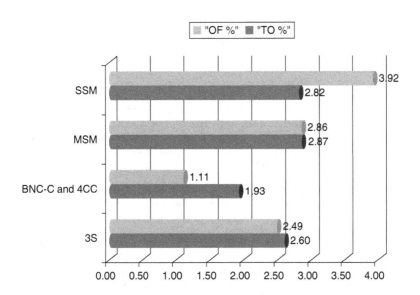

4.i The Material and Sources: Chapter 4

The research is based on three main corpora: the BBC Reith Lectures from 1948 to 2011, the LSE Public Lectures from 2006–2013 and Public Lectures on artworks held by National Museums Liverpool (NML) between 2006 and 2011. Furthermore, a variety of transcripts from a number of public events and presentations held by a variety of organisations over the last decade have been added, to have a further, less heterogeneous sub-corpus. The total number of tokens across all corpora is 1,449,718 items. Apart from the sources, the corpora are further divided into sub-corpora along the following criteria:

1. Sources: BBC, LSE, NML and VAR (Various)
2. Type of Speech: (a) single-speaker lecture, (b) multiple-speaker lecture plus Q&A sessions after a lecture.

Further subdivisions will be described below.

This section describes the three main sources – BBC, LSE and NML – and gives details where to find the originals and describes the sets of text involved.

Furthermore, the sub-corpus VAR will be described and the main sources of the corpus will be named here.

4.ii   Sub-corpus: BBC Radio

The BBC Reith Lectures, in honour of the founder of the Corporation, were started in 1948 and initially broadcast on the *Home Service* and later moved to its current home, *BBC Radio 4*. It has been transmitted every year since, though both 1977 and 1992 lectures are not available. The latest transcript ready for download is from the year 2011. Each year, a chosen speaker – usually a public figure, a philosopher, historian or scientist – delivers a series of speeches over a period of several weeks. The number of lectures vary – there are only two by Aung San Suu Kyi (in 2011), while John Zachary Young delivered eight lectures in 1950. The majority of the lecturers provide six sessions. In order to have a fair distribution, two lectures were chosen, at random, by each of the speakers for each year. The majority of the speakers are British, a number are from the US and a minority come from overseas with English not necessarily being their first language. Speeches usually lasted 30–45 minutes.

One thing that could not be randomised, however, is the distribution of speakers by gender: early transcripts are reflecting a clear bias towards male speakers, while more recent recordings show that the BBC is striving to invite women as well as men to give a Reith Lecture.

The BBC website provides access to all the Reith Lectures given and makes transcripts of each lecture in PDF format (and often as .MP3s, too) available for download at http://www.bbc.co.uk/radio4/features/the-reith-lectures/transcripts/2011 (last accessed August 20, 2013).

The format stayed uniform in both delivery, length and in the manner of the transcription from the inception of the programme until the year 2005.

Starting with the year 2006, however, the transcripts have become more comprehensive. There is a transcription of the introduction and, more importantly, a full transcription of the ensuing Question-and-Answer (Q&A) sessions, giving the full names of those asking questions and their queries are also recorded in full. Because of this, the files used here have been split into two parts: one which has only the lecture itself and another, second file which has only the Q&A section. The discussion of results will show in what way this division is necessary and relevant.

As the Reith Lectures span a long period of time, they can also be used (though, as there is no direct comparator corpus, only to a certain extent) to track changes in use over time. A broad 2-part division has been made to enable a tentative look at chronological change: 1948–1989 (the first 40 years, covering the Cold War period) and 1990–2011 (the most recent two decades, mirroring current experience of language use. There is, also, a sub-group to reflect most recent use and which can also be used to directly compare the use as found in both the LSE and the NML data: the 2006–2011 transcripts which, as described above, provide both transcripts of the lectures given and the discussions had in those years.

Reith Lectures 1948–2011	Total tokens	TO	OF
single speakers	500,490	14,084 (2.81%)	21,890 (4.37%)
Q & A	47,346	1,447 (3.06%)	1,206 (2.55%)

4.iii   Sub-corpus: London School of Economics: LSE Public Lectures and Events

These are the transcripts of speeches delivered to staff, students and anybody interested as arranged by the LSE, covering a period from October 2006 up to March 2013. The subject matter shows a clear bias towards economics, though there are also a large number of speeches concerned with national and international politics as well as some that look at the area of arts and humanities. Given the kind of background under which these lectures have been arranged, the vast majority (in fact, there are very few exceptions) of the presenters are male. There are a large number of politicians – either British or international – economists and heads of central banks. Even if English is not their native language, they are well-versed in using the language proficiently as their language of business. Prepared speeches, furthermore, will have been worked on by adept specialists. Speeches vary in length. No times are advertised, but the transcripts can be as short as five and as long as 20+ pages. A number of them have been given in tandem with a PowerPoint presentation (which the LSE also makes available for download). There is also clear evidence that a large number of the lectures delivered are *not* transcripts but the written text of prepared speeches. Some of the downloads have a note warning "check against delivery" and a very small number even say "embargoed until" – showing that public figures use the LSE event as a forum to announce policies with the probably aim to make headlines. The speeches given by employees of the *Bank of England* are meant for wider dissemination and can also be found on the Bank's on website. On the other hand, some of the PDFs downloaded look less like official documents – this can mean that the speaker either made his prepared notes available or that these are actual transcripts. It must be noted that, unlike in Reith, NML or VAR, there is no multiple-speaker sub-corpus in LSE and the Q&A sessions are available for only four of the lectures.

All speeches are downloadable in PDF format form the LSE website, which also provides audio files (.mp3) and slides of presentations. http://www.lse.ac.uk/assets/richmedia/webFeeds/publicLecturesAndEvents_iTunesRssAudioPdfAllitems.xml (last accessed August 20, 2013).

LSE Public Lectures 2006–2013	Total tokens	TO	OF
single speakers	467 506	13,859 (2.96%)	17,272 (3.69%)
Q & A	13 766	383 (2.78%)	399 (2.90%)

4.iv   Sub-corpus: National Museums Liverpool

In the time between May 2006 and February 2011, National Museums Liverpool recorded their public lectures held regularly on pieces of their collection. The podcasts vary in length considerably: the shortest is just over ten minutes, the longest nearly 70 minutes long. The majority last between 30 and 45 minutes. All podcasts have been transcribed and made available at http://www.liverpool-museums.org.uk/podcasts (last accessed August 20, 2013).

Since then, however, no new podcasts have been added, though the lectures continue. The majority of the lectures were given by senior employees (curators, head of education) of NML, though a sizable amount has been given by guest speakers. The selection ensures that there is only one transcript per speaker (as a number of NML staff have presented multiple lectures). Transcripts of poetry or drama were not added to this corpus. Furthermore, as this represents the Arts, rather than the field of Economics and Politics, there is a larger proportion (just above 50 per cent) of female speakers represented in this corpus. Single-speaker lectures use a fairly uniform frame – they start with the speaker introducing themselves and almost always end with a "thank you" note.

This corpus has been split two ways: single speaker presentations, multiple-speaker presentations (nine NML-sourced transcripts and a tenth is from a BBC Radio Merseyside transcript). In these presentations, the speakers present consecutively, rather than in a round-table discussion, followed by a Q&A with the public.

NML Public talks 2006–2011	Total tokens	TO	OF
single speakers	159,290	3,967 (2.49%)	5,177 (3.25%)
Q & A	63,508	1,621 (2.55%)	1,206 (3.31%)

4.v   Sub-corpus: Various Sources (VAR)

This is a random collection of material rendered through a basic trawl through websites with the search "podcast transcripts UK" and "presentation transcripts UK" which resulted in wide-ranging sources, including a podcast from a cancer research foundation and a transcript of a presentation given to web-developers. It has been found, however, that a large number of search results returned either transcripts which are quite short (covering 1–5 minutes of speech) or representing panel and group-discussions rather than lecture-like longer exhibitions.

The VAR corpus is also unevenly split: in the corpus, the multiple-speaker transcripts are around one-third larger than the (28 texts) single-speaker corpus. This sub-corpus therefore acts very much as a control group. The largest single source here are transcripts from a BBC Radio 4 programme. A total of 11 transcripts, representing one piece by each of the presenters listed. These have been transmitted between 2011 and 2013. Unfortunately, the majority of the presenters are male again (only three females). *A Point of View* is very much a slot-filler, lasting for about 10 minutes of broadcasting time. This makes it far shorter than the public lectures used here in other sub-corpora, yet it fits broadly in with the material collected, overall, in the *Various* selection. These can be found at http://www.bbc.co.uk/news/magazine: *Previously on a point of view* (last accessed August 20, 2013). The second-largest group here are seven transcripts of the British Library (BL) *Breaking the Rules* exhibition (2007–2008) where transcripts are made available in PDF format: www.bl.uk/onlinegallery/features/breakingtherules (last accessed August 20, 2013). These seven texts are the closest to the NML presentations in style and subject-matter, albeit shorter. The third selection have been taken from public lectures held by Gresham College: shorter than the LSE lectures, yet equally written to be spoken material, more varied in their content, more focussed on the Arts/Humanities but equally biased towards male speakers. Podcasts can be found here: http://www.gresham.ac.uk/lectures-and-events. Other texts come from the British Library (BL) , Transport for London (TfL), a museum and a web-developer conference.

Amongst the multiple-speaker sources, the largest group is from the Digital R&D Fund for the Arts (http://www.artsdigitalrnd.org.uk/) amounting to six out of 21 files. A number (5/21) have been taken from the *International Museum of Women* (http://www.imow.org). Three are podcasts from the *Guardian* (http://www.theguardian.com/global-development/series/global-development-podcast) and one is from the BBC Radio 4 show *You and Yours*. The remaining transcripts come from a variety of other sources. All transcripts have been provided by the sources and any obvious noise (headers, quotes) have been removed.

Various sources ca. 2007–2011	Total tokens	TO	OF
Single speakers	75 637	2,057 (2.72%)	2,821 (3.73%)
Q & A	122 225	3,646 (2.98%)	3,420 (2.80%)

British Academic texts:

- BASE (British Academic Spoken English):

http://www2.warwick.ac.uk/fac/soc/al/research/collect/base

The recordings and transcriptions used in this study come from the British Academic Spoken English (BASE) corpus (http://www2.warwick.ac.uk/fac/soc/celte/research/base/). The corpus was developed at the Universities of Warwick and Reading under the directorship of Hilary Nesi (Warwick) and Paul Thompson (Reading). Corpus development was assisted by funding from the Universities of Warwick and Reading, BALEAP, EURALEX, the British Academy and the Arts and Humanities Research Council.

- BAWE (British Academic Written English):

http://www2.warwick.ac.uk/fac/soc/al/research/collect/bawe

The research project *An Investigation of Genres of Assessed Writing in British Higher Education*, undertaken in the period 2004–2007 at the universities of Warwick, Reading and Oxford Brookes, was funded by the ESRC (project number RES-000-23-0800).

5.i The Material and Sources: Chapter 5

(All URLS below last accessed 06 January 2015)

COLT. 1993. *The Bergen Corpus of London Teenage Language* (COLT). Details at http://clu.uni.no/icame/colt/cd

LANCASTER. 2003. *The Lancaster Speech, Writing and Thought Presentation Spoken Corpus* (SWAT), comprising data taken from the British National Corpus and from archives held at the Centre for North West Regional Studies (CNWRS),

Lancaster University, UK. Project supervised by Professor Mick Short, Dr Elena Semino and Professor Tony McEnery, Department of Linguistics and Modern English Language, Lancaster University. Corpus construction by Carol Bellard-Thomson, John Heywood, Tony McEnery, Dan McIntyre, Elena Semino and Mick Short, Department of Linguistics and Modern English Language, Lancaster University.
Details at http://www.lancaster.ac.uk/fass/projects/stwp/handbook.htm

LIVERPOOL. 2010/2014. Material based on SCO (Pace-Sigge, 2013) and transcripts of conversations recorded between 2012 and 2014 which have been kindly provided by Amanda Cardoso and Marten Juskan.

LONDON. 2009. Hackney and Havering material are part of the *Linguistic Innovators Corpus* (LIC). Details at http://www.lancaster.ac.uk/fass/organisations/galsig/costas.pdf (Gabrielatos, C., Torgersen, E., Hoffmann, S.& Fox, S.) University of Lancaster. Part of the Kerswill and Cheshire project – details at http://www.lancaster.ac.uk/fss/projects/linguistics/innovators
Material kindly provided by Paul Kerswill.

NEWCASTLE. 2001/2004. Material taken from: *Newcastle Electronic Corpus of Tyneside English.* A Linguistic 'Time-Capsule' (NECTE). Corrigan, Karen; Moisl, Hermann; Beal, Joan. Funded through university grants and funding from the Arts and Humanities Research Council (AHRC); British Academy; Catherine Cookson Foundation. Newcastle upon Tyne School of English Literature, Language and Linguistics, Newcastle upon Tyne.
Details at http://research.ncl.ac.uk/necte

6.i Bigrams and trigrams for all sub-corpora: OF

R	OF BNC-F 2w	N	%	R	OF 19C 2w	N	%	R	OF BNC-F 3w	N	%	R	OF 19C 3w	N	%
1	OF THE	85631	25.46	1	OF THE	99341	26.91	1	OUT OF THE	6409	1.91	1	ONE OF THE	4615	1.25
2	OF A	16959	5.04	2	OF A	20553	5.57	2	ONE OF THE	5919	1.76	2	OUT OF THE	3636	0.98
3	OUT OF	16425	4.88	3	OF HIS	19202	5.20	3	IN FRONT OF	2948	0.88	3	PART OF THE	1680	0.46
4	OF HIS	15150	4.51	4	OF HER	11918	3.23	4	THE END OF	2459	0.73	4	THE END OF	1503	0.41
5	OF HER	14415	4.29	5	OUT OF	10223	2.77	5	A COUPLE OF	2437	0.73	5	**A SORT OF**	**1383**	**0.38**
6	ONE OF	12250	3.64	6	ONE OF	9864	2.67	6	A LOT OF	2384	0.71	6	OF THE HOUSE	1310	0.36
7	OF COURSE	9872	2.94	7	OF MY	8156	2.21	7	SIDE OF THE	2223	0.66	7	SIDE OF THE	1264	0.34
8	OF THEM	7084	2.11	8	OF IT	6734	1.82	8	THE REST OF	2092	0.62	8	SOME OF THE	1242	0.34
9	OF IT	5972	1.78	9	OF THAT	5313	1.44	9	END OF THE	2087	0.62	9	OF HIS OWN	1183	0.32
10	SORT OF	4397	1.31	10	OF THIS	5019	1.36	10	THE BACK OF	2073	0.62	10	IN SPITE OF	1144	0.31
11	OF MY	3982	1.18	11	OF THEIR	4721	1.28	11	SOME OF THE	1555	0.46	11	OF THE WORLD	1103	0.30
12	KIND OF	3804	1.13	12	OF THEM	4616	1.25	12	PART OF THE	1362	0.41	12	END OF THE	1100	0.30

R	OF MSM 2w	N	%	R	OF SSM 2w	N	%	R	OF MSM 3w	N	%	R	OF SSM 3w	N	%
1	OF THE	1706	24.14	1	OF THE	11913	25.42	1	A LOT OF	262	3.71	1	ONE OF THE	627	1.34
2	ONE OF	318	4.50	2	OF A	1913	4.08	2	ONE OF THE	224	3.17	2	PART OF THE	333	0.71
3	KIND OF	280	3.96	3	ONE OF	1083	2.31	3	IN TERMS OF	202	2.90	2	OF THE WORLD	333	0.71
4	SORT OF	270	3.82	4	OF THIS	818	1.75	4	SOME OF THE	154	2.21	3	SOME OF THE	324	0.71
5	LOT OF	269	3.82	5	OF OUR	780	1.66	5	PART OF THE	71	1.01	4	A LOT OF	302	0.64
6	OF A	250	3.35	6	PART OF	684	1.46	5	OF THE THINGS	71	1.01	5	IN TERMS OF	285	0.61
7	SOME OF	249	3.35	7	KIND OF	655	1.40	6	OF THE WORLD	46	0.65	6	THE END OF	225	0.48
8	PART OF	206	2.91	8	SOME OF	629	1.34	7	THE END OF	40	0.57	7	A NUMBER OF	161	0.35
9	OF THAT	157	2.22	9	OF COURSE	592	1.27	8	LOT OF THE	38	0.52	8	**A KIND OF**	**147**	**0.31**
10	OF COURSE	146	2.07	10	OF THESE	501	1.07	8	**THE SORT OF**	**38**	**0.52**	9	OUT OF THE	144	0.31
11	OF THIS	138	1.95	11	OUT OF	496	1.05	9	THE KIND OF	35	0.50	10	THE IDEA OF	137	0.30
12	ALL OF	134	1.90	12	OF THEIR	491	1.05	10	A BIT OF	34	0.48	11	THE REST OF	133	0.28
								11	FIRST OF ALL	33	0.47	12	END OF THE	132	0.28
								12	TERMS OF THE	31	0.43				

(continued)

Continued

R	OF BNC-C 2w	N	%	R	OF 4CC 2w	N	%	R	OF BNC-C 3w	N	%	R	OF 4CC 3w	N	%
1	OF THE	6197	14.65	1	OF THE	2507	15.24	1	A LOT OF	1833	4.33	1	A LOT OF	1085	6.60
2	SORT OF	4517	10.68	2	SORT OF	1822	11.07	2	A BIT OF	1081	2.49	2	ONE OF THE	328	1.96
3	ONE OF	2878	6.80	3	LOT OF	1184	7.20	3	A COUPLE OF	796	1.88	3	A BIT OF	258	1.55
4	OF THEM	2501	5.91	4	OF THEM	829	5.04	4	ONE OF THE	738	1.74	4	A COUPLE OF	241	1.47
5	OUT OF	2388	5.64	5	ONE OF	811	4.93	5	ONE OF THEM	649	1.53	5	LOT OF PEOPLE	200	1.22
6	LOT OF	2065	4.88	6	OUT OF	699	4.25	6	THE END OF	593	1.40	6	**SORT OF THING**	196	1.20
7	**OF IT**	2029	4.80	7	OF COURSE	660	4.01	7	OUT OF THE	486	1.15	7	**WHAT SORT OF**	183	1.11
8	**OF A**	1626	3.84	8	OF A	590	3.59	8	**ONE OF THOSE**	481	4.14	8	AND OF COURSE	171	1.04
9	**BIT OF**	1585	3.75	9	KIND OF	584	3.57	9	**SORT OF THING**	410	0.97	9	SOME OF THEM	170	1.04
10	OF COURSE	1310	3.10	10	OF IT	519	3.16	10	CUP OF TEA	389	0.92	10	THE END OF	146	0.89
11	SOME OF	1222	2.89	11	SOME OF	405	2.46	11	BIT OF A	369	0.87	10	THAT SORT OF	146	0.89
12	OF THAT	1201	2.80	12	OF PEOPLE	385	2.34	12	A CUP OF	339	0.82	11	ONE OF THEM	138	0.84
								12	ONE OF THESE	339	0.82	12	OUT OF THE	130	0.79
								13	END OF THE	337	0.82	13	MOST OF THE	124	0.75

6.ii Longer clusters for all sub-corpora: OF

R	OF BNC-F 4w	N	%	R	OF 19C 4w	N	%	R	OF BNC-F long	N	%	R	OF 19C long	N	%
1	THE END OF THE	1317	0.39	1	AT THE END OF	641	0.17	1	AT THE END OF THE	605	0.18	1	AT THE END OF THE	254	0.07
2	THE REST OF THE	1166	0.35	2	THE END OF THE	593	0.16	2	IN THE MIDDLE OF THE	547	0.16	2	IN THE MIDDLE OF THE	245	0.07
3	AT THE END OF THE	1068	0.32	3	THE REST OF THE	553	0.15	3	THE OTHER SIDE OF THE	541	0.16	3	THE OTHER SIDE OF THE	228	0.06
4	IN THE MIDDLE OF	1018	0.31	4	IN THE MIDST OF	532	0.14	4	ON THE OTHER SIDE OF	416	0.12	4	A QUARTER OF AN HOUR	215	0.06
5	THE EDGE OF THE	867	0.26	5	IN THE COURSE OF	502	0.13	5	ON THE OTHER SIDE OF TH	357	0.11	5	ON THE OTHER SIDE OF	198	0.54
6	THE BACK OF THE	854	0.25	6	FOR THE SAKE OF	467	0.13	6	ON THE EDGE OF THE	298	0.09	6	IN THE COURSE OF THE	171	0.05
7	THE TOP OF THE	791	0.24	7	OF ONE OF THE	453	0.12	7	AT THE TOP OF THE	294	0.09	7	ON THE OTHER SIDE OF THE	152	0.04
8	IN FRONT OF THE	741	0.22	8	A GREAT DEAL OF	430	0.12	8	AT THE BACK OF THE	242	0.07	8	IN THE DIRECTION OF THE	145	0.04
9	THE MIDDLE OF THE	712	0.21	9	IN THE MIDDLE OF	395	0.11	9	OUT OF THE CORNER OF	240	0.07	9	AT THE HEAD OF THE	130	0.04
10	THE OTHER SIDE OF THE	649	0.19	10	THE MIDDLE OF TH	369	0.10	10	THE FAR END OF THE	221	0.07	10	THE OTHER END OF THE	123	0.03
11	THE SIDE OF THE	646	0.19	11	IN A STATE OF	360	0.10	11	THERE WAS NO SIGN OF	221	0.07	11	AT THE BOTTOM OF THE	123	0.03
12	OTHER SIDE OF THE	545	0.16	12	ONE OF THE MOST	358	0.10	12	AS A MATTER OF FACT	220	0.07	12	WHAT DO YOU THINK OF	120	0.03

(continued)

Continued

R	OF MSM 4w	N	%	R	OF SSM 4w	N	%	R	OF MSM long	N	%	R	OF SSM long	N	%
1	ONE OF THE THINGS	50	0.71	1	THE END OF THE	110	0.24	1	ONE OF THE THINGS THAT	26	0.37	1	AT THE END OF THE	49	0.10
2	OF THE THINGS THAT	39	0.54	2	AT THE END OF	96	0.21	2	I THINK ONE OF THE	14	0.20	2	IN THE MIDDLE OF THE	33	0.07
3	A LOT OF THE	38	0.52	3	ONE OF THE MOST	80	0.17	3	AT THE END OF THE	13	0.19	3	THE REST OF THE WORLD	30	0.07
4	IN TERMS OF THE	31	0.43	4	IN THE CASE OF	77	0.16	4	SOME OF THE THINGS THA"	8	0.11	4	IN THE CASE OF THE	25	0.05
5	IS ONE OF THE	21	0.30	5	THE REST OF THE	75	0.16	4	THAT A LOT OF THE	8	0.11	5	ONE OF THE THINGS THAT	23	0.05
5	THE END OF THE	21	0.30	6	ON THE BASIS OF	61	0.13	4	ONE OF THE THINGS WE	8	0.11	6	AT THE HEART OF THE	17	0.04
5	A LOT OF PEOPLE	21	0.30	7	IS ONE OF THE	60	0.13	5	AND ONE OF THE THINGS	7	0.10	7	AS A RESULT OF THE	15	0.03
6	AT THE END OF	19	0.27	8	IN TERMS OF THE	59	0.13	5	A LOT OF THE TIME	7	0.10	7	THAT'S ONE OF THE	15	0.03
6	ONE OF THE MOST	19	0.27	9	AS A RESULT OF	58	0.12	5	ONE OF THE THINGS I	7	0.10	7	ONE OF THE MOST IMPORTANT	15	0.03
7	THAT A LOT OF	18	0.25	10	IN THE FACE OF	55	0.12					8	AT THE TIME OF THE	14	0.03
8	THE REST OF THE	17	0.24	10	IN THE MIDDLE OF	55	0.12					8	THE FREEDOM OF THE WILL	14	0.03
8	A BIT OF A	17	0.24	11	OF THE UNITED ST	53	0.11					9	THE OTHER SIDE OF THE	13	0.03
9	WAS ONE OF THE	16	0.23	12	WAS ONE OF THE	50	0.11					9	OTHER PARTS OF THE WORLD	13	0.03
9	A LITTLE BIT OF	16	0.23									9	IN THE FACE OF THE	13	0.03

R	OF BNC-C 4w	N	%	R	OF 4CC 4w	N	%	R	OF BNC-C long	N	%	R	OF 4CC long	N	%
1	A BIT OF A	301	0.71	1	A LOT OF PEOPLE	189	1.15	1	AT THE END OF THE	166	0.40	1	AT THE END OF THE	50	0.30
2	THE END OF THE	293	0.69	2	A BIT OF A	95	0.57	2	IN THE MIDDLE OF THE	90	0.21	2	WANT A CUP OF TEA	29	0.18
3	A CUP OF TEA	259	0.61	3	IT'S A LOT OF	93	0.57	3	THE END OF THE DAY	78	0.18	3	THE END OF THE DAY	28	0.17
4	AT THE END OF	256	0.61	4	QUITE A LOT OF	84	0.51	4	AT THE END OF THE DAY	73	0.17	4	AT THE END OF THE DAY	26	0.16
5	A LOT OF MONEY	178	0.42	5	AT THE END OF	83	0.51	5	THE OTHER SIDE OF THE	69	0.16	5	AND THAT SORT OF THING	26	0.16
6	A LOT OF PEOPLE	175	0.42	6	A LOT OF THE	79	0.48	6	IT'S A BIT OF A	61	0.14	5	THE PICTURES OF A SUNDAY	25	0.15
7	IN THE MIDDLE OF	162	0.38	7	THE END OF THE	78	0.47	7	A HELL OF A LOT	52	0.12	6	TO THE PICTURES OF A	25	0.15
8	GOT A LOT OF	149	0.35	8	THAT SORT OF THII	75	0.46	8	I CAN'T THINK OF	50	0.12	6	TO THE PICTURES OF A SUNDAY	25	0.15
9	THAT SORT OF THING	130	0.31	9	A LOT OF MONEY	63	0.38	8	WANT A CUP OF TEA	50	0.12	6	BEEN WAITING OF A BUS	24	0.15
10	THERE'S A LOT OF	119	0.28	10	DO YOU THINK OF	61	0.37	9	HAVE A CUP OF TEA	42	0.10	7	I'VE BEEN WAITING OF A BUS	24	0.15
11	A LITTLE BIT OF	117	0.28	11	A CUP OF TEA	60	0.36	10	HELL OF A LOT OF	40	0.10	7	IN OTHER PARTS OF THE	23	0.14
12	IT'S A BIT OF	116	0.27	12	A LOT OF THEM	58	0.35	11	YOU WANT A CUP OF	39	0.09	7	IT'S A BIT OF A	23	0.14
13	THE MIDDLE OF THE	106	0.25	13	OF THINGS DO YOU	56	0.35	11	WHAT DO YOU THINK OF	39	0.09	8	WHAT SORT OF THINGS DO YOU	22	0.13
14	ALL OF A SUDDEN	101	0.25	14	WAS A LOT OF	51	0.33	12	IT'S A LOT OF MONEY	37	0.09	8	THE OTHER SIDE OF THE	22	0.13

6.iii Bigrams and trigrams for all sub-corpora: TO

R	TO BNC-F 2w	N	%	R	TO 19C 2w	N	%	R	TO BNC-F 3w	N	%	R	TO 19C 3w	N	%
1	TO THE	48098	11.57	1	TO THE	40974	11.51	1	BACK TO THE	2864	0.69	1	TO GO TO	1545	0.43
2	TO BE	29125	7.00	2	TO BE	28751	8.08	2	WAS GOING TO	2505	0.60	2	TO BE A	1527	0.43
3	TO HER	13329	3.21	3	TO ME	10845	3.05	3	BE ABLE TO	2481	0.60	3	BE ABLE TO	1216	0.34
4	GOING TO	11892	2.86	4	TO HER	10447	2.93	4	TO GO TO	2420	0.58	4	WAS TO BE	1212	0.34
5	TO DO	10552	2.54	5	TO HIM	8457	2.38	5	ON TO THE	2347	0.56	5	TO SPEAK TO	1198	0.34
6	HAVE TO	10218	2.46	6	TO HIS	8417	2.36	6	TO BE A	2166	0.52	6	NOT TO BE	1134	0.32
7	TO SEE	9429	2.27	7	TO HAVE	7694	2.16	7	I WANT TO	2147	0.52	7	UP TO THE	994	0.28
8	TO GET	9408	2.26	8	TO SEE	7168	2.01	8	TO TALK TO	1880	0.45	8	SEEMED TO BE	992	0.28
9	TO GO	9326	2.24	9	TO A	7041	1.98	9	TO DO WITH	1831	0.44	9	TO SAY THAT	950	0.27
10	WANT TO	9288	2.23	10	TO DO	6933	1.95	10	GOING TO BE	1742	0.42	10	TO ME TO	949	0.27
11	BACK TO	8726	2.10	11	HIM TO	6522	1.83	11	SEEMED TO BE	1735	0.42	11	AS TO THE	938	0.27
12	HAD TO	8335	1.98	12	AND TO	6494	1.82	12	YOU WANT TO	1524	0.37	12	TO BE THE	917	0.26

R	TO MSM 2w	N	%	R	TO SSM 2w	N	%	R	TO MSM 3w	N	%	R	TO SSM 3w	N	%
1	TO BE	577	8.13	1	TO THE	3604	10.71	1	GOING TO BE	106	1.49	1	BE ABLE TO	258	0.77
2	TO THE	526	7.41	2	TO BE	2666	7.93	2	BE ABLE TO	97	1.37	2	IN ORDER TO	240	0.71
3	GOING TO	495	6.97	3	TO A	763	2.36	3	I'M GOING TO	79	1.13	3	WE NEED TO	233	0.69
4	TO DO	312	4.39	4	TO DO	709	2.11	4	WE NEED TO	79	1.13	4	I WANT TO	199	0.59
5	HAVE TO	296	4.17	5	HAVE TO	668	1.99	5	YOU HAVE TO	68	0.96	5	TO BE A	171	0.51
6	WANT TO	290	4.08	6	TO MAKE	616	1.83	6	TO BE ABLE	66	0.93	6	WE HAVE TO	150	0.45
7	TO HAVE	202	2.85	7	AND TO	610	1.80	6	I WANT TO	63	0.89	7	TO TRY TO	148	0.41
8	TO GET	198	2.79	8	NEED TO	588	1.75	6	WE HAVE TO	63	0.89	8	TO BE ABLE	132	0.39
9	TO MAKE	193	2.72	9	WANT TO	575	1.71	7	TO GO TO	62	0.88	9	HAVE TO BE	120	0.36
10	NEED TO	177	2.48	10	IS TO	558	1.66	8	ARE GOING TO	50	0.82	10	WOULD LIKE TO	109	0.32
11	TO GO	172	2.42	11	GOING TO	550	1.62	9	TO MAKESURE	46	0.62	11	TO SAY THAT	103	0.31
12	ABLE TO	156	2.20	12	TO HAVE	534	1.59	10	TO TRY TO	44	0.60	12	TO BE THE	101	0.30
								11	YOU WANT TO	43	0.59	12	GOING TO BE	101	0.30
								11	IN ORDER TO	43	0.59				
								11	IS GOING TO	43	0.59				
								12	WE'RE GOING TO	41	0.58				

R	TO BNC-C 2w	N	%	R	TO 4CC 2w	N	%	R	TO BNC-C 3w	N	%	R	TO 4CC 3w	N	%
1	HAVE TO	6015	8.19	1	USED TO	3808	15.65	1	I'VE GOT TO	1890	2.57	1	WE USED TO	692	2.84
2	TO GO	4916	6.69	2	TO THE	1677	6.89	2	I'LL HAVE TO	1457	1.98	2	I USED TO	625	2.57
3	TO THE	4861	6.61	3	TO GO	1660	6.88	3	TO GO TO	1275	1.73	3	TO GO TO	569	2.34
4	TO DO	4759	6.48	4	TO BE	1619	6.65	4	YOU HAVE TO	1087	1.48	4	USED TO GO	485	1.99
5	TO BE	4474	6.09	5	TO DO	1247	5.12	5	YOU WANT TO	1057	1.42	5	THEY USED TO	439	1.80
6	GOING TO	4327	5.89	6	GO TO	1242	5.11	6	BE ABLE TO	928	1.26	6	USED TO BE	398	1.64
7	TO GET	4304	5.81	7	HAVE TO	1013	4.16	7	YOU'VE GOT TO	870	1.18	7	USED TO HAVE	348	1.42
8	GOT TO	3541	4.82	8	TO GET	981	4.03	8	TO DO IT	809	1.10	8	I WENT TO	334	1.37
9	WANT TO	3496	4.76	9	WENT TO	979	4.03	9	I SAID TO	806	1.10	9	HE USED TO	307	1.25
10	USED TO	2864	3.90	10	HAD TO	924	3.80	10	I WANT TO	724	0.99	10	YOU USED TO	300	1.23
11	GO TO	2800	3.81	11	GOING TO	780	3.21	11	GO TO THE	646	0.88	11	GO TO THE	290	1.21
12	TO HAVE	2483	3.38	12	TO HAVE	758	3.12	12	YOU'RE GOING TO	641	0.87	12	YOU HAVE TO	262	1.08

6.iv Longer clusters for all sub-corpora: TO

R	TO BNC-F 4w	N	%	R	TO 19C 4w	N	%	R	TO BNC-F long	N	%	R	TO 19C long	N	%
1	I DON'T WANT TO	859	0.21	1	I SHOULD LIKE TO	577	0.16	1	WANT TO TALK TO YOU	171	0.04	1	I SHOULD LIKE TO KNOW	113	0.03
2	TO BE ABLE TO	794	0.19	2	TO BE ABLE TO	453	0.13	2	WHAT ARE YOU GOING TO	164	0.04	2	I WANT TO SPEAK TO	108	0.03
3	HE WAS GOING TO	650	0.16	3	I AM GOING TO	321	0.09	3	DON'T WANT TO GO	152	0.04	3	I AM SORRY TO SAY	100	0.03
4	TO GO TO THE	614	0.15	4	FROM TIME TO TIME	306	0.09	4	I WANT TO TALK TO	148	0.04	4	IT SEEMS TO ME THAT	95	0.03
5	SHE WAS GOING TO	502	0.12	5	WAS NOT TO BE	276	0.08	5	ARE YOU GOING TO DO	146	0.04	5	I WANT TO SPEAK TO YOU	84	0.02
6	NOTHING TO DO WITH	487	0.12	6	TO GO TO THE	269	0.08	6	DO YOU WANT ME TO	145	0.04	6	I SHOULD LIKE TO SEE	84	0.02
7	GOING TO HAVE TO	471	0.11	7	TO SPEAK TO YOU	262	0.07	7	WAS GOING TO HAVE TO	140	0.03	7	AS MUCH AS TO SAY	83	0.02
8	ARE YOU GOING TO	469	0.11	8	IT SEEMS TO ME	233	0.07	8	THERE'S NO NEED TO	140	0.03	8	YOU DON'T MEAN TO	79	0.02
9	TO GO BACK TO	454	0.11	9	I DON'T WANT TO	208	0.06	9	DON'T WANT TO BE	136	0.03	9	I WANT TO SPEAK TO YOU	78	0.02
10	TO TALK TO YOU	442	0.11	10	I WANT YOU TO	203	0.06	10	IT'S GOING TO BE	135	0.03	10	HAVE NOTHING TO DO WITH	78	0.02
11	I WANT YOU TO	434	0.11	11	TO ME TO BE	200	0.05	11	WHAT ARE YOU GOING TO DO	132	0.03	11	DON'T MEAN TO SAY	74	0.02
12	WAS GOING TO BE	429	0.11	12	IT SEEMED TO ME	192	0.05	12	HAD NOTHING TO DO WITH	127	0.03	12	MADE UP MY MIND TO	73	0.02

R	TO MSM 4w	N	%	R	TO SSM 4w	N	%	R	TO MSM long	N	%	R	TO SSM long	N	%
1	TO BE ABLE TO	66	0.93	1	TO BE ABLE TO	130	0.39	1	IT SEEMS TO ME THAT	11	0.16	1	SEEMS TO ME TO BE	18	0.05
2	TO MAKE SURE THAT	34	0.47	2	I WOULD LIKE TO	73	0.22	2	I'M GOING TO TAKE A	10	0.14	2	I WANT TO T ALK ABOUT	15	0.04
3	I DON'T WANT TO	24	0.33	3	IT SEEMS TO ME	41	0.12	3	I'M GOING TO CALL IN	8	0.11	3	I'M GOING TO TALK	14	0.04
4	I WOULD LIKE TO	21	0.30	4	WHEN IT COMES TO	38	0.11	3	LIKE TO HEAR FROM YOU	8	0.11	4	I'M GOING TO TALK ABOUT	12	0.04
5	IS GOING TO BE	21	0.30	5	TO DO WITH THE	35	0.10	3	NEED TO MAKE SURE THAT	8	0.11	5	IT SEEMS TO ME THAT	11	0.03
6	TO GO TO THE	20	0.28	6	IS GOING TO BE	35	0.10	4	WE NEED TO MAKE SURE THAT	7		6	THE EXTENT TO WHICH THE	9	0.03
7	GOING TO HAVE TO	18	0.25	7	WILL BE ABLE TO	34	0.10								
8	IT SEEMS TO ME	17	0.24	8	IF WE ARE TO	33	0.10								
9	ARE GOING TO BE	15	0.21	9	I AM GOING TO	31	0.09								
9	IF YOU WANT TO	14	0.20	10	TO ME TO BE	28	0.08								
10	THAT'S GOING TO	14	0.20	11	WE RE GOING TO	27	0.08								
10	THAT WE HAVE TO	13	0.18	11	THE EXTENT TO WHICH	27	0.08								
10	DO YOU WANT TO	13	0.18	11	IN RELATION TO THE	27	0.08								
11	WHEN IT COMES TO	13	0.18	12	THAT WE NEED TO	26	0.08								
11	TO GO BACK TO	12	0.17	12	TO DEAL WITH THE	26	0.08								
11	I JUST WANT TO	12	0.17	12	IT IS IMPORTANT TO	26	0.08								
11	THAT WE NEED TO	12	0.17												

(continued)

Continued

R	TO BNC-C 4w	N	%	R	TO 4CC 4w	N	%	R	TO BNC-C long	N	%	R	TO 4CC long	N	%
1	DO YOU WANT TO	356	0.48	1	USED TO GO TO	180	0.74	1	DO YOU WANT ME TO	180	0.24	1	FOR TO TALK TO YOU*	64	0.26
2	TO GO TO THE	330	0.45	2	WE USED TO GO	135	0.55	2	DON'T KNOW WHAT TO	89	0.12	2	USED TO GO TO THE	50	0.21
3	I DON'T WANT TO	295	0.40	3	TO GO TO THE	126	0.52	3	DO YOU WANT TO GO	77	0.10	2	THERE USED TO BE A	50	0.21
4	ARE YOU GOING TO	294	0.40	4	USED TO HAVE TO	120	0.49	4	DON'T KNOW WHAT TO DO	58	0.08	3	I'M GOING TO READ OUT*	38	0.16
5	YOU DON'T HAVE TO	244	0.33	5	AND WE USED TO	104	0.43	4	YOU'RE GONNA HAVE TO	58	0.08	3	TO TALK TO YOU ABOUT*	38	0.16
6	WE RE GOING TO	239	0.33	6	AND I USED TO	99	0.42	5	YOU WANT TO GO TO	54	0.07	4	WOULD JUST LIKE TO KNOW*	33	0.14
7	YOU WANT ME TO	232	0.32	7	WE USED TO HAVE	91	0.37	5	GO TO THE TOILET	54	0.07				
8	IF YOU WANT TO	231	0.32	8	AND THEY USED TO	89	0.36	5	I DON'T KNOW WHAT	54	0.07		(*intervewer form ulae)		
9	TO BE ABLE TO	224	0.31	9	I USED TO GO	81	0.33	5	I'M GOING TO GET	53	0.07				
10	DO YOU WANT ME	187	0.25	9	DID YOU USED TO	81	0.33	5	I DON'T KNOW WHAT TO	52	0.07				
11	I SAID TO HIM	176	0.24	9	USED TO BE A	81	0.33	5	YOU WANT ME TO DO	52	0.07				
12	I WAS GOING TO	156	0.21	10	TO TALK TO YOU	78	0.28	5	WHAT ARE YOU GOING TO	50	0.07				

Notes

1   Introduction

1. See Appendix 1.i for an overview that presents percentages for all three genres.
2. This is a reference to Lewis Fry Richardson's *Coast Line Paradox*, which states that landmass tends to have fractal-like properties which means that the smaller the ruler applied to determine length, the longer the coast (or border) becomes.

2   The Background: From Historical Descriptions of *TO* and *OF* to Contemporary Corpus-Based Evidence

1. A search for *wireless* in the BNC brings up *the wireless* – a synonym for *radio*. The later use for wireless connectivity between computational devices is not yet recorded. *Gay* (as, for example, *gay abandon*) meaning "bright" or "care-free" is quoted to have been in use, according to the OED, as recently as 2003. In 2014, most readers will link *gay* to "*good as you*" – a homosexual, originally US slang, according to the OED.
2. This does not mean that the author has not viewed the literature: it has been felt to detract from the aim of this book as a corpus-driven investigation of the items *of* and *to* to focus too much on a particular role that such items can play – that is, the category of *preposition*. What the reading of this the research on the topic has revealed is that there is (a) a great deal of disagreement – sometimes writers insist that the same item has to be either only a particle or a preposition – and (b) a wealth of detailed investigations, though it is often not clear whether these are based on sets of examples made up of, found in, say, literary texts, or found to be a prominent feature – that is, being present in the majority of texts viewed.
3. Hill's *interim classification – semantic, structural and graded,* despite dating from 1968, has been chosen as it is more targeted and comprehensive in listing and describing the uses for these items than any of the following: Cambridge Grammar of English, Collins COBUILD Grammar, Longman Grammar of Spoken and Written English.
4. Palmer presents, first of all, prepositions as usage for *of* and *to*.
5. This mirrors Michael Hoey's idea of a *personal grammar* (2005:15). Hoey himself refers to Hopper: My argument here also follows a similar line to that of Hopper (1988, 1998), who argues that grammar is the output of what he calls 'routines', collocational groupings, the repeated use of which results in the creation of a grammar for each individual. [Hopper] terms this process 'emergent grammar' and importantly every speaker's grammar is different because every speaker's experience and knowledge of routines is different; Hopper also makes use of the notion of priming, though as a less central notion." (Hoey, 2005:9).

6. For a comprehensive background of the concept, its origins and the research undertaken to support that the claims of *(lexical) priming* can be deemed valid, please see Pace-Sigge (2013).

3   *OF* and *TO* Usage in Fiction

1. See BNC-F Index – which can be found, for example, here: http://www.uow. edu.au/~dlee/home/corpus_resources.htm.
2. The small ANC-F was used mainly because of its ease of use and because a previous selection that is downloadable has been made available. This was deemed to be sufficient as the I otherwise do concentrate on British English material. A better source is COCA, which has not been used here as its material is not downloadable – making direct comparisons slightly awkward. See http://corpus.byu. edu/coca/compare-ANC-F.asp in how far COCA and ANC-F material compare.
3. *Her* occurs 326,667 times – meaning that *of her* and *to her* are used in about 8 per cent of all uses of *her*.
4. Furthermore, there is also *of an*, which is clearly less frequent – reflecting that an occurs only with a frequency of 0.26 per cent.
5. "X" stands for a wildcard search – any item.
6.

Key term	Freq.	Bigram	% of key term
End	12,430	End of	46.46
Rest	7,682	Rest of	39.46
Middle	2,958	Middle of	62.81
Top	5,291	Top of	52.60
Edge	3,009	Edge of	64.81
Back	50,003	Back of	5.15
Side	15,208	Side of	35.61
Bottom	2,319	Bottom of	48.56
Centre	2,208	Centre of	54.40

7. *In front of the* is proportionally more frequent in BNC-F (but ranks lower) and is overall less frequent in 19C.
8. *Of the people* in ANC-F should be discounted as it is part of *of the will of the people* which is used repeatedly in one of the 11 novels.
9. Note, also, the use of these phrases as discussed in chapters 4 and 5.
10. In the ANC-F, *from time to time* occurs only 31 times in 100,000 words.

4   *OF* and *TO* in Semi-Prepared Speech

1. To the point where the LSE does not make available transcripts but the written speech – and there are many indications (see Section 4.3) that these were published, in written form, before the actual spoken speech was delivered.
2. Another trait that becomes apparent in comparing the highest-occurring clusters of various corpora is to distinguish different forms and genres.

3. The use of *have to* and *need to* is interesting here also when compared to one-to-one exchanges. Glass (2014) writes that *you need to* is employed by people who have an interest in the well-being of the addressee. Furthermore, "*you need to* will be more appropriate, thus [used more often as is] more common [coming] from people with knowledge about subject matter, people in a mentoring role; people with power" (Glass, 2014)

4. The one exception here is Reith and VAR where the *to* 3-grams are very similar in both ranking and percentage of occurrence. Statistical testing shows only a slightly significant difference concerning both *in order to* and *to be able*, which is fractionally less frequent in Reith than could be expected.

5. In the case of Reith and NML, the proportional percentage of use of *be able to* are broadly similar for the single- and multiple-speaker corpora.

6. In the NML single-speaker sub-corpus, *to go to* is it found to be in rank eight, with 26 occurrences: 0.65 per cent of all *to* uses.

7. The nicest example of this comes from David Fleming, the NML director: "The world is full of things that are free **to do that** people don't do. You know, they might not go to parks, they might not go for walks along the promenade, they might not go wandering around historic buildings. It's all free – people have lots of things to do with their time and in order to get them to come to museums just being free won't really attract anybody."

8. *A lot of* is a clear exception here as regards the NML sub-corpus: it is the most frequent 3w *of* cluster. This issue will be discussed in detail below.

9. Please also see Hoffmann (2005) for his discussion of *in terms of*. Chapter 2.3.2 contextualises the use of this phrase, too.

10. The reader may have noticed that *a kind of* is fairly frequent in single speaker corpora; yet it is *the kind of* in multiple speaker corpora. Looking at VAR, where those two items appear roughly equally frequent, a curious thing became apparent: in the single speaker sub-corpus, both *a kind of* and *the kind of* are followed by a rather negative noun phrase. In the multiple-speaker sub-corpus, however, both variants are followed by a noun phrase that carries a positive prosody.

11. 99.9th percentile; 0.1 per cent level; $p < 0.001$; critical value = 8.40 for LSE and 13.84 for NML.

12. VAR lies in between, though is not much more significant in its divergence than NML. Looking at the use of *have to be* in LSE and NML, there is no degree of difference in their proportional use. A direct comparison of *to be able* highlights that it is significantly more used in NML (99.9th percentile; 0.1 per cent level; $p < 0.001$; critical value = 13.64 for NML) than in Reith.

13. Here and in Tables 4.12, 4.13 and 4.14, the total number of files where the target n-gram occurs is divided by the total number of files per sub-corpus. Thus the spread is calculated.

14. This phrase is, however, much rarer in VAR than the other three sub-corpora.

5 *OF* and *TO* Usage in Spoken Texts

1. A selection of around half the *COLT* (http://clu.uni.no/icame/colt) transcripts, leaving out the longest and shortest ones.

2. Hackney and Havering will, below, simply be referred to as "London". As the project recorded both young and elderly speakers, a further distinction can be made and comparisons drawn to the earlier COLT (London teenage) corpus.

3. Andrew Hardie (Lancaster University) points out that, as verb-phrases are more frequent than noun-phrases, *to*-Infinitive can be expected to be more frequent than *to* as preposition (which is usually followed by a noun).

4. In the BNC-C there is also "load of", which reflects the non-standardised transcription of "lot of" which only exists to a minimal extent in 4CC. 221 of the 268 concordance lines are the trigram *a load* of. The combined figure would be 2,333 – 5.6 per cent of all *of* uses.

5. When the clusters are tested against the total of tokens, there is no statistically significant difference between *bit of a* and *a couple of*. However, *a bit of, one of those* and *one of these* are significantly less used in 4CC, while all other trigrams are significantly more used than expected in 4CC. The discussion below is based on statistical testing, based on the total tokens for *of* in the respective corpora.

6. Interestingly, *one of these people* occurs only four times in BNC-C. The 3.5 times smaller 4CC records it five times – three times by a Liverpool speaker. The BNC-C also only offers the construction *one of the people that – that* or – *who* occurs equally in 4CC.

7. *A cup of tea* occurs, proportionally, one-third more frequently in BNC-C than it does in 4CC. Katie Patterson points out that the phrase is to be seen in the context of a host offering to makes this – a social ritual throughout Britain. The host can be both the recorder or the informant. The use of the phrase reflects the immediacy of the utterance, which is usually followed by the appropriate action.

8. Twelve out of 17 occurrences of *want a cup of tea* have been recorded in the Tyneside corpus; all instances of *have a cup of tea* come from the London corpus.

9. While *to do* appears significantly less often in 4CC, it is included here as the ranking is similar.

10. This may also explain the higher frequency of *got to*. *Got* appears in 0.68 per cent of all words in BNC-C, but the figure is only 0.43 per cent. *Got to* appears in 12.4 per cent of *got* in BNC-C, but only 8.3 per cent in 4CC. This seems to indicate that there are more occurrences of *got* as *got to* more often employed.

11. The next most frequent, *used it* (BNC-C) and *used with* (4CC – exclusive to Tyneside speakers) is found in 0.1 per cent.

12. In Liverpool, *used to* is in 352 concordance lines, *to be* in 345, *I went to* in 61 and *we used to* in 60.

13. There is one concordance line in BNC-C that indicated both movement and an event in the future, showing how closely linked these can be when the *going to* form occurs: "And tomorrow, she's going to this thing at the chapel."

6   Discussion: Usage Patterns for *OF* and *TO* in British English

1. This also means: that there are only around a quarter of the files, while the size of the corpora is roughly comparable.

2. *Used to* is, however, employed in less than one-third of all occurrences of *used* in both academic spoken and academic written English. It is, however, the dominant bigram: *used in* occurs in only 12.2 per cent of all uses of *used* in BASE and 14.8 per cent in BAWE. In BAWE, furthermore, the second-most frequent *used* bigram is *be used* which occurs in one-fifth of all times *used* is found.

3. To be precise, 71.60 per cent in the Q&A and panel data; 75.56 per cent in the single-speaker data.

4. It occurs most strongly in the multiple-speaker podcasts (43 per cent) and least in BNC-C (11 per cent). However, the figures from the other sub-corpora in the genre level these closer to the average, which are best represented by the fiction texts.

5. "My lot" was uttered by the same speaker in VAR, 2007. There is also the use of "fell to *the lot of my* anxious hosts" which occurs in Reith Lecture No. 6 of 1948 and is a singular usage. Overall, *lot* is rare in Reith – used maybe only once or twice per speech until 1991. VAR speakers, however, appear to use them very frequently in their utterances.

6. *Course* is only 0.01 per cent of the counted tokens in BAWE. This is the lowest count in all the sub-corpora investigated here. BASE, by contrast sees *course* occurring in 0.12 per cent of all tokens. That *of course* appears in BAWE at all might be due to the fact that part of the material consists of student essays.

7. *I* and *you* (and, in BNC-C, *it*) are more frequent.

8. "*In front of* has taken over a substantial part of the semantic territory at one time associated with *before* ... As the lexeme front – derived from Old French – supplanted the indigenous *before*..." (Tyler and Evans, 2003: 156).

9. *Will to*, with *will* as L1 quite often employs will as a noun (either the "testament" or "desire").

10. Least frequent in BNC-F (2.3 per cent); most frequent in 4CC (3.25 per cent).

7 Implications for the Teaching of English

1. Nattinger, J. 1980. A lexical phrase grammar for ESL. *TESOL Quarterly*, 14, pp. 337–344.

2. Robert Shiller (2015: 179), who is an economist and not a linguist, highlights how important the spoken word is: "The human mind is the product of evolution almost entirely in the absence of the printed word, e-mail, the Internet, or any other artificial means of communication. ... Look around you. Everywhere you go, when two or more people are not working or playing or sleeping (and, in some cases, even when they do these things) they are talking."

3. *The sort of thing* (ten concordance lines) and *this sort of thing* (seven) can be found – yet only fairly rarely.

4. It must be noted that *in terms of* has been single out as a key *of* phrase by Sinclair and Sebastian Hoffmann, amongst others. The data presented here underlines that it is usually found in more formal or institutional forms of spoken English.

5. *It seems to me* is even more prominent in SSM, where it is the fourth-most frequent 4w *to* cluster.

Bibliography

Aarts, Bas. 1989. Verb-preposition constructions and small clauses in English. *Journal of Linguistics*, 25, pp. 277–290.

Arnon, Inbal and Neal Snider. 2010. More than words: Frequency effects for multi-word phrases. In: Journal of Memory and Language, 62, pp. 67–82

Baker, Paul. 2011. Times may change, But we will always have money: Diachronic variation in recent British English. *Journal of English Linguistics*, 39:1, pp. 65–88.

Biber, Douglas. 2000. Investigating language use through corpus-based analyses of association patterns. In: Michael Barlow and Suzanne Kemmer (eds) *Usage Based Models of Language*. Stanford, CA: CSLI Publications, pp. 287–314.

Biber, Douglas, Sue Conrad, and Randi Reppen. 1998. *Corpus Linguistics*. Cambridge: CUP.

Biber, Douglas, Stig Johansson, Geoffrey Leech, Susan Conrad, and Edward Finegan. [1999] 2007. *Longman Grammar of Spoken and Written English*. Harlow, Essex: Pearson Education.

Brorström, Sverker. 1963. *The Increasing Frequency of the Preposition* about *During the Modern English Period*. Stockholm: Almqvist & Wiksell.

Brorström, Sverker. 1965. *Studies on the Use of the Preposition* of *in the 15th Century Correspondence*. Stockholm: Almqvist & Wiksell.

Bybee, Joan. 2003. Mechanisms of change in grammaticization: The role of frequency. In: Brian D. Joseph and Richard D. Janda (eds) *The Handbook of Historical Linguistics*. Malden, MA: Wiley-Blackwell Publishing, pp. 602–623.

Bybee, Joan. 2006. From usage to grammar: The mind's response to repetition. *Language*, 82, pp. 711–33.

Cappelle, Bert. 2004. The particularity of particles, or why they are not just "intransitive prepositions". *Belgian Journal of Linguistics*, 18:1, pp. 29–57.

Carter, Ronald. 2004. Grammar and spoken English. In: C. Coffin, A. Hewings and K. O'Halloran (eds) *Applying English Grammar*. London: Arnold, pp. 25–39.

Carter, Ronald and Michael McCarthy. 2001. Ten criteria for a spoken grammar. In: E. Hinkel and S. Fotos (eds) *New Perspectives on Grammar Teaching in Second Language Classrooms*. Mahwah, NJ: Lawrence Erlbaum Associates, pp. 51–75.

Carter, Ronald and Michael McCarthy. 2006. *Cambridge Grammar of English: A Comprehensive Guide*. Cambridge: CUP.

Cheng, Winnie. 2012. *Exploring Corpus Linguistics. Language in Action*. London: Routledge.

Collins, Beverly, and Inger Mees. 2009. *Pratical Phonetics and Phonology*. London: Routledge

Cruttenden, Alan. 2001 [1962]. *Gimson's Pronunciation of English*. Sixth Edition, revised. London: Arnold.

Denison, David. 1985. Why old English had no prepositional passive. *English Studies*, 3, pp. 189–204.

de Mornay Davies, Paul. 1998. Automatic sematic priming: The contribution of lexical and semantic-level processes. *European Journal of Cognitive Psychology*, 10:4, pp. 358–370.

De Smet, Hendrik and Hubert Cuyckens. 2005. Pragmatic strengthening and the meaning of complement constructions: The case of like and love with the to-infinitive. *Journal of English Linguistics*, 33:3, pp.3–34.

Dolón Herrero, Rosanna and Fuster Márquez, Miguel. 2012. Technology implementation in second language teaching and translated training: New tools, new approaches. *A Corpus-Driven Study of Ideology-Driven Discourse Practice: The University Language Learner as Researcher of Prepositions in Use*. Forthcoming.

Fischer, Olga. 2000. Grammaticalisation: Unidirectional, non-reversable? The case of *to* before the infinitive in English. In: Olga Fischer, Anette Rosenbach and Dieter Stein (eds) *Pathways of Change. Grammaticalization in English*. Amsterdam/Philadelphia: John Benjamins, pp. 149–169.

Flowerdew, Lynne. 2009. Applying corpus linguistics to pedagogy: A critical evaluation. *International Journal of Corpus Linguistics*, 4:3, pp. 393–417.

Flowerdew, Lynne. 2012. *Corpora and Language Education*. Houndmills, Basingstoke: Palgrave Macmillan.

Francis, Gill. 1993. A corpus-driven grammar. In: Mona Baker, Gill Francis, and Elena Tognini-Bonelli (eds) *Text and Technology: In Honour of John Sinclair*. Amsterdam: John Benjamins, pp. 137–156.

Glass, Leila. 2014. Need to vs. got to/have to: Deriving social meaning from semantic meaning. Presentation given at NWAV 2014, Chicago, USA.

Gries, Stefan Th. 2003. Towards a corpus-based identification of prototypical instances of constructions. *Annual Review of Cognitive Linguistics*, 1, pp. 1–27.

Gries, Stefan Th. 2009. *Statistics for Linguistics with R: A Practical Introduction*. Berlin: Walter de Gruyter.

Guéron, J. 1990. Particles, prepositions, and verbs. In: J. Mascaro and Marina Nespor (eds) *Grammar in Progress*. Dordrecht, The Netherlands: Foris.

Heaton, J. B. 1965. *Prepositions and Adverbial Particles*. London: Longman.

Hill, Leslie Alexander. 1968. *Prepositions and Adverbial Particles*. London: Oxford University Press.

Hoey, Michael. 1995. The lexical nature of intertextuality: A preliminary study. In: B. Warvik, S.-K. Tanskanen, and R. Hiltunen, (eds) *Organization in Discourse*. Proceedings from the Turku Conference 1995. Anglicana Turkuensia, 14. pp. 73–94.

Hoey, Michael. 2003. Why grammar is beyond belief. In: University of Liège. *Belgian Association of Anglicists in Higher Education: Belgian Essays on Language and Literature*, pp 183–96.

Hoey, Michael. 2005. *Lexical Priming. A New Theory of Words and Language*. London: Routledge.

Hoey, Michael. 2014. Old Approaches, new perspectives: The implications of a corpus linguistic theory for learning the English language. Plenary Talk presented at the 48th Annual International IATEFL Conference, Harrogate, 4 April.

Hoffmann, Sebastian. 2005. *Grammaticalization and English Complex Prepositions*. London: Routledge.

Hoffmann, Thomas. 2011. *Preposition Placement in English: A Usage-based Approach*. Cambridge: Cambridge University Press.

Hook, J.N. 1975. *History of the English Language*. New York: The Ronald Press Company.

Hunston, Susan, Gill Francis, and Elizabeth Manning. 1997. Grammar and vocabulary: Showing the connections. *ELTJournal*, 51:3, pp. 208–216.

Hunston, Susan and Gill Francis. 1999. *Pattern Grammar: A Corpus-driven Approach to the Lexical Grammar of English*. Amsterdam/Philadelphia: John Benjamins.

Jacobsson, Bengt. 1977. Adverbs, prepositions, and conjunctions in English: A study in gradience. *Studia Linguistica*, XXXI:I, pp. 38–64

Johns, Tim. 1991. Should you be persuaded – two samples of data-driven Learning materials. *English Language Research Journal*, 4, pp. 1–16.

Knowles, Gerald. 1987. *Patterns of Spoken English: An Introduction to English Phonetics*. London: Longman.

Lebas, Franck. 2002. The theoretical status of prepositions. In: S. Feigenbaum and D. Kurzon (eds) *Prepositions in Their Syntactic, Semantic, and Pragmatic Context*. Amsterdam/Philadelphia: John Benjamins, pp. 59–76.

Lindkvist, Karl-Gunnar. 1972. *The Local Sense of the Prepositions OVER, ABOVE and ACROSS. Studied in Present-Day English*. Stockholm: Almqvist & Wiksell International.

Lindkvist, Karl-Gunnar. 1976. *A Comprehensive Study of Conceptions of Locality in which English Prepositions Occur*. Stockholm: Almqvist & Wiksell International.

Linzen, Tal, Sofya Kasyanenko and Maria Gouskova. 2013. Lexical and phonological variation in Russian prepositions. *Phonology*, 30, pp. 453–515.

Longman Dictonary of Contemporary English (LDOCE) [1978] 2006. 5th Edition. London: Longman.

Mair, Christian. 1997. The spread of the *going-to*-future in written English: A corpus-based investigation into language change in progress. In: R. Hickey and S. Puppel (eds) *Language History and Linguistic Modelling: A Festschrift for Jacek Fisiak on His 60th Birthday*. Language History. I, Volume 2. Berlin: Walter de Gruyter, pp. 1537–1544.

McCarthy, Michael. 1998. *Spoken Language and Applied Linguistics*. Cambridge: CUP.

McDonough, Kim and Pavel Trofimovich. 2009. *Using Priming Methods in Second Language Research*. New York: Routledge (Taylor and Francis).

McEnery, Xiao and Tono. 2006. *Corpus-Based Language Studies*. London: Routledge.

Mindt, Ilka. 2013. Gesprochene Korpora des Englischen und ihre Anwendung in der Grammatikforschung. In: Iva Kratochvílová and Norbert Richard Wolf (eds) *Grundlagen einer sprachwissenschaftlichen Quellkunde*. Tübingen: Narr Francke Verlag, pp 111–120.

O'Dowd, Elizabeth M. 1998. *Prepositions and Particles in English. A Discourse-functional Account*. New York/Oxford: Oxford University Press.

O'Keeffe, Anne, Brian Clancy and Svenja Adolphs. 2011. *Introducing Pragmatics in Use*. London: Routledge.

O'Keeffe, Anne; Michael McCarthy, and Ronald Carter. 2007. *From Corpus to Classroom*. Cambridge: CUP.

Pace-Sigge, Michael. 2009. *Why TO is a Weird Word*. Available from www.academia.edu/4107981/Why_TO_is_a_weird_word (last accessed November 10, 2013)

Pace-Sigge, Michael. 2013. *Lexical Priming in Spoken English Usage*. Houndmills, Basingstoke: Palgrave Macmillan.

Palmer, Harold, E. [1924] 1976. *Grammar of Spoken English*. Revised by Roger Kingdon, 1969. Cambridge: CUP.

Palmer, Harold E. [1938] 1961. *A Grammar of English Words*. London: Longmans, Green and Co. Ltd.

Partington, Alan. 2003. *The Linguistics of Political Argument. The Spin-Doctor and the Wolf-Pack at the White House*. London: Taylor and Francis.

Patterson, Katie J. 2014. The analysis of metaphor: To what extent can the theory of Lexical Priming help our understanding of metaphor usage and comprehension? *Journal of Psycholinguistic Research*. Available online: http://link.springer.com/article/10.1007/s10936-014-9343-1#page-1 (last accessed December 8, 2014)

Pawley, A. and F. H. Syder, 1983. Two puzzles for linguistic theory: Native like selection and native like fluency. In: J.C. Richards, and R. W. Schmidt (eds) *Language and Communication*. London: Longman, pp. 191–226.

Plank, F. 1984. The modals story retold. *Studies in Language*, 8, pp. 305–364.

Quirk, Randolph, Sidney Greenbaum, Geoff Leech and Jan Svartvik. 1985. *A Comprehensive Grammar of the English Language*. London: Longman.

Rayson, Paul. nd. Log-likelihood calculator. UCREL University of Lancaster webpage: http://ucrel.lancs.ac.uk/llwizard.html (last accessed 23/01/2015)

Rayson, Paul, D. Berridge and B. Francis 2004. Extending the Cochran rule for the comparison of word frequencies between corpora. In: Volume II of G. Purnelle, C. Fairon, A. Dister (eds) *Le poids des mots: Proceedings of the 7th International Conference on Statistical Analysis of Textual Data (JADT 2004)*, Louvain-la-Neuve, Belgium, March 10–12, 2004, Presses universitaires de Louvain, pp. 926–936. ISBN 2-930344-50-4.

Renouf, Antoinette and John Sinclair. 1991. Collocational frameworks in English. In: Karin Aijmer and Bengt Altenberg (eds) *English Corpus Linguistics*. New York: Longman, pp. 128–143.

Rice, Sally. 1999. Patterns of acquisition in the emerging mental lexicon: The case of to and for in English. *Brain and Language*, 68, pp. 268–276.

Rudanko, Juhani. 1998. *To* infinitive and *to ing* complements: A look at some matrix verbs in late Modern English and later. *English Studies*, 79:4, pp.336–348,

Saint-Dizier, Patrick. 2005. *PrepNet: A Framework for Describing Prepositions, Preliminary Investigation Results*. IWCS: Tilburg.

Scott, Mike. 2012–2015. *Wordsmith Tools Version 6*. Liverpool: Wordsmith Tools.

Scott, Mike and Christopher Tribble. 2006. *Textual Patterns: Key Words and Corpus Analysis in Language Education*. Amsterdam: John Benjamins Publishing.

Shiller, Robert J. 2015. *Irrational Exuberrance*. Princeton, NJ: Princeton University Press.

Sinclair, John M., Susan Jones and Robert Daley. [1970] 2004. *English Collocation Studies: The OSTI Report*. London. Continuum.

Sinclair, John M. 1989. *Collins CoBuild Dictionary*. London/New York: Collins CoBuild.

Sinclair, John M. 1990. *Collins CoBuild English Grammar*. London/New York: Collins ELT.

Sinclair, John M. 1991. *Corpus Concordance Collocation (Chapter Six)*. Oxford: OUP.

Sinclair, John M. [1996] 2004. The search for the units of meaning. In: J. Sinclair (ed) *Trust the Text*. London: Routledge.

Sinclair, John M. [1998] 2004. The lexical item. In: J. Sinclair (ed) *Trust the Text*. London: Routledge, pp. 9–23.

Sinclair, John and Anna Mauranen. 2006. *Linear Unit Grammar: Integrating Speech and Writing*. Amsterdam: John Benjamins.

166   *Bibliography*

Snider, Todd. 2010. The semantics of prepositions: An exploration into the uses of "at" and "to". *Dietrich College Honors Theses*. Paper 61. http://repository.cmu.edu/hsshonors/61. Last Accessed 15/07/2013.
Stubbs, Michael. 1996. *Text and Corpus Analysis. Computer-assisted Analysis of Language and Culture*. Oxford: Basil Blackwell.
Stubbs, Michael. 2001. *Words and Phrases. Corpus Studies of Lexical Semantics*. Oxford: Basil Blackwell.
Swan, Michael and Bernhard Smith (eds.). 1987. *Learner English*. New York: Cambridge University Press.
Traugott, E.C. 1993. Subjectification and the development of epistemic meaning: The case of promise and threaten. In: T. Swan and O. Jansen Westwik (eds) *Modality in Germanic Languages*. Berlin: Mouton de Gruyter, pp. 185–210.
Tyler, Andrea and Vyvyan Evans. 2003. *The Semantics of English Prepositions. Spatial Scenes, Embodied Meaning and Cognition*. Cambridge: CUP.
Van der Gucht, Fieke, Klaas Willems and Ludovic De Cuypere. 2006. The iconicity of embodied meaning. Polysemy of spatial prepositions in the cognitive framework. *Language Sciences*, 29, pp. 733–754.
Visetti, Yves-Marie and Pierre Cadiot. 2002. Prepositions in their syntactic, semantic and pragmatic context. Starting from the case of prepositions. In: S. Feigenbaum and D. Kurzon (eds) *Prepositions in their Syntactic, Semantic and Pragmatic Context*. Amsterdam/Philadelphia: John Benjamins, pp. 9–39.
Weisbuch, Robert. 1986. *Atlantic Double-Cross: American Literature and British Influence in the Age of Emerson*. Chicago: University of Chicago Press.
Wray, Alison. 2002. Formulaic language in computer-supported communication: Theory meets reality. *Language Awareness*, 11:2, pp.114–131.
Wray, Alison and Michael R. Perkins. 2000. The functions of formulaic language: An integrated model. *Language and Communication*, 20, pp 1–28.

Index

GPSR Compliance
The European Union's (EU) General Product Safety Regulation (GPSR) is a set
of rules that requires consumer products to be safe and our obligations to
ensure this.

If you have any concerns about our products, you can contact us on

ProductSafety@springernature.com

In case Publisher is established outside the EU, the EU authorized
representative is:

Springer Nature Customer Service Center GmbH
Europaplatz 3
69115 Heidelberg, Germany